CAMBRIDGE LATIN AMERICAN STUDIES

EDITORS

MALCOLM DEAS CLIFFORD T. SMITH
JOHN STREET

22

LETTERS AND PEOPLE OF
THE SPANISH INDIES
SIXTEENTH CENTURY

THE SERIES

TRANSCRIPTION AND TRANSLATION OF
LETTER ILLUSTRATED OVER

señora hermana

en otra sin esta e suplicado a v. md me haga md de me mandar aca a su yerno y a vna de sus hijas la donçella pues v. md sabe que yo no tengo a quien pueda dejar en esta tiera lo que tengo sera justo que para que no goçe dello quien no es suyo que v. md lo anime a que venga y trayga a su muger que yo lo quedare con que biva muy descansado y si se quisiere bolver bien puede que yo le dare con que se pueda mantener en esa tiera y si determina de venirse procure por marcos de sandoval en sevilla en casa de don jorje de purtugal que de alli lo encaminaran y le daran lo que vuiere menester v. md no haga otra cosa porque en ello me hara muy gran md de la muerte del señor andres perez me peso muy mucho nro s^{or} perdone su anima y v. md de salud para que por ella y las demas haga bien — de la nueva españa i de la puebla de los angeles seis de diçiembre de iMdlxxv años

a serviçio de v. md

ana maçias

Lady sister:

In another letter aside from this one I have implored you to do me the favor of sending to me here your son-in-law and one of your daughters, the unmarried one. Since you know that I have no one in this land to whom I can leave what I have and it would be just that someone should not enjoy it to whom it did not belong, encourage him to come and bring his wife, and I will see to it that he lives in great repose, and if he should want to return, he can very well, for I will give him the means to maintain himself in that land there (Spain). And if he decides to come, let him arrange it through Marcos de Sandoval in Seville, in the house of don Jorge de Portugal; they will set him on his way from there and give him what he should need. Don't do differently, because therein you will be doing me a great favor.

I was grieved by the death of Mr Andrés Pérez; may our Lord pardon his soul and give health to you to do good for it and the souls of others. From New Spain and Puebla de los Angeles, 6th of December of the year 1575.

At your service,

Ana Macías

Letter by Ana Macías, in Puebla, to her cousin María Deza in Talavera, Badajoz, 1575. (Published in Otte, 'Cartas privadas de Puebla'.)

LETTERS AND PEOPLE OF THE SPANISH INDIES

SIXTEENTH CENTURY

Translated and edited by

James Lockhart and Enrique Otte

CAMBRIDGE UNIVERSITY PRESS

CAMBRIDGE

LONDON • NEW YORK • MELBOURNE

Published by the Syndics of the Cambridge University Press
The Pitt Building, Trumpington Street, Cambridge CB2 1RP
Bentley House, 200 Euston Road, London NW1 2DB
32 East 57th Street, New York, NY 10022, USA
296 Beaconsfield Parade, Middle Park, Melbourne 3206, Australia

Library of Congress catalogue card number: 75-6007

ISBN 0 521 20883 1 hard covers
ISBN 0 521 09990 0 paperback

First published 1976

Printed in the United States of America
Type set by Computer Productions, Inc. New York, printed and bound by
R.R. Donnelley & Sons Co., Crawfordsville, Indiana

CONTENTS

PREFACE

I have written you so many times and sent so many letters by whoever has left here . . .

Melchor Verdugo, in Trujillo, Peru,
to his mother in Spain, 1536

Letters abound in the records of early Spanish America. Or at least, public correspondence does. Members of all of the different official hierarchies were constantly writing to higher authority, and especially to the Spanish crown, petitioning, proposing, polemicizing. All corporations and interest groups did the same, and so did individuals when aggrieved or desirous of favors. The strident texts produced by this activity were long the main corpus with which historians of the Spanish Indies worked, first taking them at face value, then learning to appreciate their conventions, their propagandistic nature, their systematic distortions when compared with other types of evidence. New evidence emerged in many forms, from tax lists to notarial records, but rarely indeed, until recently, in the true counterpart of official correspondence, that is, private correspondence.

Were there no private letters? Scholars were long inclined to think so, and they even incorporated the supposed lack of intimate written expression into theories of the Spanish character. But in fact there were, and today's scarcity is only the result of the vulnerability of private correspondence to loss. From the examples that have been coming to light one can deduce that letter-writing among private individuals was a well-established custom in both Spain and the Indies (as the Spaniards persisted in calling America). Correspondents acknowledge previous letters, complain of lack of mail, speak of the cheapness of paper and ink, and in other ways betray that it was customary to write letters to absent relatives and friends. The genre was mature, with a complete set of salutations and courtesy endings, and certain conventions of vocabulary and structure, such as for example the frequent use of the word *razón* ('right,' 'reason') somewhere in the beginning sentences.

Letters must have originated in all areas and gone in all directions, but in general only those which found a place in some official repository have been preserved. Most to appear so far were written from the Indies to relatives and associates in Spain. Of letters directed from Spain to the Indies we know little more than what we can deduce from the replies of the settlers, namely that they contained frequent appeals for money. As to the settlers' letters, they are often written with an eye to recruitment; they praise the opportunities and plenteousness of the new land in terms that would do justice to a Pole or Italian in the United States of 1910. Stereotypes and bias are no less evident in letters like these than in official reports, and must be equally discounted, or rather taken as such. Even so, there is much immediacy, reality, sobriety and simple informativeness in them. They are very human documents, in which the Spaniard of the Indies appears in roles intuitively familiar to us, as son, brother, immigrant, tradesman, European, anything but some exotic 'conquistador' 'thirsty for gold.'

The greatest cache of such letters is in the records of the Casa de la Contratación, the clearing house in Seville for departures to the Indies, where emigrants brought the correspondence as proof that they had connections at their declared destinations.[1] Other letters are incorporated as evidence in litigation, as when there was a dispute over inheritance, or the investigation of an official's conduct. Among such papers one often comes upon a somewhat different kind of private correspondence, the letters that merchants wrote back and forth across the Atlantic. These appear going in both directions, for the headquarters of the exporting firms was in Seville, which in some senses was almost a part of the Indies and was drawn into the latter's judicial-documentary web. Merchants' letters lack some of the biases of other settler correspondence, but have their own predispositions; though quite technical in vocabulary, in the end the commercial letters are as fresh, personal and informative as the others, covering somewhat different ground.

In this volume we bring together a structured selection of these three types of letters, with unabashed emphasis on the more personal ones, trying to give as nearly complete a panorama of sixteenth-century Spanish American settler society and its genres of correspondence as we can achieve. The wide spread of social types and functions will speak directly to the reader. The humanity and the familiar sentiments of the writers will also readily make themselves felt. But these people were deeply embedded in a complex and rapidly evolving society, at a specific point in time; now removed from us by some centuries, that society calls for a certain amount of explanation. With an understanding of the context, the regularity and universality of the processes come home to us even more (a universality not at all inconsistent with the unique flavor of the individuals, the time and the culture). Rather than supply this context in disembodied form in a long introduction, we have adapted it more specifically to the letters themselves, arranged in three large sections – Conquest, The Variety of Life in the Indies, and Officials and Clerics – which we imagine as best read consecutively, in the same order as presented, since the comments are cumulative, and there is structure in the arrangement of the letters as well.

In this preface, then, we will make only a few very general remarks on early Spanish America. The letters in this book throw light on many trades, functions, offices and social mechanisms, but one might not get from them a sufficient sense of the overriding importance of cities, unless perhaps by noting that most are written *from* cities. Spanish America was built on an Indian base, and without fail more Spaniards went where there were more Indians, but the great majority of Spaniards themselves resided in widely dispersed cities that they would found almost as soon as they set foot in a country. In these all the elements of Spanish life soon took root, and there all Spanish organizations, whether commercial, governmental, or ecclesiastic, had their center. Even the estate structure centered on the cities. There all Spanish people of rank, wealth and influence were to be found, only subordinates and recent arrivals being stationed in the country, and they principally to channel things towards the cities.

Cities were also the units into which entire regions were divided. Each city included a vast district stretching all the way to where the jurisdiction of the next began. Where Indian provincial organization would allow it, and in all the more densely populated areas it did, the district was subdivided into encomiendas, ideally one encomienda per Indian provincial unit, the labor and tribute of which was assigned for a lifetime to one Spaniard, the encomendero. Though the encomienda was in the countryside, the encomendero, following the general principles of the organization of the society, was a citizen of the city and maintained his principal establishment there. The encomenderos indeed long dominated Spanish city society, as heads of retinues, members of town councils, and the chief patrons of merchants, artisans and clerics. During the sixteenth century and long after, most parts of the Indies could be described as consisting of Spanish cities and Indian towns which formed their hinterlands.

The first area of Spanish impact was the Caribbean, where many lasting patterns were set, but that area itself soon faded to relative insignificance with the exhaustion of precious metals and catastrophic demographic loss among the Indian population. The Spaniards proceeded from Hispaniola and Santo Domingo, the main Caribbean center, towards the mainland in two roughly simultaneous streams, one to Cuba and then Mexico, the other to the area of the Isthmus of Panama, then called Tierra Firme, and from there on to Peru. Peru and Mexico, with their large Indian populations, rich agriculture, strong provincial structures, and vast silver deposits, constituted the real substance of sixteenth-century Spanish America. The rest of the mainland was a fringe and dependency, conquered and to some extent ruled from these two truly central regions, with their capitals of Lima and Mexico City, which quickly became the seats of the only two viceroys of Spanish America. Our letters, mainly from Mexico, Peru, and the approaches thereto, reflect this situation.

As the central regions became consolidated, with substantial Spanish immigration and continuing productivity in silver, there grew up a fleet system which figures in some of the correspondence here. With a regularity which was something less than mechanical, a fleet would leave Seville carrying merchandise and people. Following the precedent of the original conquest, it split in the Caribbean, one part going to Mexico's port of Veracruz, and the other to the Isthmus. Here things were a bit more complicated. From the Caribbean port of Nombre de Dios (and later Portobello), a mere shell most of the time, goods were carried to the more developed center of Panamá on the Pacific side, and thence to Peru. Essentially Tierra Firme was Peru's port as Veracruz was Mexico's. The fleets then returned to Seville carrying silver, some Spaniards on their way home to a wealthy retirement, and letters like the ones which make up our book.

The reader will encounter quite a few unfamiliar terms in succeeding pages. In almost every letter appear the denominations of the money of the time. In the Indies, the primary unit was the peso, containing eight silver reales or gold tomines. In Spain, one spoke more often in terms of ducats. Both were reducible to the pure denomination of account, the maravedí, used especially by merchants and treasury officials in keeping records. The usual 'peso of good gold' of the sixteenth century was worth 450 maravedís, the ducat 375; thus the ratio was 6 : 5. In fact, in view of inflation in the Indies, there was some tendency to think that a peso there was equivalent to a ducat in Spain, a view in which one of our correspondents (Letter 17) concurs.

[1] A much more detailed statement on the nature and origin of the letters is in Otte, 'Die europäischen Siedler und die Probleme der Neuen Welt,' *Jahrbuch für Geschichte von Staat, Wirtschaft und Gesellschaft Lateinamerikas,* VI (1969), 1-40.

Map: The Spanish Indies, Sixteenth Century

PART I: CONQUEST

> Having few prospects in Nicaragua, we came to
> this district, where there's more gold and silver
> than iron in Biscay, and more sheep than in Soria,
> and great supplies of all kinds of provisions, and
> fine clothing and the best people that have been
> seen in the whole Indies.

> Gaspar de Marquina, Cajamarca, Peru, 1533

Since conquest and settlement were one single ongoing process
in Spanish America, we are a little reluctant to emphasize the
distinction between them by devoting a separate section to conquest alone. Yet only in this way can we illustrate to what an
extent the conquerors were acting like immigrants, businessmen
and settlers. Then too, the creation of Spanish cities, governmental jurisdictions and encomiendas took place at the time of
the conquests, as a direct reflection and integral part of them.
Spaniards tended to take their new cities – the framework of
their world – for granted, but the encomiendas and governor-
ships, being the great rewards of the enterprise, engendered
strife and comment; whole genres of conquest correspondence
grew up to brag, complain or petition about these matters.

We also wish to give some notion of the often down-to-earth
first reports on new areas, whether private (Letters 1, 6), official (Letter 2), or mercantile (Letters 4, 5). It is enlightening to
compare these with texts written some years after the occupation, such as Letter 3, or the last pages of Letter 36, both good
examples of incipient legend formation. Finally, in the accounts
of the conquest one gets an impression of the vast geographical
spread of the movement, the differences between regions, and
the varying success of the conquerors, who achieved quick victory and large rewards in the most densely settled areas of the
Andes and Mexico, but experienced long struggles and relative
poverty elsewhere.

1

1. Conquest in the personal view

Gaspar de Marquina, in Cajamarca, Peru, to his
father Martín de Gárate in Mendaro, Biscay,
1533[1]

> ... When he arrived where we were, the Governor
> rushed out with all his men and we attacked them
> and seized the lord and killed many of his people ...

To match the hundreds of extant reports to the crown that
governors and captains wrote about their conquests, there remain very few of the many letters the conquerors sent from the
scene to family and friends. Most of these – and it is a characteristic worth noting – stick close to personal matters (the
writer's fortunes, his prospects of coming home, his plans for
relatives and for himself), hardly mentioning the progress of the
conquest or the nature of the country. So the present letter is
doubly rare, since the impressionable young man who wrote it
did devote some space to the land of the Inca empire and the
climactic event of the capture of its emperor, Atahuallpa, in
which he took part. What he says is as fresh and direct as
conversation, and with the complete honesty of a person who
has no need to extol or excuse. Most accounts of the episode at
Cajamarca give prominence to the dramatic parley in which a
Dominican friar told Atahuallpa of Christianity and the Spanish
king, with the fighting beginning only when the emperor broke
off the talk. Gaspar skips over this as though it had never happened – not that it did not, but in his eyes it was an unimportant detail. What really happened was a great display of Indian
wealth and numbers, followed by a sudden, total reversal when
the Spaniards attacked. Gaspar bears the Indians no ill will and
appreciates their accomplishments, indeed more than many
other Spaniards of his time, but no need to justify the conquest
ever occurs to him, nor is he concerned about the Indians'
conversion (though he takes permanent Spanish government for
granted).
     An aspect that Gaspar lays bare more fully than do many

reports by leaders, who enlarge on their own bravery and skill, or keep silent, is the overwhelming Spanish military superiority. When fighting nomads, the Spaniards faced military near-equals. Even in the more settled areas, confined situations could cause them difficulty (like Mexico City, with its island situation, its maze of canals and stone buildings); but on flat land and against sedentary peoples, European steel and horses regularly produced results like those seen here. 'We killed 8,000 men in about two hours and a half.' Gaspar tends to attribute it to a miracle, while we may prefer the advantages of Eurasian weaponry and animals as an explanation. In any case it is a fact of capital importance, allowing the Spaniards to forget about the Indians much of the time and devote themselves to their own internal affairs and rivalries to a degree that never ceases to surprise.

Even in this letter, after all, the Indians and the fighting are mentioned almost in passing. They are relevant because they were instrumental in Gaspar's attaining wealth. That is what the letter is about: how Gaspar has gained wealth and success and can start doing something for his family, both past and future generations.

Note that Gaspar does not use the word 'soldier' for himself and his fellows; nor does it appear in our Letter 2, an official conquest report, nor in any of the other contemporary letters in this section. Only in the posterior, already myth-creating account of a lady in Paraguay (Letter 3) is the word to be found. The conquerors were free agents, emigrants, settlers, unsalaried and ununiformed earners of encomiendas and shares of treasure, and a great many other things that do not fit well with today's concept 'soldier.'

We will present a few details about Gaspar beyond those he gives in the letter. The use of a different surname in the Indies – in this case Marquina rather than Gaspar's father's name, Gárate – was a quite common phenomenon, particularly with the Basques, who were happy enough to let themselves be called anything the other Spaniards could pronounce. Gaspar was born out of wedlock, but recognized by his father and brought up carefully, so that he had strong family roots, as indeed the letter itself shows. In his early twenties at the time of the letter, apparently acting as Governor Pizarro's page, he was still one of the expedition's least influential members. After this, he soon bought a horse and began to acquire some business connections, but later in 1533 the Spanish vanguard imprudently went single file up a long steep slope not far from Cuzco, losing more men than in all the fighting up to that time, and Gaspar de Marquina among them.

Dear Sir:

It must be about three years ago that I got a letter from you, in which you asked me to send some money. God knows how sorry I was not to have anything to send you then, because if I had anything then there wouldn't have been any need for you to write; I've always tried to do the right thing, but there wasn't any possibility till now. You also told me to remember my homeland; God knows if I remember my homeland or not, but as I said, till now there hasn't been time to think of it. I give you my word that I never had a penny the whole time since I came to these parts until six months ago, when God was pleased to give me more than I deserved, and now I have over 3,000 ducats; please God that it will be for his holy service.

Sir, I'm sending you 213 pesos of good gold in a bar with an honorable man from San Sebastián; in Seville he'll have it turned into coin and then bring it to you. I'd send you more except he's taking money for other people too and couldn't take more. His name is Pedro de Anadel, I know him, and he's the kind of person who will get the money to you, so that's why I asked him to do me a favor and take you the money.

Sir, I would like to be the messenger myself, but it couldn't be, because we're in new country and haven't been here long, and they aren't giving license to leave except to married men who have been in these parts for a long time. I expect to be there with you in two years with the aid of our Lord; I swear to God that I have a greater desire to be there than you have to see me, so that I can give you a good old age.

Sir, I'll tell you something of my life since I came to these parts; you must know how I went to Nicaragua with Governor Pedrarias as his page, and I was with him till God was pleased to take him from this world. He died very poor and so all of his servants were left poor too, as the carrier of this letter can very well tell you when he sees you. Then a few days after he died we got news of how Governor Francisco Pizarro was coming to be governor of this kingdom of New Castile and so, hearing this news and having few prospects in Nicaragua, we came to this district, where there's more gold and silver than iron in Biscay, and more sheep than in Soria, and great supplies of all kinds of provisions, and fine clothing and the best people that have been seen in the whole Indies, and many great lords among them; one of them rules over 500 leagues. We have him prisoner in our power, and with him prisoner, a man can go by himself 500 leagues without getting killed, instead they give you whatever you need and carry you on their shoulders in a litter.

We took this lord by a miracle of God, because our forces wouldn't be enough to take him nor to do what we did, but God gave us the victory miraculously over him and his forces. You must know that we came here with Governor Francisco Pizarro to the land of this lord where he had 60,000 warriors, and there were 160 Spaniards with the governor, and we thought our lives were finished because there was such a horde of them, and even the women were making fun of us and saying they were sorry for us because we were going to get killed; but afterwards their bad thoughts turned out the opposite. The lord came with all his armed men within two shots of a crossbow from where we were camped and pitched his camp there, and then from there he came to see the governor and what kind of people we were, with about 5,000 men all dressed in his livery, and him in a litter covered with gold, with a hundred nobles carrying him and sweeping the ground in front of his litter, and all of them singing in unison, and when he arrived where we were, the governor rushed out with all his men and we attacked them and seized the lord and killed many of his people, most of the ones that came with him, and then we went out where all the rest of the warriors were, all armed with lances 15 feet long, and we routed them all. In the rout we killed 8,000 men in about two hours and a half, and we took much gold and clothing and many people. It would be too long to tell if it all were told; the bearer of the present letter can inform you, and I won't say more because as I say, it would be too long to tell.

Give my greetings to Catalina and my brothers and sisters and my uncle Martín de Altamira and his daughters, especially the older one, because I am much in her debt, and also to my cousins Martín de Altamira and Marina de Gárate and my uncle San Juan de Gárate and my uncle Pedro Sánchez de Arizmendi and all the rest of my relatives, because I've already forgotten many of their names. I really want you to greet them all from me and tell them that I greatly desire to see them, and pleasing God I'll be there soon. Sir, the only thing I want to ask you is to do good for the souls of my mother and all my relatives, and if God lets me get there, I'll do it very thoroughly myself. There is nothing more to write at present except that I'm praying to our Lord Jesus Christ to let me see you before I die. From Cajamarca, in the kingdom of New Castile, 20th of July, 1533.

Your son who would rather see than write you,
        Gaspar de Gárate

[On the outside is a memorandum to Anadel, bearer of the letter:]

Sir, I implore you to write me with the first people who come, and if by chance God our Lord has been pleased to take my father from this world, give the 213 pesos to my uncle Martín de Altamira and to San Juan de Gárate, jointly to both, and if one of them is dead, to either of them, so that with 100 pesos they can do good for the souls of my parents Martín de Gárate and María Ramírez de Altamira, and divide the other 113 pesos among my brother and sisters, and in case both my uncles are dead, to my brother Jorge de Gárate with a guardian, who as I say should do good for my parents with the hundred

and divide all the rest between himself and his and my brothers
and sisters, all equally.

      Gaspar de Marquina

[1] Published in Spanish and English in Appendix I of Lockhart, *The Men of
Cajamarca*, which also includes further biographical material on Gaspar.

2. A standard conqueror's report

Pedrarias de Avila, governor of Tierra Firme, in
Panamá, to the emperor, 1525[1]

    We hear news of great wealth.

It is a shame, in a way, that the best-known early official
reports from the Indies are Columbus' hand-waving Italianate
pictures of an island paradise, and Cortés' university prose,
elegantly magnifying himself and his conquest. As fine and
informative as these writings are, they are not representative of
the scores of reports that Spanish leaders sent the crown every
year from new areas rich and poor, important and unimportant.
There, sobriety and woodenness ruled. Yes, there were bows to
the king, and some talk of spreading Christianity, far more than
in private letters, and even some mention of marvels of nature
and divine intervention, but all in few words, one item after the
next, in matter-of-fact, unexcited language corresponding well
to the conquerors' generally Spartan temperament. The message
usually went to the basics of whether or not the climate was
tolerable for Europeans; whether the Indians were settled and
agricultural, capable of sustaining encomiendas and Spanish
cities; and whether there was gold, silver or some other product
that could subsidize imports from Europe and pay the crown
the revenues it desired.

We have chosen the present letter because it has a little of
everything; it illustrates the points above, and more. In the
second and third decades of the sixteenth century, Tierra Firme
and its capital Panamá were the clearing house for exploration
and conquest in both directions along the South Sea (the Pacific, with the North Sea in this context being the Caribbean).
Thus two major conquests appear underway in this letter, that

of Nicaragua led by Francisco Hernández de Córdoba and others, and that of the 'east' or Peru led by Pizarro and Almagro. The relay system of conquest, with each new area conquered by people and resources from the immediately preceding one, is seen very clearly here, as well as the tensions that grew out of it. The governor would aid some important citizens in outfitting expeditions which he sent out in his name to add new territories to his own jurisdiction. But the subordinates, who usually took much of the initiative and bore most of the expense, invariably sought independence, and often attained it. In this letter Gil González de Avila, a former quasi-subordinate of Pedrarias, is causing trouble in Nicaragua, but that was only the beginning, for Pedrarias would later have to come there in person to quell a rebellion; before many years both Nicaragua and Peru would be independent of Tierra Firme. Thus it is by no means atypical that this report speaks more of conflicts among Spaniards than of fighting with Indians, or that notaries should be spilling ink, taking and authenticating evidence against fellow Spaniards, at the ends of the earth.

Famous names abound in the letter. Two, Benalcázar and Soto, evoke careers which illustrate the continuity of personnel and the repeating cycle of tension in the Spanish conquests. Both men came to prominence under Pedrarias in Tierra Firme, then moved to Nicaragua, as the most important new area then being opened up. From Nicaragua they later went as quite major leaders to the far wealthier Peru, where their very influence made them unacceptable to the Pizarros, so with riches gained in Peru they undertook further conquests, Benalcázar in Quito and New Granada, Soto in North America. The person referred to as 'an Oviedo' is Gonzalo Fernández de Oviedo, the voluble and sharp-tongued chronicler. Fray Francisco de Bobadilla, who is here being gently nominated for bishop (conquerors would try to have the most prominent of their ecclesiastical companions named bishop of their area), did not attain that dignity, but did later appear in Peru. He figures again in Letter 25.

We have left geographical names as they are in the original

text and will not attempt to identify them further, since the important thing here is the generic aspect, the sheer variety of strange new names written down with as little explanation as if they were Seville and Toledo.

Sacred Catholic Caesarean Majesty:

On the tenth of this month of April of '25 there arrived here in this city of Panamá a messenger from the west, named Sebastián de Benalcázar, who has taken part in everything that has been done there, and was sent by my lieutenant Francisco Hernández with a letter in which he reports the following things:

At the Doubtful Strait a town called Bruselas was founded, at the site of Urutina, which has plains on one hand, and the sea on the other, and good fisheries. The land is fertile, with good orchards, and the Indians are peaceful. The town is in the midst of all the people of those provinces. It is a very good region with good waters and air and hunting and fishing in quantity and rich land with good orchards, well suited for the native grain, which it bears in abundance.

From this settlement to the province of Nequecheri is thirty-five leagues. The land up to there is very populated and abundant. In this province there is a populated area of more than three leagues, and in the middle of it they founded and settled the new city of Granada. In the surrounding region are up to 8,000 native households; it has good rivers, gardens, fishing and hunting. The city is on the banks of the fresh-water sea. In this city they made a very sumptuous church, which is well served and adorned. No town was founded in the province of Nicaragua because though it is very large in itself, it is only the beginning of the land, and there was no necessity to settle there.

From this New Granada they went down to the province of Ymabite, in the midst of the great and very populated province of Masaya; and in the province of Endevi and Managua next to this province of Masaya there is a great fiery crater that never ceases to burn; at night the great fire seems to touch the skies and lights up everything as clear as daytime for fifteen leagues around. In this province of Ymabite, in the middle of it, the new city of León was founded; in the surroundings are 15,000 native families. They built the best church there that has been erected in these parts. Near this city of León is another high mountain, with fire coming out above its peak from five mouths, clearly visible day and night; around the mountain there is a great quantity of sulfur. All this land is very level, and there are very large rivers in it, though in some parts there is a lack of water. Some of the rivers are very hot, so that they can hardly be crossed for the heat of the water; there is a fountain so constantly boiling that if they put in a fowl or something else raw it is immediately cooked, and if they want to roast something it can be roasted quickly by the heat of the water. This city is also not far from the fresh-water sea, and has many large orchards and groves.

The fresh-water sea has two arms, one of them thirty leagues wide; going from one to the other is a strait through which the water flows, and between the two arms is a small lake in which there are many populated islands. On this sea they launched for my lieutenant a brigantine that can be carried in pieces, and using it they explored and circumnavigated the entire sea. They found an outlet or river through which it is drained, but the brigantine was not able to navigate it because it is very rocky and has a strong current besides two very large rapids, so they explored it in a canoe, but could not find its mouth. It is thought to flow into the North Sea.

In the interior of this land another captain went with some men eighty leagues farther and found the country very populated, with large groves of sandalwood, citrine, cedar and pine, oaks of different kinds, and cork trees in great quantities; they have been making a great deal of pitch from the pines.

From this city of León they went ahead discovering and pacifying as far as the great city of Nequepio, which they said was the same as Melaca where Alvarado had arrived with Cortés' men; they saw where he had had his camp, and they saw some of the things he left there, especially a cannon and some footwear. From there the men turned back, and while they were quartered in a city called Toreva, Gil González arrived with some horsemen, musketeers and crossbowmen in the middle of the night, shouting 'St Gil, death, death to traitors,' and at the noise the captain ran out with the men he had and fought without knowing against whom, and some cavaliers and horses were killed, and then Gil González, after the men and horses were dead, called out loudly saying 'Peace, sir Captain, peace in the name of the king,' and Captain Soto answered 'peace, in the name of the emperor.' Believing the peace was real and not feigned, Captain Soto withdrew his men; although his companions told him that Gil González was acting deceitfully in the expectation of more men, he still turned aside with his men. Then when Gil González was stronger, more of his men having arrived, and the other side trusting in peace, seeing his advantage he started the fighting again and took from them 130,000 pesos of local low-carat gold and some other spoils, as though they were his enemies. When Gil González saw the error he had made, and that he could not maintain his position, he abandoned his men, leaving behind the banner and some halberds and a folding chair and some other stores, and went away with ten horsemen and twenty foot. My lieutenant sent me sealed and authenticated evidence of all this; I am sending your majesty a signed copy and keeping the original, thinking that because of the bad ink with which it is written, after such a long journey it might be illegible when it arrives there.

He also says that more than 400,000 souls have been converted to our holy Catholic faith of their own free will, and more continually come to request baptism, because the Indians in one town where a wooden cross had been set up tried to burn it and never succeeded, and then all the people of the town died of pestilence without an Indian remaining, and seeing this miracle and other miracles that have occurred, the Indians of the region around came to be baptized and request crosses, which are given to them with the greatest ceremony possible. Also certain mosques that had not yet received images of Our Lady were struck by lightning and burned, and seeing this the people of those towns come to request images and crosses and baptism, and as there are few priests, the Indians themselves, seeing the acts the priests perform, cross themselves and sprinkle water on each other.

He also says that he has sent people in the direction of the North Sea to look for gold mines, feeling sure they exist; and they have written asking for permission to melt down and distribute the gold they have taken and what they should take or get from the mines in the future; I will write granting it as soon as possible.

Royal treasurer Alonso de la Puente will leave, with the aid of God, at the end of May, or by the end of June at latest, with all the gold he has and whatever more should come or could be obtained; he is not going now because this ship goes unescorted. When he goes he will take everything that should be here, as well as a full accounting of the royal treasury which has been and is under his care.

This then is what has been done toward the west along the South Sea by the expedition that went under my lieutenant Francisco Hernández. It was done without touching your majesty's royal treasury; some individuals in this your majesty's kingdom gave me their aid, because my own estate is not sufficient for the great expenses that present themselves every day.

Toward the east along the South Sea, as I have written your majesty, I sent another expedition under Captain Pizarro, my lieutenant in the east, with very good people and good equipment. We daily expect good news from them which will please God and your majesty and ennoble these kingdoms, because we hear news of great wealth. May our Lord guide it all so that it can in some way serve your majesty. For this expedition to the east the reverend father Maestrescuela don Fernando de Luque and Captain Pizarro and Diego de Almagro have aided me with their own means, showing the good will that true vassals of your majesty should.

I am busying myself with building ships and doing what is necessary to bring back spices from the islands, as pilots assure me can be done. I implore your majesty, since expenses here are so great and for this enterprise of the spice islands your majesty's aid is necessary, that you order me given favor and aid for

it, and also that you have friars and learned persons sent to
instruct the Indians in the things of our holy Catholic faith,
because they are much needed here. The reverend father fray
Francisco de Bobadilla, provincial superior of the order of St
Mary of Mercy in this kingdom, is going to inform your majesty
of this matter, and I humbly beg you to give him audience,
because he is a person whose example and teaching have borne
much fruit in the conversion of the Indians, and he has given
much consolation to the Christians with his preaching; he has
founded some houses of his holy order here, and knows of
matters here as an eyewitness. Order him to return forthwith,
because his teaching is greatly needed by both Indians and
Christians, and order him favored so that he can bring back
friars with whom to augment the holy faith of Jesus Christ,
since that is the principal thing your majesty has charged me
with in your service.

I have been informed that Captain Gil González, forgetting
the benefits he received from me in this kingdom and how
much I, trying to serve your majesty, helped him with the expedition under his command, has departed from the truth and
told falsehoods to your majesty and those of your very high
council. And also they say that an Oviedo who was here filling
certain offices for Secretary Lope Conchillos and fled secretly
in fear of the punishment his crimes merited has presented
certain charges against me, and since any guilt on my part
should be punished more severely than in another, I humbly beg
your sacred majesty, in remuneration for the services I have
performed since my childhood and that I did for the blessed
Catholic Monarchs of glorious memory, for your grandfather
and your father and for your majesty, that you appoint a judge
above suspicion to come and review my performance, because I
feel sure that then your majesty will be informed of my services, and I will be freed from the iniquitous accusations the
above two have made against me. Also I beg your majesty to
give me license to come and kiss your royal hands and feet,
because in respect to your majesty no one should dare tell you
an untruth, and whoever does not do right by his own good

name will not do right in the service of God and your majesty.[2]

[1]Published in Spanish in Raúl Porras Barrenechea, ed., *Las relaciones primitivas de la conquista del Perú*, pp. 59–62.

[2]The concluding formulas and signature are missing.

3. The woman as conqueror

Doña Isabel de Guevara, in Asunción, Paraguay,
to Princess doña Juana, regent in Spain, 1556[1]

... The men became so weak that all the tasks
fell on the poor women ...

The heroic woman in the style of early North American history is not really a central figure of the Spanish conquests. Mainly Indian servant women accompanied the conquerors. Most expeditions set out with no Spanish women at all; at most one or two camp followers or mistresses of leaders, like the well-known Inés Suárez in Chile. But in the relay system of conquest, at the more established base from which the expedition left there would always be wives and female relatives of the conquerors, who would begin to appear in the new country almost before the fighting was over. And legends formed around them. In the rich central regions the first women became known as grain goddesses and bearers of European civilization, each reputed to have introduced wheat and other European foods and amenities. On the periphery, tales were told of the hardships and battle prowess of the once humble women who came with the conquerors, Inés Suárez again being a good example.

The present letter pertains more to the second phenomenon, though with some differences. The Plata region was indeed the periphery of the periphery, one of the most difficult and, in sixteenth-century terms, economically hopeless regions into which Spaniards ventured. However, this was not known in Spain when don Pedro de Mendoza, expecting another Peru, bypassed the step-by-step series of conquests and brought a great expedition directly from Seville, including no small number of women who were not camp followers; some were ladies with the title of *doña* and noble surnames like Guevara. As to the rest, doña Isabel tells it, not untruly, but in legendary and heightened form, twenty years after the fact and with the urgency of a disappointed claimant.

Very high and powerful lady:

Several women came to this province of the Río de la Plata along with its first governor don Pedro de Mendoza, and it was my fortune to be one of them. On reaching the port of Buenos Aires, our expedition contained 1,500 men, but food was scarce, and the hunger was such that within three months 1,000 of them died; it was such a famine that the one of Jerusalem cannot equal it, nor any other be compared to it. The men became so weak that all the tasks fell on the poor women, washing the clothes as well as nursing the men, preparing them the little food there was, keeping them clean, standing guard, patrolling the fires, loading the crossbows when the Indians came sometimes to do battle, even firing the cannon, and arousing the soldiers who were capable of fighting, shouting the alarm through the camp, acting as sergeants and putting the soldiers in order, because at that time, as we women can make do with little nourishment, we had not fallen into such weakness as the men. Your highness will readily believe that our contributions were such that if it had not been for us, all would have perished; and were it not for the men's reputation, I could truthfully write you much more and give them as the witnesses. I believe others will write this story to your highness at greater length, so I will cease.

When this so perilous turbulence was over, the few who were still alive decided to ascend the river, weak as they were and with winter coming on, in two brigantines, and the weary women nursed them and looked after them and cooked their meals, carrying firewood on their backs from off the ship, and encouraging them with manly words not to let themselves die, that soon they would reach a fertile land, and carrying them on our shoulders to the brigantines with as much tenderness as if they were our own sons. And when we came upon a kind of Indians called Timbues who are great fishermen, again we served the men in finding different sorts of dishes so that they wouldn't get sick from eating fish without bread when they were so weak.

Afterwards they decided to ascend the Paraná in search of provisions, in which voyage the unfortunate women underwent such hardships that God gave them life miraculously because he saw that the men's lives depended on them, for they took all the tasks of the ship so to heart that a woman who did less than another felt affronted; they worked the sail, steered the ship, sounded the depth, bailed out the water, took the oar when a soldier was unable to row, and exhorted the soldiers not to be discouraged, that men were meant for hardships. And the truth is, no one forced the women to do those things, nor did they do them out of obligation; only charity obliged them. Thus they arrived at this city of Asunción, which though today it is very rich in provisions, was then greatly in need of them, and the women had to turn to their tasks anew, making clearings with their own hands, clearing and hoeing and sowing and harvesting the crop with no one's aid until such time as the soldiers recovered from their weakness and began to rule the land, acquiring the service of Indian men and women, until the country at last attained its present state.

I wanted to write this and bring it to your highness' attention to let you know how ungratefully I have been treated in this land, because recently most of it was distributed among the Spaniards here, both the first-comers and the new arrivals, without any consideration of me and my hardships, and I was left out without being given the service of a single Indian. I greatly wish I were free to present myself before your highness and tell you the services I have done his majesty and the injustices they are now doing me, but that is not in my power, since I am married to a gentleman of Seville named Pedro de Esquivel, who, through serving his majesty, was the reason my hardships were forgotten and now are renewed, because three times I have taken the executioner's knife away from his throat, as your highness may know. So I beg you to order that my encomienda be granted to me in perpetuity, and that in gratification of my services my husband be appointed to some office suiting the quality of his person, since for his own part, his services merit it. Our Lord prolong your royal life and estate for many years. From this city of Asunción, 2nd of July, 1556.

 Your highness' servant who kisses your royal hands,
   Doña Isabel de Guevara

[1] Published in Spanish in *Cartas de Indias*, pp. 619–21.

4. The merchant and the conquest of Peru

Martín de Zubizarreta, Basque merchant, in Nombre de Dios, Tierra Firme, to his employers Juan Sáez de Aramburu, Francisco de Churruca, Martín Pérez de Achotegui and company, in Seville, 1526[1]

 . . . There was some breakage in the olive oil . . .

The conquests would have been impossible without the European equipment, metal and supplies that Spanish merchants delivered to America; nor, without the prospect of a European-style life that the merchandise held out, would the conquerors have had as strong a motivation for their campaigns. Thus merchants are woven into the fabric of the conquest as one of its characteristic phenomena, and their letters are most informative, throwing the process into quite a different light, with their talk of horseshoes and nails, casks of wine, or considerations of currency and credit. Sometimes a merchant would actually accompany an expedition, but his more usual station was at the base of operations, where he would receive shipments from Spain, sell them or send them on to the conquerors, and send remittances back. When the focus of conquest in Tierra Firme shifted to Panamá and the west coast, the merchants stayed for a while in Nombre de Dios on the Caribbean, where we find Martín de Zubizarreta, writer of the present letter. It may be viewed as a sequel to Letter 2, which is from the same region a year earlier. By now Governor Pedrarias has gone to assert his authority in Nicaragua, but the limitations of Nicaraguan wealth are already becoming apparent, and attention is shifting towards Peru, Pizarro and Almagro. A little later, as Peru becomes dominant, the merchants will make Panamá their base, and subsequently Lima as well.

Import merchants in the Indies at this time were usually representatives of trans-Atlantic commercial networks with headquarters in Seville. Sometimes the merchants in America were partners, having made an investment; or sometimes, as here, they were factors who were paid a salary or commission. In either case they were junior men, quite dependent on the senior figures in Seville for their advancement. They could not make too many decisions independently, and they were under pressure to sell quickly and send a steady stream of money back. Their letters show this state of things in their often wavering tone and extraordinarily weak statements: 'I believe that pleasing God I will sell everything . . . as quickly as I can.' The general content of the messages is reporting on local demand and conditions, so that the people in Seville can decide what to invest in, and registering in great detail all remittances, with promise of more. The local man is always apologetic for the present, hopeful for the future. In such letters conditions are generally painted as bad at the moment, while untold riches are to be expected within a few days.

Mercantile companies were fluid, transitory arrangements; underlying continuity and security came from ties of blood, marriage and region. In this case, though the company headquarters was in Seville, all the members were from Biscay, indeed all from the single town of Azcoitia, and Francisco de Churruca was Martín de Zubizarreta's (doubtless older) brother. A personal note is characteristic of merchant letters, and often, as here, the local man asks favors for wife and children back in Spain. Senior partners were well aware of the loyalty this assured, and when ties were lacking they sometimes arranged marriages so that the departing factor would, so to speak, leave a hostage. Zubizarreta had already been representing his brother and other Basques in the Caribbean for some nine years, and continued to do so for another three before returning to Castile, apparently for good.

This letter has some very technical passages describing gold remittances. To understand the conquest and settlement of Spanish America generally, it is necessary to have an adequate notion of the role of precious metals. The subject tends to be buried under myths and stereotypes of a 'thirst for gold.' One gains a bit better perspective by thinking of precious metals simply as money, and indeed the merchants often referred to gold or silver shipments in just those terms, as *dineros*. But the core of the matter is that precious metals were an export product, the only viable one, to trade for the equipment that fed the conquests and the clothing and accoutrements that would make life in the European manner possible. Neither conquerors nor merchants cared anything for the metal itself, which they traded immediately; they cared for the value and buying power in it. And so, with metal of varying quality in circulation, both merchants and settlers had to become experts in its evaluation; the character of a commercial transaction was altered completely if the value of the metal was miscalculated. In this game, the merchants stayed ahead, because they kept in touch with the money markets in Spain, as this letter shows, and they had greater experience with the very empirical methods of assaying. Observe Zubizarreta's statement: 'I received the 16-carat gold as being 12-carat, in exchange for merchandise.'

As to the technicalities, 'good gold,' pure or practically so, was worth 450 maravedís a peso, and *oro de minas* or gold as it came from the mines, what we have called 'mine-gold,' was accepted at this value. The peso and its subdivisions the tomín and the grain were not values but weights, properly speaking, and pesos of lower-carat gold had to be converted mentally into good gold to obtain the true value, an operation Zubizarreta carries out each time.

Noble sirs:

On the 30th of July of the present year of 1526 I received from shipmaster Alonso Buenaño your letter dated the 29th of May of the present year from the city of Seville, and I also received the merchandise you gentlemen sent me with Buenaño.

All arrived, praise to God, in very good condition, the wines as well as the flour, and all the boxes and the rest contained in Alonso Buenaño's receipt, though there was some breakage in the olive oil and the jars of honey and the vinegar, as will appear in the bill of payment I made out to Buenaño. I paid the freight in good gold as the receipt stipulates, and the truth is that he deserved it, because he delivered the merchandise in good shape, though very little of it has been sold up to now on account of there being few people in the land. Aside from there being few already, Governor Pedrarias de Avila took with him to Nicaragua all the men he could remove from the country, because he went after Francisco Hernández, his captain, who they told him had rebelled. We think that, God willing, he will soon be back with the people he took. I believe that pleasing God I will sell everything, this shipment as well as what I had before, as quickly as I can. And I think that we will earn money with it, even if the sale is somewhat delayed, because until now we have been awaiting a captain called Diego de Almagro, who went exploring along the eastern shore of the South Sea. We thought he was going to bring back an infinite amount of gold, to judge by the richness of the land, but now it seems that the Indians have defended themselves against him, and leaving all his men there he has founded a town. He has arrived now, and brought about 10,000 pesos in gold, for which reason I am about to leave for Panamá, because the members of his company owe me more than 500 gold pesos, and I am going there to collect it. Because of that, and because they will quickly melt down what he brought back, and the ships are ready to leave again, I am not sending you gentlemen an account of what has been sold up to now, but pleasing God in the first ship that should leave this city of Nombre de Dios I will send an account of everything sold and what remains unsold. Also I will send you all the gold I can, and I believe we will earn a great deal of money on the goods. Although at present there is little money, the land is so disposed that there soon may be, because we are expecting Pedrarias de Avila with much gold. And we expect the people

Diego de Almagro left behind will send the same, since that was the agreement among them. He is coming for horsemen, because they have found the local people, I mean the Indians, to be very strong, and for that reason he has not brought much gold. May it please God to remedy it all as he knows is needed; certainly we expect much wealth from that land.

With Juanés de Astigarraga I sent you gentlemen 296 pesos and 2 grains in the following manner:

167 pesos and 4 tomines in mine-gold;

38 pesos, 2 tomines, in 14-carat gold, which is, in good gold, 23 pesos, 6 tomines, 5½ grains;

13 pesos, 4 tomines, 6 grains, in 16-carat gold, which makes 9 pesos, 5 tomines, 5 grains;

133 pesos, 4 tomines, in 16-carat gold, which makes 95 pesos, 5½ grains;

all of which gold pesos I trust you gentlemen will receive. Truly at present I could not send you more money, because the country is somewhat exhausted; but pleasing God I will supply money as soon as I can. I think we will make a profit on the gold I am sending you, because it is good. I received the 16-carat gold as being 12-carat, in exchange for merchandise.

I sent you gentlemen 600 pesos of good gold by Fernán Gómez, citizen of Palos. I am sure that, pleasing our Lord, you will have received it by now. May it please God that it has arrived safely in your city as I desire. Also I am sending you 71 pesos in the form of some mine-gold and some necklaces with designs. I beg you, when you receive the gold from Juanés de Astigarraga, to sell the mine-gold, and when converted into coin you send it with a person of confidence to milady wife in the town of Azcoitia. Also send her the necklaces; but should you gentlemen think best, sell it all and send it all in coin, as indeed I expect you will do. My wife has need of the money, as you know, to pay a certain debt.

Also I am sending you a receipt made out by shipmaster Juan Pérez de Menchola for the amount of 19 pesos of 20-carat gold in the form of a large medal. I gave it to him to take to Seville and sell, and when converted into coin to send it to my wife. It appears that since he died on the way, he never sent it. I implore you gentlemen, since you have the power to act for me, to collect it from the estate of this Juan Pérez de Menchola, may God rest his soul. And when you have recovered it, send it to my wife with the rest. If you can't recover it there, send the receipt to my wife, so she can collect it in Azcoitia. Also I sent you by Francisco González, pilot, 269 pesos, 5 tomines, 8 grains of good gold:

> 221 pesos of 20-carat gold, which makes 196 pesos, 6 tomines, 7½ grains;
>
> 18 pesos, 4 tomines, 6 grains in 18-carat gold, which makes 15 pesos, 4 tomines;
>
> 86 pesos in 15-carat gold, which makes 57 pesos, 3½ tomines;

all of which makes as I say 269 pesos, 5 tomines, 8 grains. May you receive it together with the rest. The gold is good, and I think you will make a profit on it. When there are grains over and above the carats, each grain is worth 5 maravedís, because any gold with grains in addition to carats is assayed gold, and as I say is worth 5 maravedís per grain. Take care to look closely at the gold with grains. And if you think best, you can mix the gold assayed at 20 carats with the 16-carat gold, then have it assayed and see how it turns out. Send to tell me the result, so that I can know what to do here about the different kinds of gold, though I think that from now on there will be no bad gold at all.

The receipts made out by Juanés de Astigarraga, Francisco González, and Juan Pérez de Menchola go along with this letter. Don't neglect to send the goods I wrote to request of you through Fernán Gómez, because there is money to be earned with them, despite the country's being quite flooded with merchandise at the present. But with the arrival of Pedrarias de Avila and his people, and the arrival of the caravel of Diego de Almagro, all will be sold, and it might arrive at a time when everything is selling well. And Alonso Buenaño will inform you gentlemen of what goes on here. As I say, because of the departure of the ships I am about to leave in order to be at the melting down and distribution in Panamá, and am not sending you an account of everything. But with the first person who leaves here I will send you a complete account and write you at great length. I think that some people are going with the intention of shipping merchandise back here. If you gentlemen decide to send something, then let it be before any of the others do, and we will steal the fodder from the horse. Alonso de Buenaño will advise you of everything.

Also I send you a decree the governor has had made out to me, giving me as a citizen of this city permission to bring four blacks here without paying any duties in Spain. This is part of the grant his majesty made to this land to import five hundred blacks freely without paying any duties. And you gentlemen can buy these four blacks and send them to me for me to sell them here, and we will earn money with them. They must be from eighteen to twenty-five years old, and should be new from their homeland and strong, for those are the ones needed here, to get gold in the mines. And in the shipment, if you gentlemen send one, don't send me lances, because they have no price at all here, nor any more iron nor horseshoes, except perhaps some shoes fitted for mules with plain nails, which should have a good shaft even though it costs somewhat more. And send me four or five thousand loose nails, because here nails wear out quicker than shoes. And send me cinches with their hooks, for mules, since I greatly need them for my beasts, and also some fine serge, which should be from Carmona. And some common linen if it is very good, and some heavy carter's thread, and some long packing-needles with good-sized eyes, and two or three dozen cattle bells, and some things like that. And as to earthenware, don't send any at all, because it is a waste, except perhaps some stewpots and casseroles; and two or three dozen small hampers for carrying things, and two or three dozen bundles of cordage fiber, and let there be a good quantity of that.

Our Lord guard and increase the life and honor of your noble persons for a very long time as I desire. In Nombre de Dios, the

28th of September 1526.

Your very faithful servant,

Martín

And gentlemen, don't forget to send that money of mine to milady wife because, as you know, she has need of it. And I ask you as a favor always to take charge of supplying my household, since I am so far away and there is no one else who could do it for her.

[1] Published in Spanish, with comment, in Otte, 'Mercaderes vascos en Tierra Firme a raíz del descubrimiento del Perú,' *Mercurio Peruano*, nos. 443–4 (1964), 81–9.

5. The merchant and the conquest of Mexico

Hernando de Castro, in Santiago, Cuba, to his senior partner Alonso de Nebreda in Seville, 1520[1]

... This Cortés is in that city, some sixty or seventy leagues from the sea ...

Until all are at peace, it is clearly no time to do business ...

Having been introduced to some aspects of mercantile organization and correspondence in Letter 4, the reader will perhaps be prepared for this letter, written earlier but longer and more complex. Here, in addition to the characteristics seen before, we glimpse the operation of a large-scale commercial network with branches and representatives in several places at once. In the letter, names fly by bewilderingly. Without trying to be exhaustive, let us detail some of the most important figures. All were from Burgos, Old Castile, the town whose merchants, in the period before the discovery of America, long shared dominance of Spanish international trade with the Genoese.

(1) Alonso de Nebreda, recipient of the present letter, based in Seville, the head of interests trading towards both Flanders and the Caribbean.

(2) Juan de Ríos, Nebreda's brother-in-law as well as long-standing factor and partner, based in Santo Domingo.

(3) Hernando de Castro, writer of the present letter, from a prominent Burgos family, important investor along with Nebreda and Ríos in a new venture to sell goods in Cuba and 'Yucatán'; yet acting as factor and junior partner, based in Santiago, Cuba.

(4) The Herrera brothers: (a) Francisco, referred to here sometimes as 'Herrera' and 'young Francisco,' Castro's chief aide, who despite intentions to leave eventually succeeded Castro as the company's factor in Santiago. (b) Juan, working for Juan de Ríos, the Santo Domingo representative; in Ríos' name, he took merchandise to Mexico, selling it to:

(5) Pedro de Maluenda, Hernando de Castro's cousin, not part of the Nebreda-Castro enterprise at the moment, but in Mexico as a representative of Cuban governor Diego Velázquez.

(6) Fernando de Santa Cruz, nephew of Castro, killed in a shipwreck on his way to Mexico, taking merchandise for his father,

(7) Juan Fernández, in Seville, who was Castro's cousin, as well as his associate in selling black slaves.

All of these people maintained close personal and commercial connections, investing in joint enterprises or more individual ones, working for each other or for themselves as it best suited them at the moment, but still somehow within the framework of the larger group. Nebreda, Castro and Ríos also invested in a ship (in Cuba at the time of the letter), saving freight costs but earning themselves much worry and trouble, as the reader will see.

Perhaps two more names will bear a little explanation. 'Villalón' is a reference to the Fair of Villalón; Nebreda and Castro had bought a large part of the goods for the new venture on credit, and the debts fell due at the time of the fair. 'Baltasarejo' is the Spanish-speaking black slave Castro so praises and considers indispensable; nevertheless, he ran away shortly after the letter was written.

In this letter we see the importance for conquest-period commerce of the *fundición* or melting down of metals. The practice was that at the conquest of a new area, and for some time thereafter, all precious metals that accrued in any way were brought together into a common pile (or were supposed to be), then at irregular, widely-spaced intervals melted down, evaluated, and redistributed to the whole body of conquerors, following criteria that are too complex to go into here. This procedure did not last long, but while it did, it gave commerce a stop-and-go, highly speculative quality, with merchants constantly forced to extend credit, and not for a fixed term, but for the first melting down (which might come late or never), or even for the second one. If the amount melted down proved small, disaster ensued; if large, a time of great demand and high prices would follow immediately.

Another frequent practice illustrated in the letter is the seizing of goods to pay debts. The world worked on credit; with great distances and unsettled conditions so unfavorable to debt collection, the creditors demanded bondsmen, who as often as not were merchants. Despite the merchants' great skill in avoiding seizure and their great resentment when it happened, having a part of one's stocks confiscated for debts, one's own or someone else's, was a normal part of a merchant's life.

In this letter Hernando de Castro evinces not only a charmingly different perspective on the conquest of Mexico, but a very good grasp of the course of the conflict between Governor Diego Velázquez of Cuba and the subordinate he had helped outfit, Hernando Cortés, who was now declaring independence (another situation of the type discussed in relation to Letter 2). At this time Velázquez has already sent the second large contingent under Narváez to bring Cortés to submission, but Castro expects further trouble – 'all seems to be the passion, anger and vengeance that impoverish men.' He sees the potential of the Mexican market, feels it will still be there when the Spaniards have resolved their conflicts, and is inclined to wait.

In the present case, the times proved more propitious for the Burgos merchants' goods than for their lives. The melting down in Cuba produced better results than those who had already left for Mexico would have imagined, and Castro sold his goods at a profit level approaching 200 percent, including even the flour that he is so pessimistic about in the letter. But within a very few years all the merchants of this group on the American side, except Castro, were dead in shipwrecks and other calamities. Castro himself went back to Spain after a year, then later returned to Cuba as royal factor and member of the town council of Santiago.

Jesus *Cuba, last day of August, 1520*

Very virtuous sir:

Francisco Vara left here on the 27th of last month, and I wrote by him of our arrival. After that Ambrosio Sánchez came and gave me a letter from you, and though he gave it to me when I was in bed being purged of some persistent fevers, I was very glad to receive it, and will now answer and tell what else is happening.

As to the shipment, I kept the ship loaded for twelve days, mainly to make arrangements with the sales tax collector; I said I wanted to go on to Tierra Firme, since I was registered for that destination, and I thought surely I would make him do the courteous thing. But then Mr Maestre Donato came, and because the deputy ordered him to present the decree the judges of the House of Trade issued, he brought it and it was read; then I had to unload, and I lost 100 pesos in duties because of it, but there was nothing else to do. And also there was no sign of Diego Velázquez coming, nor any news from Yucatán, and the men were all ailing, and the leaks in the ship were worrying me. And so I unloaded, and thank God, everything is in good condition, except the wines. If it weren't for the iron hoops I wouldn't have a drop left; I don't know what caused it, but I think bad hoops, and it has been a great worry. During unloading, one cask of the new white wine leaked out; and another half cask of red wine, not being fully matured, fermented in the cask and burst. But the rest, thank God, is in good shape, though there will be wastage as always. And so I have it all unloaded and here with me, and do not much regret not having gone farther for now, because of what I will now tell you.

One of the eighteen ships Diego Velázquez sent in his expedition has arrived back here, the flagship itself, which left from San Juan de Uloa on the 4th of May, and from the many letters it brought from people there, and from the men on the ship themselves, we have heard about everything that is going on, with full particulars. First they say that Hernando Cortés, the person who was there, before he knew that a fleet was coming from this island, left the coast and went inland to a very great city that they now call Venice. They say it has 80,000 citizens, and they call it Venice because of its greatness and because it is all surrounded by water, with drawbridges. This Cortés is there with all his men, fortified and at peace with the Indians, while he awaits the reply from a message he has sent to the king, and refuses obedience to the captain whom Diego Velázquez just now sent there. As I say, this Cortés is in that city, some sixty or seventy leagues from the sea. They say he is extremely rich in gold and silver, and those with him the same, and in great peace with the Indians, and he awaits, as I say, a reply from Castile. And so there he is with all this wealth. The other expedition that left later under Captain Narváez arrived on the 19th of April, but found no place to make camp, because at the port they came to there was neither house, hut, water nor firewood: only sandy beaches. For this reason he thought he would return with the fleet to the river of Grijalva, twelve leagues away, and disembark and make camp there, since the place was well suited for it. So things there up till now are not so smooth and peaceful as would be best, either for them or for merchandise. Those who have the gold have retired with it to that city, and those who hold the port, that is, those who just went there, are without a penny and are now seeking a share for themselves and vengeance on this Cortés. As to the merchandise that went in the fleet, six ships were lost, with forty Christians, among them my nephew Fernando de Santa Cruz, as I am writing to Juan Fernández; some of the merchandise aboard was saved, but it didn't fit on the other ships. So I give thanks to God for all, and am not sorry I did not go ahead from here myself, nor am I concerned about the decree from the gentlemen of the House of Trade. Until all are at peace, it is clearly no time to do business nor to put in an appearance there. It cannot last long thus; one person must command the country, not two. If, as they now write, Diego Velázquez should go there, all will turn out well; he is coming from Trinidad, 150 leagues from here, and some believe he is sure to go. I would like that, because I could either go with him or give him what I have left. I feel sure he will go, because if there was already much talk of that country before, now there is much more, about its great wealth and abundance in all things; and to be lord and rule in such a land would be a grand affair. Diego Velázquez will be here within twenty-five or thirty days to see to the melting down of the gold, which was not done for eighteen months, and to carry out the distribution of encomiendas; I hope to God this will help me in the sale of merchandise. And if the land of Yucatán is as they say, it will be just as good a time for me to take advantage of it after six months; then there will be more money than now, and they don't yet know even where they will be living. Whatever happens or should happen is by the will of God, and we must consider it good or even the best thing; content yourself with what God does, and that will be a great favor to me.

As to the sale of the merchandise, I can tell you, sir, that if they had set fire to this country on purpose it could not have been consumed so quickly, because 1,200 men have left this island for Yucatán and bought up the bulk of everything that had come from Castile. And though gold has been gathered in reasonable quantities, there are few people to sell to. So you must have double patience, first because I did not go on, and second because of the small sales. But I expect through God to do better than average in the end. And though I send you no money now, because there is none, one day you will receive more than you are expecting. May God give us good weather and health, amen. What troubles me most is that I and others have so much flour that the country is full of it. I have sold 5 casks at 7½ pesos on credit and have sold no more. It concerns me because, as you know, we could lose on it if time goes by and no demand for it develops. I am sending along a memorandum of what I have sold on credit; truly I have no need of instruments to test gold, since even if there were gold to test, they aren't in use here now. So I ask you many times, please have patience. With the arrival soon of Adelantado Velázquez and with the melting down, which will take place between now and Christmas, I expect to sell a great deal of it. And if not, we expect news from Yucatán any minute, and if it is as we believe, either everything will be sold here or we can reload. You can rest assured that there is no lack in me of diligence and desire to obtain good sales; instead my will to face what is coming only grows.

I wouldn't want to forget to write that at present you should not send me any merchandise whatever, even if they gave it to you gratis on the steps of the Exchange, because you cannot retrieve the money as quickly as you would think, no matter to what lengths you go. And so I beg you under no conditions send goods; indeed I will not receive them, to avoid giving a bad account of them.

When I got here I was told that Francisco de Garay, of Jamaica, had discovered another land sixty leagues beyond that of Diego Velázquez; they say it is all one, and one part as rich as the other. There chanced to be a brigantine here going to Jamaica, and I wrote Garay thinking that he would have money, and I might sell him the whole shipment. He answered me with a letter, a copy of which I'm sending along. You may well believe that if the goods were loaded now, I would go there with everything, but that could not be, because he was slow in replying, and the sailors pressed me to unload. Take a look at the letter, for two purposes. First, so you can tell Dr Matienzo the good news that there is gold in his abbacy, and at the melting down they expect to have 12,000 or 15,000 pesos of very fine gold, through which his income will be augmented. And the other thing is that I hope, God willing, to do business with Francisco de Garay as governor and captain, so that, as I have written, you and I would supply all the merchandise from Castile necessary for that island. If this is done, I promise you it will be profitable. Please God that it be for his service, amen.

I am sending out a ship that will go to the savannas for meat, with an Alonso Lucas, citizen of Jamaica, as captain; on the strength of this letter I mentioned, and since he issued a written obligation, I gave him 373 pesos worth of merchandise for Garay, as described in the memorandum, to be paid at the time gold is melted down in Jamaica, or in any case by next feast of Ash Wednesday. I would have liked to sell it at different prices and with better security, but I did this to begin cleaning up such a large stock, and also to begin doing business with him, since he is the best and most truthful person in this land. Please be happy with this as I am; I'm as sure that he will pay as if it were you who owed it. Do write me your clear opinion on this.

I already wrote that Hernando Gallego was going with his ship, which God preserve, to Yucatán. In it Francisco de Herrera, as he is writing you, shipped twenty-six casks of flour, two casks of red wine, and olive oil and vinegar, as appears by the receipt, all of which cost him 300 gold pesos. The ship left this port on the 17th of August. May God take it safely, amen. If you want to insure some of this, you can do as you please on the basis of the receipt and what he is writing. (I have nothing to do with it, nor any say in it.)

I have sold two of the blacks for 135 pesos, to be paid when gold is next melted down; one of them is for Juan Fernández and the other for us. I think that although I will not get such a price, since these were the best specimens of all, I will be able to sell the others too when the time of melting down comes, God willing; I don't want to sell them on credit. The one I brought who speaks Spanish does everything for me, since Francisco fell ill; it seems this land doesn't agree with Francisco, and he is returning in the ship, God save it. The black woman fell ill too, but is well again now; may God guide all for his service, amen. I have sold all the velvet at 3 pesos, to be paid at the time of melting down. I have a yard and a half left. This was good business, it seems to me.

Herrera fell ill as soon as he arrived, but through God, with treatment he recovered. Now he has had a relapse of tertian ague, and is being treated again. May God give him health as I desire; his illness certainly troubles me.

As to the merchandise that Juan de Herrera took from Santo Domingo to Yucatán for Juan de Ríos in this ship I mentioned, Juan de Herrera has written at length about it to Juan de Ríos. If I can, I will send you a copy along with this. The paragraph he writes on the subject is in substance this:

> Sir, I have come to terms with Pedro de Maluenda on 90 percent profit for all undamaged goods, and for what is damaged irreparably, whatever it cost in Santo Domingo. I consider this a good arrangement, sir, and would rather give it to him in this way than have it continue as mine. I don't know where we'll go from here, and if you knew what difficult navigation we have, and might even have to turn back, you would consider it much better than one might think. The terms are payment within six months, and if Alonso García should send the caravel back with money, Maluenda will send neither more nor less than I am able to. I have done this, so approve it; I swear to God that if I had not made this arrangement, I would have had to sell for much less. Not a man in the camp would have dared buy any of it, if I hadn't given it to him. That was the reason he took it because, our Lord willing, however bad things go, he will not lose, as he is in charge of all of the Adelantado's business here, things having to do with the expedition as well as money going to Diego Velázquez as his share, and so he has opportunity. And since he supplies the whole expedition, sailors and landsmen, with goods, in this way he can find an outlet for everything, and can collect from the first money that accrues. For this reason he dared take what no one else would come within a hundred leagues of taking. I consider it a very good sale, sir, and I have begun to hand over

the goods. I have had a good deal of trouble in the ships, because they say that this merchandise belongs to the Adelantado. If I don't seal this letter before settling with Maluenda, I will write about this in detail. As to wastage, of olive oil and of wine, it is impossible that there should not be much wastage. In everything I will try to do what is best for us. Since I know that Maluenda is a man who will not let gossip or troublemakers come between him and us, I would rather have 90 percent with him than 120 with someone else.

The letter is dated the first of May. The reason for this sale was that, as Captain Narváez seized Licentiate Ayllón and the notary and constable from Santo Domingo, and ordered them sent here as prisoners in the ship in which these goods were loaded, he had no choice but to unload. As six ships were lost, the others took on the goods that were salvaged, and so he had to do this, more from necessity than voluntarily. It will be all right; I am sure they will pay. I don't know what the profit will be, because freight is high, and there will be much damage to the merchandise and other costs. The best thing will be for him to remain there along with another employee of Juan de Ríos and then, when they get the first money, to bring it back. This is all I can tell you and that appears through his letter. I think you should approve it, sir, as I would, and though you don't see a penny now, someday it will come. I consider all that country extremely rich, though I am afraid the discord between this Hernando Cortés and Diego Velázquez will bring it to ruin. If no remedy comes from Castile, the country is no place for business; all seems to be the passion, anger and vengeance that impoverish men. May God send his mercy, or if not, then his justice; both are much needed. A mare or horse sells for 320 pesos, to be paid when there is money. It is an illustrious rich land, level and abundant, with peaceful people and many cities. May God direct all to his service, amen.

As to the flour I brought here, I'm afraid there will be little or no profit, because there is as much flour hereabouts as water, selling at 5½ or 6 pesos. Let us hope to do well with the other things, because there will be little gain in this.

In the matter of the ship now returning to Seville (God save it, amen), if I could only find the means of selling it and a buyer with the money, I would be willing, because having it with no one aboard to take care of it is total ruin. For that reason I'm sending you powers to sell it, even though that might seem unnecessary, but since I was so empowered I did it. It seems to me that the best thing would be to try to sell half interest to someone in whom you have full confidence, and he would pay for half, because there is no point in selling a smaller share. And I would rather give him two thirds than one third, because then he will show greater concern. As long as I am here I can take care of my part, and also that of Juan de Ríos, it seems to me. And if you sell half interest, the price would be 250,000 maravedís at cost, more or less, if so it seems to you. Or if you don't care to do this and could find someone to buy all of it, that would also be very well, but by no means let it be or come back this way. Do as you think best, but I would greatly prefer selling half, because in two voyages there would be a profit, and besides, this country of Yucatán is so extremely rich that it will be of great advantage to us. Sir, do as you please, but by all means do one of these two things; I know you will find a way to do one or the other. The memorandum of what it originally cost in Spain is in the book, in my hand, and there is no other cost, except I think they bought four guns in Cádiz for 12 ducats, as they wrote me. And Herrera bought two for 39,740 maravedís, and in Sanlúcar he spent 6,409 on the topsail and other things, which cost 6,898 above what we wrote. On this voyage, which God willing will finish well, the ship has made 40,000 or 60,000 maravedís. If we were going to Yucatán, we would still do all right, since the freight is 6 pesos a ton from here to there. May God guard it and give it a good voyage; I would rather return with it than not. May God save it, amen.

The ship's crew all fell ill, as you already know, sir. There is a sailor among them called Domingo, and since I know him and he wants to continue to serve with the ship, I gave him 1,600 maravedís, as you will see by this acknowledgment, which he will pay forthwith and put on my account. I know you will say it is a fine bar of gold, this first one I'm sending, but one thing will come after another, God willing. Try to see that this Domingo serves in the ship, since he is a very fine sailor.

I already wrote you from Santo Domingo that I had finished up accounts with that young fellow, and that I collected 60 pesos in cash, while I refrained from collecting another 70 from Mr Juan de Ríos. I brought the 60 pesos along with me, not wanting to send it in case it should be necessary here for freight. I have decided to send it to you, 63 pesos, going in a bag saying '63 pesos for Mr Alonso de Nebreda.' With it I beg you to do me the favor of buying the goods mentioned in an accompanying memorandum and send them to me in a case in the first ship or in ours, God willing. Be sure the merchandise is what I ask for, and above all that it is very good. And if the money is not enough to pay for it, since you are there perhaps you will be so good as to make it up. You could send me some satin and damask that people have been asking for, and some hats, since I have none, and some leather footwear, all of which I believe will find good sale. So aid me, as I see you aided by God and the Virgin Mary. As to the insurance that I wrote you from Santo Domingo to take out for me at 25 ducats per ship, I entreat you to do it, and I say again it will be a favor to me, and I run the risk. Let the goods be very good, and let them come in good condition under the quarterdeck to avoid rain. And make sure the case has no holes; one before had a hole that the mice got into and destroyed thirty pairs of sandals on me.

Please send this letter I'm writing to Alonso Hernández in Córdoba with the first person going there, and please pay him the some 13,000 maravedís that the six riding saddles will cost him, or whatever is needed. And I beg you to do it quickly.

In the matter of the 162 ducats that Pablos Mejía was to pay with our ship as security, what has happened is that he was confident Diego Velázquez would pay that much for him and more, but he is not here, and there was nothing left for him to do but find someone who would lend him money, the royal treasurer

50 pesos and another local citizen 50 pesos, to be paid at the time of melting down, and he asked me to wait for the rest, 42 ducats, until he can pay. I considered it a bad arrangement, but took the two promises that I mentioned for 100 pesos, believing they will pay me duly, but I don't believe the 42 ducats will be paid until Yucatán. This is what comes of doing good deeds. I am so angry that I would rather be a friar than receive such annoyance for such little profit. What happened was that I was never able to convince the person who represents Mr Perona not to seize goods for the debt; yesterday he did it, and I indicated the goods he could take. What a reward for pleasing someone! Be sure you thank Mr Perona for it there, I just ask you that. So I consider the 100 pesos sure, the 42 ducats not till Yucatán, though I will do what I can to get him to pay. Since he appears not to have means, there is a limit to what I can do. No matter how much I offered Perona's representative security or guarantees, nothing I said could convince him not to have goods seized. Again I tell you to reward him for it, now and other times.

I'm not writing to Mr Diego Díaz; he should consider this letter his, and if you think best, you or he might send this letter to Mr Cristóbal de Haro.

They gave me a kind of little cat in Hispaniola that I sent to Juan Fernández' wife, since Mr Juan de Ríos sent you another one while I was there, and one is enough to torment the parrots. But I will try to send another. There are no yams on this island, as is only just, because where there is no health there should not be good things.

I paid the master and his associates the freight costs, as they will tell you. The master is a good man, but not cut out for this position, which he doesn't know how to handle and should not hold. We settled accounts, and his share for his work was 10,000 maravedís. He has already spent that much, and an additional 3,635 deficit he has incurred, on good eating and drinking. He is a good man, but you will never collect the deficit from him; put it on my account. Here is the written obligation. Take into account the ship and tackle, as will appear in the book there and the memorandum they gave me when I bought it. May God save it, amen.

In the matter of what is owing for Villalón, don't think I've forgotten it. To this day I have sold 700 pesos worth of goods, 370 owed by Francisco Garay, and the rest here, 320 or 330 pesos, which we can count on when the gold is melted down. And some more will be sold between now and then, God willing. Don't think I will be without anxiety until I can send the money, much less that I would decline sales. I hope through God to be able to send it by Christmas. And if you should not believe it and want to sell the ship, I leave it up to you. But I do expect through God that things will turn out so I can send it to you in time.

It would be well if when the ship arrives, God willing, you would go straight to it and station some trustworthy person there to guard it so the sailors and others won't take whatever is on it, and this I beg of you.

While writing this I sold 3⅓ yards of crimson satin, at 3 pesos cash. Consider what a price! I wish it had all gone that way. I have sold 14 yards of the fine scarlet for breeches at 3 pesos on credit; I did it to sell it, since the cloth is perishable. I think the rest will have to be closed out in Yucatán, or more properly speaking San Juan de Uloa. May God give me good sales for this and for everything, amen.

Young Francisco is returning in the ship. May God bear him safely. He fell ill, as the land didn't seem to agree with him, and after that he didn't want to stay with me except on a monthly basis. Besides that, he was thinking of going to Yucatán, and might leave me when I need him. And also business is not what it might be, and I wanted to reduce costs. So I settled accounts with him and paid him; you help him there as much as you can. If we hadn't brought Baltasarejo, we would be in fine shape.

I already told you that when the ship is registered you should put a very trustworthy person on it so they won't rob it. They are all very cunning, and you will prevent them from taking a thousand trifles and filling up their houses for Christmas. I'm sending along a memorandum of what is on the ship, aside from what is in the book. I do not yet know who the passengers will be, so you will have to find out there who they were in order to take your part. I think the ship will carry some from here to la Yaguana, and also from la Yaguana to Seville. Don't let them take more from us, it was enough with the thousand damages they have done; I am missing .13½ arrobas of olive oil, worth 13½ pesos, and 7 arrobas of vinegar. The master owes 3,635 maravedís, from which you should deduct, sir, 1,560 for the candles he bought for the ship.

Herrera here is also writing you about the ship of Hernando Gallego, and I refer you to what he is writing. May God give it a good voyage, amen. This is being sealed on the 15th of September.

At your service,
                    Hernando de Castro

The ship has been kept here more than twenty days because Diego Velázquez, who has been in Trinidad for ten months, has left to come here and wants to use it to send messages to Castile. And for the same reason they will not let Ambrosio go, because such is the custom in this land. They say that gold will be melted down by Christmas, and at the same time the Indians will be distributed and when that is done, Diego Velázquez will go to his Yucatán. If all this occurs, I think I will have a reasonable sale of the merchandise. May God grant it as I desire, amen. So far I thank God for having given us peace. The news could not be worse from Yucatán, with this discord; while here we have peace, but not a penny. May God aid us, amen.

[1] Published in Spanish, with comment, in Otte, 'Mercaderes burgaleses en los inicios del comercio con México,' *Historia Mexicana*, XVIII (1968), 120–9.

6. The non-hero

Maestre Baltasar, on Gallo Island off Ecuador, to
his brother in Panamá, 1527[1]

> ... Two years is long enough to go about begging
> without servants...

Readers of Prescott or the Spanish chroniclers get no inkling
of what expeditions of discovery and conquest in the Indies
were like. Hardships, high mortality, and sometimes fierce fighting were indeed involved. But what the chroniclers took for
granted, and Prescott did not know, was that the expeditions
were joint economic ventures shot through with capitalism and
commercialism. The leaders were the largest investors, in ships
and supplies, to which they gave their men access – practically
always for a price; but all the men invested something, if only
their person and clothing, and the shares the conquerors won
were adjusted more than anything else to the size of their
investments. Owning a horse doubled one's share. The ships
may have left most of the import merchants behind, but commercialism and lively trading continued to be part of the picture. The wealthier expedition members took stocks to be sold
to their fellows later, when supplies would be scarcer and higher
priced. The expeditions contained blacksmiths, tailors, sur-
geons, notaries and others who charged for their services. And
trading back and forth of horses, weapons, clothing and slaves
went on constantly.

Another aspect not much spoken of, and which for lack of
sources scholars still know too little about, is the large number
of Indian and black helpers the Spaniards always took with
them on expeditions, outnumbering themselves at least two to
one. Their direct role in the fighting was not great, but they
freed the conquerors by carrying the baggage, searching for
provisions, bringing wood and water, and helping with other
tasks; the women among them were also cooks, mistresses, companions. Blacks, as highly expensive slaves, were the minority.
The bulk were Indians, who might either be informal permanent
dependents, simply commandeered somewhere, or slaves like

the blacks, though much lower priced (Indian slavery, while short-lived in the central regions, was a standard phenomenon of the conquests); in either case, they originated in areas already conquered, usually close to the expedition's point of departure. Rather than operating as a corps, the helpers in most cases belonged to the individual conquerors; each Spaniard normally expected to have two or three, an expectation that did not vanish with the culmination of the conquest.

It is not at all strange, then, to find our Maestre Baltasar at a critical juncture of a major conquest, under extreme conditions of danger and hardship, speaking of debt collection and appealing for servants. He appears to have been a barber-surgeon, and would have had even more than the ordinary need for helpers. (*Maestre* is 'master,' that is, master at a craft, and since the Spaniards loved names of two elements, those who acquired that title often lost their surnames almost entirely.) Maestre Baltasar and his brother have been selling supplies to the conquerors; with the brother and main investor back in Panamá, and Maestre Baltasar as the man on the spot almost like a factor, their arrangement is much like that of a mercantile company. They sold on credit by written obligation, payable at the first melting down of gold, the same system explained in Letter 5. The 6,000 pesos of good gold that Almagro took back to Panamá is the same amount referred to in Letter 4 by the merchant Zubizarreta.

Gallo Island is famous in the conquest of Peru as the spot where a brave few decided to persevere while the pusillanimous many gave up. There was indeed a strong division; Pizarro with his close associates wanted to continue, while a large part of the men wanted the opposite. This letter is one of several that members sent back to Panamá trying to have the whole expedition recalled or to get license to return themselves. It would be better not to think in terms of bravery and cowardice. All these people were heroic, in the sense of being willing to face death to get what they wanted. None were, in the sense of being dashing, given to unnecessary risk, or unconcerned with self-interest. The opposing groups were not so different, despite personal and regional antagonisms. Their situations were different. Pizarro and the others most closely identified with his venture stood to rule Peru if they could get to it; if they returned to Panamá they stood to be overwhelmed by their great indebtedness and see someone else rule it. The others, not enjoying Pizarro's favor, cared nothing about who ruled; they observed no immediate progress towards the source of the grand reports, but did observe that they continued to die off from disease as the majority of the expedition had done over the past months and years. Some of the very men who went back to Panamá at this time later joined the Peruvian conquest proper, once it was proved to them that there was a quick sea route, so that the venture was worth the risk for them.

Where we have put 'palisades' in the translation, the original has *barbacoas*. The Spaniards learned the word in the Caribbean, extending it from wooden grills used for smoking meat to just about anything Indians made of poles. Houses on stilts, tree houses, or something of that nature might be meant here.

Dear brother:

I wrote to you there by Captain Diego de Almagro; please, sir, if we are to remain here, finish getting what I asked for in the way of medicines, and as to the rest, you will do, sir, as you know is needed. You write, brother, that you want to go to Castile and that I should come there to render account to you; I wish to God, though it cost me a finger of each hand, that I could be there and settle accounts, since it would save my life and I would escape from great bad fortune, hunger and hardship. At present we are on an island where with much effort we go to the mainland to the palisades seeking maize among the bogs and carrying it on our backs, because I and most of the rest have no one to carry it for us, and so we live dying, not satisfied with only maize. Therefore, sir, I ask you, if you can find any way, please negotiate with the governor or the treasurer to give me license to come there, since I have done all I am obliged to, and am married, and they have held me by force for more than a year and a half. I'm very ill, and if you can't negotiate it they will get little advantage from me.

And sir, if this cannot be done, and if, which God prevent, more people come and the voyage continues, send me the things I mentioned and which you know I will need for the practice of my trade, and also someone to serve me, that is, a black or a good Indian man and woman, because if I should buy them here it would cost a great deal. Two years is long enough to go about begging without servants; and if the voyage continues, there is all the more to be gained. Sir, in the other letter I already wrote replying to I don't know what complaints that you made; I don't know why you should give credence to someone who talks gratuitously, since I have told you that between you and me there are to be no differences, though I be left naked, and let that be enough. Write me, sir, at great length what your will is, and everything that is going on there, and how you came out with Diego de Almagro about our money. You sent, sir, to tell me to give you a memorandum of the men who were still alive here. What need do you have of that for the first obligations, since the first and second lots of gold were already taken there to Panamá, over 6,000 pesos of good gold, and Diego de Almagro is in possession of it, while the obligations speak of the first gold and of whatever should be taken and carried back there, and Captain Pizarro and all the members of the company are so obliged? Watch that they don't deceive you by saying that I have given my power to anyone, as you wrote; and if anyone says that I have given it to him, let him produce the document.

Furnish me a little clothing, some linen and woolens, which should include a couple of shirts and a corslet and a couple yards of linen; and as to provisions, sir, send me the same as you did last time, and if you were even more generous you would be doing me a great favor, because the greatest evil we have is hunger.

There is no more, sir, to write you. Our Lord guard your virtuous person as you might desire. From Gallo Island, 15th of August, 1527.

At your orders, sir, your brother,
    Maestre Baltasar

[1]Published in Spanish in Raúl Porras Barrenechea, ed., *Cartas del Perú (1524–1543)*, p. 17, among other places.

7. The successful conqueror

Melchor Verdugo, encomendero and councilman of Trujillo, Peru, to Marina de Olivares, his mother, in Avila, 1536[1]

> ... I live in a place called Trujillo and have my house there and a very good encomienda of Indians, with about eight or ten thousand vassals ...

The shares of treasure that the conquerors received, where there was treasure to be had, were only the beginning of their remuneration. As a more basic and permanent reward, first conquerors received encomiendas, which led in turn to other advantages. The full complex consisted of an encomienda with numerous settled, tribute-paying Indians and a large revenue; a large house, establishment and following in the nearest Spanish city; a seat on that city's council; and farflung enterprises of various types from stockraising to silver mining. This was success; to top it off the lucky conqueror would write home the news, at the same time sending money and proof of his credentials, in return for which he hoped to receive from the royal court certain status symbols, the most frequent being a coat of arms and a royal title to his council seat. The present letter illustrates all these things quite fully, being a classic example of the 'Mother, I've made it' message for sixteenth-century Spanish America. The reader should not be too annoyed at Verdugo's transparent bragging; it was the manner of the time. As the young man says, 'I write you this so you'll be glad.' A more attractive side of him is seen in his longing for mail. And after saying he was not going to send his mother anything more, he in fact sent her 850 pesos (maybe meant for legal expenses), as well as some emeralds, a ring, a mirror, a comb, and some Indian textile things.

Except for those returning immediately to Spain, the vast

majority of first conquerors received encomiendas. But grants varied immensely. To support the kind of complex sketched above, there had to be sizable, stable Indian provincial entities with well-oiled tribute mechanisms, and even that availed little unless there was a steady supply of precious metals in the local economy so that the tribute could be turned into something of value to Europeans. Full success, then, was a rare thing indeed outside Peru and Mexico (one encomendero of Peru once said his grant was worth more than Chile). Even in the central areas encomiendas varied from some with princely incomes to others which barely produced a living for the recipient. The best grants went to the relatives and compatriots of the governors; beyond that, to the wealthiest, most senior and influential expedition members; beyond that, to those with good birth and education in Spain.

This last was Verdugo's advantage, for though young and little noticed at the time of the conquest, he was of an hidalgo family of Old Castile. Not the most illustrious, by any means. Note that his mother was not a *doña*; and his relatives and acquaintances tended to be in the urban professions. Still, the surnames on both sides of his family were well known, and he even had some relatives near the royal court. This was enough to earn Verdugo serious consideration in the distribution of grants, though his encomienda, good as it was, could not compare with the more centrally located holdings of some more senior figures. Verdugo was clearly set to become one of the potentates of the land in later years, as after some vicissitudes he in fact did, even eventually attaining the quite rare honor, at that time, of the membership in the Order of Santiago which he asks for here. (The Spaniards always spoke of it as being given the 'habit,' since to wear the habit and cross of the order was the essence of the thing.)

Lady:

I have written you so many times and sent so many letters by whoever has left here, without getting any reply, that I don't know what to tell myself except that you have forgotten me more than you should. I sent you 1,000 pesos from Jauja with a gentleman of Segovia called Juan de Rojas. Olivares, a nephew of Canon Olivares, who was here and left, knows him well. I feel certain that you have received the money and for that reason I'm not sending more, since I feel sure that you don't need any more; if I thought any different I would provide for you. If you shouldn't have received it, then I sent it consigned to Vicente de Avila in Seville. It is in the possession of one or the other. You collect it and let me know what is happening.

I am still in the town where I have always been. I live in a place called Trujillo and have my house there and a very good encomienda of Indians, with about eight or ten thousand vassals; I think there's never a year that they don't give me 5,000 or 6,000 pesos in income. I write you all this so you'll be glad and know that I live without necessity, praise our Lord.

Always write me and let me know how my lady sisters are, and all those gentlemen my relatives, and give them my greetings. I haven't had a letter from any of them either, but since you don't write me I won't blame anyone. From now on act differently, and since paper and ink cost little, write me twenty letters a day so that if one gets lost another will find its way. A gentleman called Hernando de Zavallos is the bearer of this letter, and he is to return here immediately. You can write me by him, since he is a very certain messenger, and even if you do write by him, write forty other letters, because my only desire is to receive a letter from you after such a long time. I'm in very good health, praise our Lord, and have no other source of dissatisfaction than not having heard from you, as I said.

With the bearer of the present letter I am sending to ask certain favors of his majesty, among which I'm sending to request a perpetual grant of my Indians for me and my heirs. I'm also sending to request a commission as royal captain and a perpetual seat on the council here; I have one from the governor, and it's necessary to have his majesty confirm it. I'm also chief constable, but I'm not sending to request that because there's no need, since the governor likes me so well that he always tries to favor me, and as long as that's his pleasure he's not going to take the office away from me.

Find out if you can arrange all these things that I mention, and if not, turn it over to Francisco de Soto so that when the emperor comes to Spain, if he's not there now, he should go and arrange all these things that I mention, because in that he would do me a great favor, and I implore him to do it; and if he doesn't want to occupy himself with this, then turn it over to someone who can do it very well and pay him, and send the documents to me with great precautions. If some relative of mine should want to come here and bring them, then let him come, and I will do what I can for him.

I would also like to send to request a habit of the order of Santiago from his majesty. They tell me that I have to be present, or at least send very convincing evidence of who I am. You try to take testimony, and let it be so complete and convincing that there will be no lack, but rather too much, and take very convincing witnesses, even though you have to go to the end of the earth to get them, and let the witnesses be solid and very honorable people. When the proof is complete, try to arrange with his majesty to have a habit of Santiago sent for me. And for all this get the advice of a lawyer on how to do it, or have the lawyer arrange it, and pay him very well. And so that everything can be done better, the bearer of this letter is carrying very convincing testimony that I had taken here of how much I have served his majesty in this country, and how I was in the capture of Atahuallpa and many other things, as will appear; anyone who wants to can see it.

I won't write more and I don't mean to write to you again until I receive a letter from you, except may our Lord care for your very noble person and let me see you as I desire. From Trujillo, 7th of December, 1536.

Your obedient son who kisses your hands,
     Melchor Verdugo

[1] Published in Spanish in Porras, *Cartas del Perú*, pp. 231-3. A detailed biography of Verdugo is in Lockhart, *The Men of Cajamarca*, pp. 250-5.

8. The unsuccessful conqueror

Bartolomé García, citizen of Asunción, Paraguay, to the Council of the Indies, 1556[1]

> ... And now, after twenty-one years, when I expected the reward for my efforts, you have left me without a share ...

A companion piece to letter 7, this letter illustrates the case of a conqueror *not* granted a rich encomienda, an occurrence frequent enough that the volume of these complaints to governor, viceroy or king was great. Two types of attributes come into play here, personal and regional. Let us look first at the personal. Our Bartolomé García was not close to the governor (he was from Seville, while the governor was a Basque); he was no big man in the original expedition of don Pedro de Mendoza, no leader who would have to be respected over and above politics; and by all indications he was not well born. The plebeian-sounding name is ambiguous and tells us little, but the lack in this whole complaint and petition of the slightest claim to be an hidalgo or gentleman tells us much. Low on all three counts, Bartolomé García emphasizes his services. Even through the heightening, we can see that they were great. But they were not the right kind. There were several skills and pursuits most useful in the Spanish conquests which had a public image such that accomplishments in them could not be brought to bear on encomienda grants. Great runners, scouts and spies had just as well not apply. Nothing related to the maritime profession counted. The most egregious example of this was in Mexico, where Martín López, a ship's carpenter, supervised the building of the brigantines without which the siege of Tenochtitlan might have gone on indefinitely, and for his trouble received a quite minimal encomienda, shared with a colleague. As to Bartolomé García, he was a great huntsman and a fine crossbow shot, not the stuff encomenderos were made of, no matter how many deer he bagged and big cats he brought down.

In Mexico or Peru, even those first conquerors who were

slighted had a half-tolerable situation, because their 'small' encomiendas numbered some hundreds of Indians who sustained their households handily, produced some money revenue, and gave the encomenderos a base for their own entrepreneurial activity related to the strong local city markets. On the periphery, a small encomienda was fifteen or twenty Indians (García does not exaggerate), and not sedentary tribute-paying agriculturalists, either, nor equipped with a strong and cooperative chief. On handing out the grants, the governor might well have added 'catch them if you can.' Consider also the difference in the time element. In the central regions encomiendas were granted within a year or two of the conquest, sometimes much earlier. In Paraguay this was not done for *twenty years*. Looking at the situation more closely, the remarkable thing is that encomiendas were granted even then. In the absence of strong chiefs or kings as intermediaries, the Spaniards had to establish more direct contacts with the Indians; in the absence of valuable tribute products they had to emphasize exclusively services and supervised labor (not a new development, but going all the way back to the first region the Spaniards occupied, the Caribbean, which was the original 'peripheral area'). Even the best encomiendas of Asunción were small by the standards of Peru and Mexico; they were more like large households or collections of permanent servants. The late establishment of encomiendas on the far periphery did not work to the advantage of people like Bartolomé García. Peru and Mexico too saw the invasion of latecoming immigrants, far, far more of them in fact, as well as the changing of standards for granting encomiendas. But there, the mariners and shoemakers among the first conquerors received encomiendas while their claim of priority was still strong, and they never lost them afterwards. If they had had to wait as long for the grants to be made as Bartolomé García did, they would have received little or nothing.

Very powerful lords:
    As a man who has been wronged I cannot refrain from complaining to your highness as my king. Your highness, I was born

in the town of Morón, nine leagues from Seville. I came to this province of the Río de la Plata twenty-one years ago, with the expedition of don Pedro de Mendoza, in which I suffered the hardships that your highness doubtless knows all those who came in that time have suffered, and I have striven to be first in the service of your highness in every way I could, of which I would send proof if I were so bold.

At the end of twenty years the governor of this province gave its natives in encomienda to those who are just newly arrived and to others who came after we did. Of those who conquered the land, some of them losing their sons and some their brothers, there remain, from the 1,700 men counted at the muster don Pedro de Mendoza held when he landed, about a hundred men, and to them the governor gave the worst grants and the most distant, from where one can get no service. And so, many have not wished to accept the grants, of whom I am one, since he gave me sixteen Indians eighty leagues from where we live, and he gave others fifteen, or twenty, or thirty, but for his sons-in-law, and sons-in-law of his sons-in-law, and the officials of your highness and for himself, he took the whole country, all the best part of it. And when I went to speak to him at the time when he was going to make the distribution, I gave him a memorandum of the hardships I had undergone, which goes along with this letter; he only answered, 'how many children do you have?' and said my petition had best be left unmade. Seeing how he had treated me, I asked his permission to go to the realms of Spain, and he refused me that too. I have said this so that your highness will know the treatment that has been given to don Pedro's men, and this letter is only to give an account of what is going on here and how those who strive are treated. From the city of Asunción, the day of St John, 1556.

Your vassal who kisses your royal feet,
> Bartolomé García

This is a petition and memorandum of some of my hardships that I gave to Governor Domingo de Irala.

> Very magnificent sir:
> > This is to remind you of my services and hardships

in this land because, to judge by what I see and have seen of how you have treated me up to now, I think you either do not know about them or do not want to remember them, as I have seen in your deeds. Yet you yourself are a good witness to all which I will now say, and also to other things of which, to avoid tediousness, I will not remind you, though you were a witness of all of them. You well know that after we arrived at Buenos Aires, I was one of sixteen men who went with Gonzalo de Acosta and discovered the Tembues, and on the way the Guaranís of the islands shot arrows at us, from which I was left wounded so that for five years part of a shaft stayed in my arm before it finally came out, and what I suffered from that you knew very well and saw with your own eyes, but in those five years I never failed to carry out my orders.

Our lord don Pedro, God rest his soul, ordered myself and six other men, of whom some are still alive as you know, to go hunting for him, and so we did, and, as you can witness, every day we bagged a dozen and a half partridges and quail, which don Pedro ate and gave to those he liked most. And this continued until they went to the Tembues and Francisco Ruiz asked for me and Baitos to stay behind with him to guard the ships, and don Pedro, because of promises he had made to Francisco Ruiz, left us there in Buenos Aires, while he went to the Tembues and returned, and then again I supplied him with partridge and quail to eat as I had done before, and the day he set sail they loaded over a hundred and fifty partridge and quail on the ship. You weren't present then, but Alférez Vergara can tell you, because he loaded them with his own hands.

You well know that after don Pedro left for Spain we stayed in Buenos Aires, suffering great hunger; I would go hunting with a crossbow, in great danger from Indians and lions, and I fed seventy men who were there, because every day, even Sundays and holidays, I shot two or three deer, from which the men were given rations to sustain themselves. And despite this work, I was not exempted from sentinel duty; you know that there are many witnesses of this, and that blood ran from my hands and knees from crawling to get in a position to shoot at the deer, the same as to this day is done by those who want to hunt them. You saw and know well that the lions came inside the palisade and killed our people, and from a tree outside the palisade I lay in wait for one who was doing great damage, against the will of Francisco Ruiz, but I begged and asked as a favor that I be allowed to lay in wait for it, and I killed it. And then you saw that when we were going to Buenos Aires by the river of the Tembues, the Quirandis came out to attack the ships with arrows, and because of a shot that I made and you saw, they did not hurt us very badly, as they very easily could have otherwise.

Whenever you have gone exploring or to the wars, and at the time of the general rebellion, I have always been in the forefront and at your side, and you are a witness of it. I have never been without two sets of weapons in good condition, for myself and for others who needed them because they had broken theirs or dissipated them in order to trade with the Indians for Indian women to serve them; but I never broke mine, nor wasted them, nor traded in mares and horses with the Indians as others have done, as you very well know. I have not bartered, nor spread rumors, nor ever gone against an order from you or from others, much less escaped and fled through the wilds, nor been in jails, nor been pardoned by you for misdeeds, nor, for all of these services and hardships that I have mentioned and many others that I leave unmentioned, as you can bear witness, have you ever to this day done me any good deed; the reason must be the disfavor with which you have always viewed me because I am not importunate as others have been and are. And now, after twenty-one years, when I expected the reward for my efforts in the distribution of Indians in encomiendas, you have left me without a share. Since you do not forget me when you need men, it would be right to remember me also when it is time to do favors, as you have done with others, even with those who came with Martín de Urrea, who though they have hardly arrived, already have received their encomiendas of Indians.

Bartolomé García

[1] Published in Spanish in *Cartas de Indias*, pp. 600-3.

9. The conqueror-governor

Don Francisco Pizarro, conqueror and governor of Peru, marqués and adelantado, in Lima, to Sebastián Rodríguez, his solicitor at the royal court, 1541[1]

... I will be left the governor of sandflats ...

The reward of the members of a successful expedition was an encomienda for each; the reward of the leader was the governorship of the area. If the new land was already somewhat known and the venture well planned and financed, the leader might have capitulated with the crown for the governorship in advance of the expedition. If the leader had only an ad hoc captaincy and license from the governor of the region where the expedition originated, he would proceed to apply for a royal appointment after the fact. Usually he would get what he asked for; he was in a very strong position locally, and the practice was firmly established in the customs of the Indies, so that the crown officials had little choice in the matter. They had little reason to disapprove in any case. One should not imagine a Machiavellian crown, plotting the immediate replacement of the conqueror-governors in favor of pliable bureaucrats and viceroys. Many of the first governors received lifetime appointments, which were honored. But the pressures were such that those lives were often short. The crown was well served to let the conquerors' momentum follow through to the establishment of a preliminary equilibrium, and wait for the natural course of further immigration, internal rivalries and Indian fighting to accomplish the replacement of the founder-governors quickly enough.

The whole sequence is well illustrated by the case of Francisco Pizarro and Peru. In Letter 2 we saw the origins of the venture under Governor Pedrarias de Avila of Tierra Firme; in Letter 4, indirectly, Pizarro's continued direction of the exploratory phase, and in Letter 1 the high point of the conquest, with Pizarro already styled governor on the basis of a capitulation obtained in Spain before the final expedition of 1532. He received high titles and honors. (Not the least of them was the *don*. Note that not another correspondent in this section, including Pedrarias, bore that title; today we can speak of Pizarro with propriety minus the 'don' only because, like Hernando Cortés, he had been without it for most of his lifetime.) He governed the country for nine years, presided over the establishment of its network of cities, and gave it its social-economic framework through the assigning and withholding of encomiendas. But to him and those like him, his activity was a far more personal matter than merely governing. Peru was his encomienda, to enjoy, to share with his brothers and to leave as a patrimony to his heirs. To govern Peru, the entire vast land, was all he lived for, as he says passionately in this letter. Without that, there would have been no point to the whole effort.

Others in Peru, senior and powerful men with allies, resources and followings, felt the same as Pizarro did. What of them? One could prod them off onto their own conquests, the more distant the better. This worked in the case of Soto and Benalcázar (as seen in Letter 2). But Pizarro had long had a partner, Diego de Almagro, who having been at first not much more than his steward, had over time become his near-equal, in full charge of organizing, financing and supplying the expeditions Pizarro led.[2] An outlet for Almagro was found in the governorship of an undefined area to the south of Peru. However, Chile proved poor in people and precious metals, so Almagro, with a large number of recent arrivals behind him, laid claim also to silver-rich Charcas (the area of Bolivia today) and even Cuzco. This brought on a civil war and the execution of Almagro by the Pizarrists, which in turn brought a storm of protest and a royal investigation. The 'judge at the door' referred to below was Licentiate Vaca de Castro (writer of Letter 29), who was then coming by way of Panamá and Quito towards Lima, and quite unexpectedly became governor of Peru when Pizarro was assassinated by Almagrists a few days after the present letter was written.

Very noble sir:

About six days ago the news reached me of the partition of this government, and that they are taking Arequipa and Charcas from me., which is the whole best part of the jurisdiction and where I have all my enterprises and encomiendas. And as the thing grieves me so, before the judge should arrive I am sending a ship with this dispatch carrying a letter for his majesty, a copy of which goes along with this one. Please, sir, do me the favor of looking at it and asking in my name for a solution as therein contained, because if these jurisdictions are not divided in the way I suggest, his majesty will not be served; I will be left the governor of sandflats, and whoever has Charcas and Arequipa will have the best of it. He who has not done service to merit it would be made prosperous while I who have served would be brought low. Yet I cannot believe that his majesty would do me such injustice, since he was born and bred in our pious faith and will not permit his conscience to be burdened with me after so many years of such signal services, because I have advised him of them, not for my own interest but in his service, if only he had believed me and made provisions according to my reports. Let your industry not flag in gaining what I am requesting of his majesty in the letter, and fear no effort, sir, nor disfavor either, and sweat drops of blood to express the damage that can be expected and the ingratitude that is being practiced with me, because in these negotiations the same thing is at stake for me as always has been, and to defend it I wagered my life and spent my property and placed myself in great disturbances. And consider that I, having my share in it, will profit as much when Adelantado Almagro has it, even if they take it from me; and they may give it to another to enjoy who perhaps will not have merited it nor done service and it would cost him nothing. Seeing that they prosper him and bring me low and put me in the hospital loaded down with debts for having sustained the land and brought his majesty the increase he has had, what can I feel and what can I do but appeal against it all, even if they gave it to my own brother, until such time as all the settlers can inform his majesty and justice is done to me as a first discoverer and settler? You may believe that even if I would stand for this, the citizens of this country would not permit it, because they cannot be so governed without great hardship to them, and I am shocked at the great blindness of ordering such a thing, since Quito cannot be governed from here, nor Charcas and Arequipa together with Chile. Above all inform my lord the cardinal, to whom I am writing, that it is not possible, nor can I believe that his lordship would want to make anyone's fortune by unmaking mine, although it were for his own son, since what is owed me is taken from me, burdening the royal conscience of his majesty and the cardinal's own. Try in any case to have things put off; the abruptness of the order could bring with it inconveniences that would be in disservice of God and his majesty. And since the importance of the matter is manifest, take it as your own affair. It is the thing most important to me and for which I have always clamored, since without it all my hardships and services will have been in vain, and I will be able to say that for my own damage and destruction I served his majesty and won him lands, which will be reason for me to complain to God and the world of such a great injustice and burden of conscience; even if I had only four days left to live and were disloyal, his majesty to show himself grateful would have to permit me to govern all that I won and have sustained at my own cost to the advantage of his royal crown and patrimony. And don't forget these

negotiations as you have those in the past; I have had no reply
from any of them, nor do I know what is being done. The judge
is at the door and I have had no warning from you or from
anyone else, and it seems to me that you are leaving me as a
man given up for dead, to live or die by himself, and you leave
my grave open for me. Or are you gentlemen all dead, and my
complaint is not licit? I want this business decided quickly because for my purpose I must know.

Our Lord guard and prosper your very noble person as you
desire. From Lima, 15th of June, 1541.

At your orders, sir,

The Marqués

[1] Published in Spanish in Porras, *Cartas del Perú*, pp. 402-3. An interpretation of Pizarro's life is in Lockhart, *The Men of Cajamarca*, pp. 135-7.

[2] The two in later years formalized an agreement to share everything they
had equally. Pizarro refers to this in the letter, a little puzzlingly in view of
the fact that Almagro was already dead.

10. The conqueror in jail

Hernando Pizarro, in the fortress of La Mota in
Medina del Campo, Spain, to his majordomo the
priest Diego Martín in Peru, 1545[1]

... Being in prison like this is the cause of it
all ...

As we said in introducing the preceding letter, royal official-
dom did not take too active a hand with the governors who
emerged from the expeditions of conquest. Letting nature take
its course, however, led not infrequently to the ruling conquerors murdering and committing outrages on upstart subordinates or other rivals who threatened their jurisdictions. For
these political crimes many were jailed and variously sentenced
or deprived. Sebastián de Benalcázar, for one example, died
while appealing a death sentence for having executed a rival
governor. While the early giants were thus at a disadvantage,
their enemies would descend on them with claims and suits, and
new powers would rise in the areas they ruled. The other side of

the matter was the resilience of the apparently toppled great; even in jail they were powerful figures, and if not they, then generally their families long survived with wealth, influence and high title, though sometimes in Europe rather than in the Indies (as with both the Cortés and the Pizarro descendants).

We have just seen much of the background of the present situation in Letter 9. Hernando Pizarro, Francisco's haughty brother and right-hand man, led the forces that defeated Almagro, and it was Hernando who ordered Almagro's execution. Hernando then went off to Spain (sent by Francisco) to justify the action, with the result that he was kept in jail under various kinds of legal assault for over two decades. Here we see him after a reversal, but not humbled, still browbeating and mistrusting his employees, plotting to smuggle money from his large Peruvian estates into Spain, asking for documents which he hopes will throw the blame onto his now dead brother the Marqués. Worse was yet coming for Hernando; just at this time his younger brother Gonzalo was leading Peru's most serious revolt to ultimate defeat. Nevertheless, Hernando eventually got out of prison, kept his estates in Peru and Spain, consolidated the family titles and entails, and established a lasting prominent position for the family in its ancestral Trujillo, Extremadura.

Reverend Father:

In many letters I have written you the state of my affairs and urged you to provide for me. What I have to report to you now is that the sentence has been handed down, as far as it refers to Almagro's death, and a very severe one too, for the little guilt there is. They condemned me to perpetual exile, to serve in an African border area of his majesty's choice for all the days of my life and to be removed from this fortress, but that provisionally, until the other matters of which I am accused are decided, I am to remain a prisoner here under heavy guard. Since they have conducted themselves so harshly in this trial where there is no guilt, if in the other evidence they should find some, they would do us no honor, but I think that, with God's aid, they will find no guilt if there are not false witnesses.

Hasten greatly and send the proof, and send me the order that the Marqués, rest his soul, gave me in Ica, because the copy that Diego Velázquez brought failed to mention the day it was presented in council; have it sent as it should be, and let a lawyer see it, and let there be no neglect in the copying as there was with the other one. If you could get the original, it would mean my life. Also send me two orders that the Marqués gave me there in Ica: one to arrest Almagro, and the other to arrest his captains. Also send me an authorized copy of the division of the jurisdictions, and how Cuzco was included in that of the Marqués, and don't neglect it, because much depends on it. If you delay from one day to the next, the damage here will be great. You didn't even manage to send me a copy with Castañeda, who departed from Lima there on the 24th of August of last year, 1544. Don't let a boat leave there without sending a letter in it.

Bustillo, I mean Pedro González Bustillo, wrote me that he was going to send a copy of the division of jurisdictions, but he didn't send it. The moment they arrive there, all they do is look after their own profit, while I'm here in despair, ready to put a rope around my neck and hang myself, and dying of hunger. May God give the remedy. Diego Moreno told me that there was still gold in Cuzco, and those rogues in my house are holding it back to fill their hands with it as in the past. Since I had written that nothing was to be left there, there was no reason to keep it back. By your life, leave no wretches in the house; I have been told that a great deal of rascality is going on, and even though I should not write about it, don't let anyone remain in the house who is best not there. Truly I am their enemy as much as if they had killed my father, and even more so of those who leave here fleeing and later turn everything to their own advantage. Castañeda wrote me from Valladolid that when he left, you had just come from Cuzco, you and the regent and Ampuero, that you had gone there on orders from the viceroy, and he wished that you had brought back the gold that was there, to send to me since you knew I was in need.

The silver that Juan de Zavala sent me from Nombre de Dios

when you went through there was taken and impounded at the House of Trade, which has done me great harm, because the Council of the Indies has sentenced me to pay Hernán Sánchez de Badajoz 2,000 pesos, and I had to take the money on credit to pay him, with the silver having been seized. For the love of God I ask you to succor me; I need it more than you can imagine. And if I must stand for my servants stealing and spending everything while my life and honor suffer here, then it would be better for you to sell what is there and take care of me. Consider that I have placed my hopes in you and you must help me, for now I am in greater need than ever, and require my own resources and those of others; I want what I have now. You can send me whatever you should want to by way of merchant friends. Juan Sánchez de la Sao is going to be stationed at Nombre de Dios, because Juan de Zavala is coming back; through one means or another, be sure that nothing stays behind there. Diego Velázquez is rather lukewarm about going back, I'm not sure he will return soon. I wish he would go, for your sake, but I am confident that you with your good industry will be sufficient to take care of everything.

I believe the originals of the orders I mentioned above are in the possession of Salas; don't neglect to send them, and a certified copy of the division of jurisdictions. Also don't neglect to furnish the evidence, since they will overlook nothing in our case, as I see. Again I implore you to send me my own wealth and that of others, because it is more needed than one can imagine. And realize that I am trusting in your good friendship and expecting you to perform better than those of the past, who have consumed everything and left me to suffer. Leave none of them in the house; they are my enemies and make war on me, since whoever sees me suffering and doesn't help me from my own property is abundantly my enemy. And again, be sure that you send me what you can scratch together, confidentially, by way of merchants and by way of Juan Sánchez de la Sao, and let it not be like the relief of Escalona, coming after the time of need.

Doctor Jara is suing me here for the property of his son. By your life, make his estate give strict account of my property, and if it should result that I owe anything to him, I mean to his executors, then pay it, and if he owes me, collect it, and if there are no means, then send the order to pay to me, and later it will be in my hand to do with it as I wish. Keep a lawyer to look after the suits in Lima, where the viceroy and Audiencia are, and let nothing be lost for lack of legal advice.

I have had very good tools made to order for silver mines, and am sending to Lisbon for black mining technicians. I will send them all with Diego Velázquez, if he wants to go, or with someone else if he doesn't. I will also send donkeys, both stallions and females. Be very diligent with the mines, and don't wait till next year for anything that could be mined this year. Complain to the viceroy of all the damage Vaca de Castro has done to me and my nephews, and how he has used the avenues of justice to do injustice to me.

Be sure that you pay immediately whatever I owe there, that is, what I promised to pay Alonso de Toro and others, because I don't want them coming here to ask it of me. When it is paid, write me; Toro's brothers say that he gave me money for them that was not delivered. And a brother of Pedro de Soria is also complaining that his brother gave me money for him and I am keeping it from him. Before long they will make me a thief; patience doesn't suffice for such rogueries. Being in prison like this is the cause of it all, and so again I tell you, pay off everything still unpaid that I obliged myself for when I left.

Palomino has arrived here, and I have been told that he brings money. Write if he is bringing me anything, and if they gave him anything there send me his statement of receipt so that we can ask for it. Whenever you send anything, take acknowledgments from those who bring it, so account can be taken of them. I urge you to do a thorough job on Armenta.

Send me the silver pieces and the gold alloy that I have asked for in some memoranda. May our Lord guard your reverend person as, sir, you desire. From La Mota in Medina del Campo, on the 8th day of March of the year of 1545.

At your orders, sir,

Hernando Pizarro

[1] Published in Spanish with comment in Otte, 'Los mercaderes vascos y los Pizarro,' *TILAS* (May–June 1966), 34-6. A biography of Hernando Pizarro is in Lockhart, *The Men of Cajamarca*, pp. 157-68.

PART II: THE VARIETY OF LIFE
IN THE INDIES

> There are many farmers and craftsmen here, and
> many others who make a living by their work and
> sweat.

> Fray Toribio de Motolinia, Mexico, 1555

Here is the core of our interest. Conquest, as conquest, was an
episode. True, it divided the history of the Western hemisphere
into two sharply distinguished periods, but only because of its
aspect as occupation, reorganization, foundation; there it
stretched forward without break into the following decades and
centuries. Even before the fighting was over, the Spaniards
began to fill in the framework, bare but durable, that the conquest created – the system of Spanish cities, estates to tie them
to the Indian countryside, and export of precious metals as
their economic leverage with Europe. Immigrants poured into
the richer areas (nearly all the letters of this section relate to
Mexico and Peru). Even in the first moments there had not been
an encomienda for literally every Spaniard, and before long
encomenderos were a small minority of a Spanish population
devoted to every pursuit known in early modern Europe.

Once a frame of reference is set, these people can speak for
themselves. Through their own communications they emphasize
the extent and earliness of development, the endless variety of
occupations and types. And they express even more directly the
humanity, universality and ready intelligibility of themselves
and of the whole process. There is hardly a word they say that
would not fit equally well in the mouths of immigrants – and
non-immigrants – much nearer to our time and place.

Even the humblest Spaniards wrote letters, or found someone
who could. The numerous black slaves and servants who lived

beside them did not have the opportunity; at least we have found no letters from them, though they are often mentioned in the letters of the Spaniards. As to the millions of Indians among whom the whole Spanish population was a minority, and on whom it was having an enormous destructive–creative effect, a certain number of them were already producing correspondence in the European fashion, of which we include three examples.

11. An encomendero's establishment

Andrés Chacón, encomendero of Trujillo, Peru, presently in the valley of Casma, to his brother Francisco Chacón in Los Hinojosos, New Castile, 1570[1]

> . . . so that there are twenty or twenty-five people eating there . . .

With this letter we mean chiefly, in the face of the individuality and crustiness of its writer, to give a flesh-and-blood illustration of that social-economic complex which was associated with the encomienda, and which we have alluded to before (Letter 7). Located in Trujillo, a secondary city in the Peruvian scheme of things, with far from the richest encomienda in his district, spending much time out in the country acting as his own majordomo, married to good plebeian Ana López, our Andrés Chacón is no full exemplar of an ideal, like the great lords of Cuzco or Charcas, who were always in the cities, cushioned by their two or three echelons of stewards, married to doña Isabel Manrique de Lara or some such. But in the nature of his establishment, in employing many people and having his hand in everything, Chacón is representative. Here one can see all the better that no encomendero with any reasonable source of income at all was without his sheep, goats, pigs, cows and horses, his orchards, his wheat farm and mill, his Spanish employees and black slaves, his big house in town where many people were fed. And he could be counted on to get involved in other aspects of the local economy that looked especially promising, here silver mining.

All this is not only basic to the organization of sixteenth-century society, it also points ahead, because the complex, as a pattern, would outlive the encomienda itself and survive in later estate forms. Everywhere the trend was for the encomenderos to put increasing emphasis on the more flexible, secure private aspect of their estates, which with the growth of Spanish cities often became the more lucrative part as well, so that as their rights to Indian tribute diminished under attack from non-encomendero Spaniards and crown officials, many maintained their economic position quite well. Another reason for emphasizing enterprises over tribute was the continued decrease of the tribute-paying Indian population. The rate of diminution was uniformly fastest at low altitudes and on routes much traveled by Spaniards; both attributes apply to Casma, which is on the coast and located on the main route south to the capital of Lima. Chacón is not being gratuitously benevolent to his Indians by helping them with money payments and reducing their tribute in kind. He has grasped that the tribute is not as important to him as a general dominance in the area, that it is better to have a little maize and fish and keep the Indians as potential employees in his enterprises than to push tribute demands and see them run off as servants with Spanish passers by.

The situation we see here is well advanced towards patterns typical of the mature colonial period, but it flows out of the conquest period. Chacón has been in the Indies forty years and has held his encomienda for over thirty, or since 1540. He must have been in Peru since the conquest phase, surviving far into the second generation, still pithy and plain-spoken, if now becoming a little pontifical and, in this letter, wavering comically between bragging about his affairs to impress his relatives and magnifying his expenses so that they will understand why he doesn't send money.

Sir:

For a long time no one there has written me. In this fleet that just came from Spain, I thought there might be some letters, but it seems that none came, because I inquired, and there is no trace of anything. I don't know the reason. It must be that you there don't want to write except when I send money. Truly you should write more often, or at least remember me from time to time if I am neglectful; it seems to me that would be best. Also, I suppose you haven't had letters from me for a long time, because another year I wrote and sent a gold ingot to Licentiate Montalbo who lives in Panamá, and unfortunately for you and the rest who were to have it, the fleet had already departed for Spain; only one ship was left there, and the Licentiate didn't want to send it in a single ship, for which I was very sorry, because in fact he didn't send it, and it was left behind. Later when I sent to Panamá to buy some blacks for some mines I have, there wasn't enough money, and he spent the gold ingot toward the purchase of the blacks. Now at present I don't know if I will send anything, because I am outside my house thirty leagues from Trujillo among my villages, and the messenger who is going to Spain will not touch in Trujillo, I believe, and for that reason I don't know if anything can be sent. If he should not go at present and there are ships when I go to Trujillo, I will try to send something, even if it shouldn't be much, because at present I don't have much, but with the aid of God if these mines that I'm working do well, I will make up for it, if God gives me life and health. I hope to God that these mines I'm working will yield us enough silver for here and for there both, because I have some silver mines that I think will be good, and if they are, I will make up for what was lost; if you had the money there that I've spent on them, it would take care of you very well. I have a dozen and a half blacks at the mine, and tools and things. So far I have spent more than 7,000 pesos on blacks and the rest, and with the aid of God, the mines will yield silver; until now everything has been spending.

What I would need now is what there is too much of there, which is a boy from among those nephews of mine, to ride about on horseback inspecting my properties and these mines; they need someone to take care of them, because the blacks overlook nothing they can steal, and as to the Spaniards that I have there, each one looks after himself. As I say, I have great need of someone to go about, because I am old and tired and can no longer run everywhere, and as these mines are far from Trujillo in the mountains, it is hard on me to go, and the cold up there doesn't agree with me. To avoid going I would like to have one of those boys here, though none have ever managed to come, and he would flourish and lighten my work, if he is the right person. In case one who wanted to come should be free, I have written to a friend or two of mine in Seville who will help him along his way. When they come, they should bring my letters along. I believe Juan Antonio Corso, a very rich man, will outfit them for the trip, because he wrote me here. He carries on business here, and he will get the boy passage without his paying anything. I will pay here what it should cost, as I am now writing to Corso. Let them come and leave that misery in which they are immersed. Somehow two thousand paupers manage to get here; they look for a way to come across and finally they find it. But in forty years that I have been away from home, not one person from our town has come here except Alonso de Lara, son of Rodrigo de Lara the Red, who became a priest, and he has a living now; if he had wanted to go seek his fortune before he was a priest, he would have things even better. I have written other times that if some of the boys should take to learning, they should be trained up as lawyers or priests. If everything is to be digging and plowing, they and their fathers will be at it their whole lives. And however many of them come or make something of themselves, I will do my part to support them, and I say that when the mines begin to show profit, I will send money for it every year as long as I live.

I've been awaiting news about my papers of nobility, and haven't seen a thing. It must all be a joke, or I don't know what to say, when at the end of ten years there still has been no judgment. I consider it a joke.

As to things here, I am well, and Ana López too, though we are old and tired, and in the end this is very poor country, and all the properties aren't worth two pennies any more. If it weren't for a mulebreeding business I have, I don't know what would come of us, because this has sustained me in my great expenses; to the priest who instructs my Indians and to Spanish employees and Indians, I pay 1,000 pesos for salaries alone, not counting the cost of their food. Consider what I need to keep up with costs, since I have to spend another 2,000 to maintain my household. And now there's the added cost of the mines, but with the aid of God they will yield enough for everything. As I said, I have a mulebreeding business and five or six stud donkeys; there's one they've offered me 1,000 pesos for, but I wouldn't sell him for 1,500, he's so good and so big. Most of the mules he sires are worth 100 pesos to me, and some more. The small livestock I have, sheep and goats, are worth nothing. A ewe can sell for 3 tomines or so, and a mutton brings me a peso at most. Meat is dirt cheap in this country. Every day at the mines the blacks and Christians eat up a goat or mutton. And here at Casma and in Trujillo we eat another every day, so that I have the expense of two head of stock daily and even then, truly, the blacks are not happy with it, so what am I to do with the rest, that is, the other expenses? I've said this so that you there understand that for all a man may have here, he needs it all, and hopes to God it is enough.

I know that those who have been here say that I am rich. Certainly I have more than I deserve from God. But as I said, everything goes for expenses, and at the end of the year the income only covers operations, and even sometimes isn't enough. And as the Indians give me nothing, that is, I take little from them and have expenses for priests and other things for them and they have been destroyed in past wars, since they are on the main highway and have been mistreated and destroyed, few of them remain. Once there were more than 2,000 Indians, and now there are about 200. I consider them as if they were my children; they have helped me earn a living and, as I say, I relieve them of tributes and everything else that I can. I have given them 220 pesos in income, [1?] 60 at my pleasure and 60 perpetually, and if God gives me life, I will leave them free of tributes when I die, so that whoever enjoys the tributes will not mistreat the Indians to get his revenue. Probably you there will say that it would be better to give this to my relatives than to the Indians. But I owe it to these children who have served me for thirty-odd years; it is a debt of life, and if I did not repay it I would go to hell. I am obliged to do what I can for my relatives, but if I don't, I won't go to hell for it.

I am here in this place much of the year because it is so luxuriant. To be able to stay, I have sheep, goats and pigs here, and I did have cows, but recently I sold them because they damaged the Indians' crops. I have a constant supply of milk, cream, and curds. This valley, or rather the Indians and my property, are close to the sea, where the Indians catch a thousand kinds of fish, and have many nets they fish with. And as they like me well, when they have good luck they bring fish to me. I have maize from tributes, and a mill where wheat is ground. And certainly we have very good fare, with the capons they give me as tribute, and the very fat kids and muttons; all is from the harvest and tribute, and praise to God, the excess here could feed all of those boys. I have four pounds of fish and two chickens in tribute daily. In the previous assessment they were obliged to give me 600 bushels of wheat and 500 of maize, but in this assessment that was just made the amounts were reduced by half, because I requested it of the inspector, since if I die, I want them relieved; I have more than enough with the wheat and the maize they give me now.

I have here next to the mill four or five hundred fig trees that yield a harvest of fifty hundredweight, and there are orange trees and some vines that yield grapes to eat. The Indians here suffer because the river of the valley is so variable, full of water in the winter and empty in the spring, and some years they have scarcity, but since they are fishermen, they get everything they need from the neighboring people in exchange for fish.

I have a farm in Trujillo where I grow wheat to maintain my household, and I have a mill in the middle of it to grind the wheat that is harvested and other wheat that is grown by surrounding neighbors. I have there a dozen Indian couples and two blacks, one of whom watches a flock of goats and sheep to supply the house. But since there are many livestock around the town, the animals are thin, and the milk is less abundant than here. And besides I have in Trujillo two black women who make bread and cook for everyone, and a mulatto woman who serves Ana López, embroidering and sewing and serving at table along with the Indian women and girls. There are five or six other Indian women who are laundresses and help the black women make bread, so that there are twenty or twenty-five people eating there, including the Indian women and boys and blacks serving at the house. I have said this so you will see whether or not I have much to maintain and support. You will ask why I never wrote this before. I say that since Trujillo causes it all, Trujillo is what I have written about.

Many salutations to milady sister Mari López and the gentlemen your sons. May our Lord give you the desired contentment and repose. From this valley of Casma, 1st of January, 1570.

Your servant,
Andrés Chacón

[1] Published in Spanish, with comment, in Otte, 'Die europäischen Siedler.'

12. An encomendero's opinions

Bernal Díaz del Castillo, encomendero, councilman and conqueror of Santiago de Guatemala, to the crown, 1552 and 1558[1]

... And we don't know when another boatload of Cerratos might arrive, to be given Indians ...

What encomenderos wrote to their relatives was one thing. What they wrote to governors and the crown was another. The encomenderos of the middle and later sixteenth century, many still conquerors or their direct descendants, had a well-defined public position, varying little from place to place. They were poor; their tributes had diminished to nothing; they were being displaced by undeserving newcomers to whom the governors were giving the whole land. Hidden in such words was their desire to maintain the monopoly and total dominance they had in the conquest period, and measured against that unreasonable hope, they indeed fell short and were deprived. Immigration to the central areas was strong, as we have said, and it included well-born and well-connected people who could not be denied their place. Others built up fortunes and connections on the spot, in mining or commerce, and then knocked insistently at the door. Incoming governors needed rewards for their entourage and close allies, to whom they could not give significant salaries. They cemented their base by awarding vacant encomiendas to relatives, employees and other followers, as indeed everyone expected them to do. Everywhere the governors acted the same, and everywhere the encomenderos protested. Actually, very few first conquerors or their sons had encomiendas taken away from them. Rather, between civil strife and Indian rebellions in the early time, and diseases in the later, many encomenderos died without direct heirs; it was mainly their grants that the governors gave away. The conquerors, within twenty or thirty years, had come to be a tightly knit group with innumerable nephews, nieces, or humble old friends under their wing, and it is to these that they would have had vacant encomiendas go. When this failed to happen, their response was not to fade into insignificance, but to marry their children into the new favored families, something which the newcomers desired just as greatly for the prestige and local acceptance it brought, so that from the second generation the encomenderos were an inextricable mixture of the new and the old, a situation that continued among leading families even in times and areas where the encomienda had lost its primary importance.

The above may give some perspective on Bernal Díaz del Castillo's colorful outrage in the first letter we include.[2] In the second, he illustrates a less grandiose, more realistic, but just as pervasive campaign that the encomenderos carried on, in this case more as individuals than as a group. Since the entire economy of the encomienda area, in its market- or city-oriented aspect, was exploited in an integrated fashion by the encomendero, he viewed any intrusion by other Spaniards as a threat, and acted either informally, or in the encomendero-dominated town councils, or before higher authorities, to repel the intruder. In doing so he often appeared in the somewhat improb-

able role of defender of the Indians, taking a position apparently – but only apparently – inconsistent with the rest of his
stance. A free hand for the encomendero in the area of his grant
was always the goal. Note how in the first letter Bernal is
against the general influence of friars with the high court and
the governor, while in the second he supports the two friars on
his own encomienda, who clearly support him in turn. Near
cities and in other areas of intensive development, encomenderos could not in fact long stem the economic invasion of outsiders, but they did usually manage to come to terms with it,
making the invaders to some extent their allies, distributors or
dependents.[3]

The writer of our letter is several steps above Andrés Chacón
(Letter 11) on the social scale. He is on the council of the
capital city of his region; he has impressive origins, with his
father having sat on the council of one of Spain's great cities,
and another relative a highly placed official; he is known and
can function at the Spanish royal court; in his own hand he
writes long letters to the royal council. And chronicles, as well.
Bernal Díaz is, of course, the famous chronicler of Mexico, who
in the nineteenth and twentieth centuries has often been mis-
leadingly pictured as some sort of uneducated plebeian. No, on
the face of it Bernal Díaz was the social equal of Hernando
Cortés. The puzzle is why Bernal, who in addition to his other
qualifications was a first conqueror of Mexico and had American experience even before that, did not soon become a prominent encomendero of Mexico City, rather than being shunted
off to Guatemala. Since his family's position was in a center of
Spanish commerce, he might have had mercantile origins; but
scions of established mercantile families of Spain were regularly
considered hidalgos and given high rewards in the Indies. Since
Bernal wrote so well, he might have been a notary, but that was
no impediment; so was Cortés. The crux of the matter seems to
lie elsewhere. In his chronicle, Bernal drops the remark that he
was 'somewhat related' to Diego Velázquez, governor of Cuba
(see Letter 5). An echoing statement appears in the second
letter here, where Bernal claims a relationship to Licentiate

Gutierre Velázquez. Conquest politics in Mexico for some time pitted a Cortés faction against a Velázquez faction. Bernal Díaz, however well disposed he may have shown himself towards Cortés, was a relative and compatriot of the enemy, certainly not someone to favor with a rich and centrally located Mexican encomienda.

Bernal Díaz to Emperor Charles V, 1552

Sacred Caesarean Catholic Majesty:
I believe your Royal Council of the Indies there will have heard of me and how I have served your majesty from when I was very young until now when I am in senescence. As such a loyal servant, and maintaining the fidelity to which I am obliged, and because I am your councilman in this city of Guatemala, and for many other reasons that exist, it is well to inform you what is being done in these lands as to their government and the administration of justice. I know for sure that your majesty and those of your Royal Council of the Indies believe that the orders you send are carried out and fulfilled, which orders are very just, to the benefit of the natives as well as of the Spaniards and the general good of the country. For that I kiss your majesty's sacred feet and pray to our Lord Jesus Christ that he guard your majesty and our lords the very illustrious princes and give them the reward your majesty wishes.

Your majesty, as I have said, this land stands in need of justice, because when it was completely without order it was much better managed, for the natives as well as for its proper perpetuation; and seeing this, I am so bold as to give this account, so that matters will not go further in such a fashion. I was at the royal court only a year ago, but when I left here for Spain, Licentiate Cerrato had just come to this province as president of the Audiencia, and by first appearances, he gave signs of doing justice; of course the citizens of this city and province always have been and remain such loyal servants, that with half a letter from your majesty they bow down to the ground in unison, as has always been seen in their actions, unlike Cerrato. We understand he has written to your majesty that he has worked and worked, and served and served, and we imagine that both your majesty and those of your royal council have given him credence. At any rate, he showed good signs at first, and for that reason when I was at the royal court there was nothing to report about what he had done up until then, and so I am not at fault for saying nothing at that time. But if I didn't inform you what is going on now I would be greatly at fault. Concerning the tribute quotas, your majesty ordered Cerrato that the towns be inspected as to what lands they have, what plants and animals they raise, what enterprises and trade they have, what the region is like and how many households there are in each town, and then, in conformity with the nature of each town and its special characteristics, a tribute should be assigned that the town can comfortably pay to maintain its encomendero. But your majesty, everything has been done contrary to your royal command, for none of the above things were inspected; Cerrato set the quotas sitting in his rooms here, following I don't know what account or listing, so that he did injustices to some towns, and left others unhappy. There are some towns without a third as many people and resources as others, though located next to each other, and he assigned as much tribute to the one as to the other, and did other altogether unreasonable things, by what I have been told. They say that now he is sending all the quota lists there to your majesty, as though people in Spain had experience of everything here and all the circumstances.

Your majesty orders that governors should give preference to conquerors and married settlers, and help to arrange the marriage of orphaned daughters of conquerors, and should sustain the poor with the patronage of these lands. What more just command could there be than this? But your majesty, Cerrato has acted as if when you issued that command, you had said: 'As to all the good positions that there should be or should fall vacant in those provinces, be sure you give them to your relatives.' To two brothers of his and a granddaughter whom he married off here, and to a son-in-law, and to his employees and friends, he has given the best encomiendas available in this province. In truth, any one of them alone yields more income than the total of everything that he has given in this city to conquerors. He gave one of these encomiendas I am talking about to a friend of his called Vallecillo, who, your majesty, was being sent prisoner from Nombre de Dios to Spain, and escaped along the way. They say that a Clavijo had reviewed his term in office, and for certain crimes and other faults that were found, fined him a certain amount of money, to go to the royal treasury. And then Cerrato took him in and gave him an encomienda of Indians! So he has neglected to give them to those whom your majesty orders, to give them to his relatives, employees, and friends, and he hasn't even finished satisfying them yet, since we are still waiting for him to make grants to two cousins of his, a nephew, and a grandson, and we don't know when another boatload of Cerratos might arrive, to be given Indians. If Cerrato would consider that your majesty ordered the encomiendas that the governors and royal officials once had to be taken away from them because they all get such substantial salaries, he wouldn't have given all this away with such grand flourishes. And also he should consider that your majesty granted him 500,000 maravedís more in salary than he had before, and he ought to remember that he is president of your majesty's Audiencia and that your majesty trusted in him to do justice uprightly and carry out your royal commands, as he has written he does.

I want your majesty to know how these grants of Indians that I have mentioned were made. In order that your majesty would believe it was done correctly, through the Royal Audiencia, Cerrato tried to have a Juan Rogel admitted as judge, because he had him up his sleeve. He needed his vote, since he saw that some of the other judges were not in favor of what he was doing, nor did they think it just to give Indians to his relatives who had just arrived from Castile, and take them away from poor conquerors who were loaded down with children and had served your majesty for thirty years. Although he had this Rogel expelled from the Royal Audiencia when he reviewed his term, I have heard it said that in order to make use of him Cerrato overlooked many things, saying 'you shave me, I'll shave you.'

Your majesty, one of the judges, named Tomás López, in truth is of good conscience, and he seems to have great zeal in fulfilling your royal commands; recently he inspected most of the provinces here. Because he didn't agree with Cerrato about giving Indians to a brother of his who just came from Spain, Cerrato, in order not to have him against him, sent him to Yucatán with 400,000 maravedís in salary, over and above what was assigned to him, which departure could very well have been dispensed with, since Cerrato will now be left alone. Licentiate Ramírez is also departing for Castile, so he will be left by himself, to command at his pleasure. And also, previously, he sent Licentiate Ramírez to Nicaragua with 7½ gold pesos in salary per diem, beyond his assigned salary, and with expenses paid, because the towns of your majesty feed them as they pass through, both him and López. May your majesty look closely at what Cerrato writes about his services and deeds and wanting to carry out your majesty's commands. Let me tell your majesty, from what I know of him he has such a command of rhetoric, and such prettified and savory words, that I feel sure he will know how to gild what he does with the pen; your majesty and your royal councilors will believe that it is as he has written and informed you, and that everything is being done as your majesty orders. Since he knows that in Spain he has such a reputation as a good judge, he dares do what he does. So let your majesty see what is necessary for your royal service; all these things have happened just as I say they have. If he has served in anything, it is in the way I have said, and at the expense of your royal treasury, giving Indians to his relatives and making them rich in a short time, handing out grants left and right as long as it pays off and his relatives prosper, and he gains fame and honor, with your majesty considering him the good judge he has made himself out to be. It's quite something the way he at times talks of past governors who stole and robbed and did ugly deeds, and says he is not that kind, that he doesn't take presents, not a chicken, nor has he transgressed with the citizens' wives, and in all this the good old man is saying that he does justice, as, with your majesty, he already has gained the reputation of doing; but he never considers that it is much worse to give a single one of those encomiendas to his relatives who used to work at their trades in Spain, and take them away from poor people who have richly deserved them by shedding their sweat and blood. So he gives what should go to the poor, according to your majesty's orders, to these people I have mentioned, but instead of considering this, he looks at the chickens and says other such things.

And also, your majesty, when some poor conqueror, perhaps married, with wife and children, comes to him to ask for help to maintain them, he is very indecorous in attending to his requests (and in other affairs too, for that matter), and answers with a fierce expression on his face and a way of wiggling in his chair that would detract from the presence of a man without many pretensions, much less the president of an Audiencia, and he says to him, 'Who ordered you to come to conquer? Was it his majesty? Then show me his letter. Go on with you, and let what you have already stolen be enough.' In this fashion he responds, and with other insults. When the poor miserable petitioners see such a countenance and such replies, they come away cursing their fortune and clamoring to God to send them justice in these things. And in truth, having been at the royal court a few months ago and seen what good and pure justice the presidents and judges of the royal councils dispense and how they pride themselves on it, and on the polite, agreeable replies they gave to supplicants, and then I see what goes on here, I am amazed at it, and I have even been so bold as to tell Cerrato to consider how your majesty is feared in our Spain, and the holy zeal shown there, with every last thing as it should be, and since in Spain Cerrato is considered a good judge, it appears to me that either I don't understand him or they must order him to do what he does here; he replies with beautified words, but no deeds at all.

Oh, if your majesty only knew what goes on here concerning

the little order that exists now among the natives of the land, how they go about as vagabonds and loiterers! Now when they should be advanced in matters of our holy faith, instead they are falling behind. They should be priding themselves on it, and seeking a better polity, and planting larger fields and raising livestock; it is all for themselves and their wives and children. But everything proceeds in great disorder, because Cerrato has no understanding of it.

And I also wish your majesty knew of the arrangement Cerrato has with two young friars and an employee of his, relator of the Audiencia, to assemble all the Indians of this province. This is something that he hides and is doing secretly in a town called Zumpango, so that all of them will unanimously and voluntarily appeal to your majesty to give them Cerrato as their perpetual governor. There would be much to say about this, but since I am not in your majesty's presence I will not say it. I only want your majesty to know that the people of these lands are of such a nature that for a drink of wine you can make the greatest chief say that he wants Barbarossa for governor, much less Cerrato, especially when those two young friars advocate it, for these people do not know of honesty and dishonesty, nor whether a request is good or bad. Here we see Cerrato telling us every day that he has written to your majesty requesting permission to return, and then he turns around and convokes people to ask for him as life-time governor. If it is true that he has written for permission to return, it is so your majesty will think he wants to leave and is not involved in convoking these people, and to give more foundation for his reputation there as a good judge. I tell your majesty, he is an old man of many stratagems, devices and tricks.

Oh sacred majesty, how just and good are the royal orders you send to this province, and how officials mold them here and do what they wish! I say this because I see how the friars are ambitious to rule and command in this land, and Cerrato desires to enrich himself and his relatives while keeping his fame as a good judge, and some of the judges have been involved in some deceits in I don't know what accounts, and they know that the friars have heard about and know their motives, so they don't want them to inform your majesty, but to write praising the members of the Royal Audiencia as good judges. The upshot is that the judges let themselves be ruled, and friars decree your royal justice and jurisdiction, and in this fashion things continue. Therefore let your majesty order something to be done, and do not consent to such a thing.

Sacred majesty, I well understand and know for sure that Cerrato will have written and informed you that the encomiendas he has given to his relatives are of little profit, and he will have glossed it over with gilded words. Your majesty, those are all the best grants there have been in this province. The least of them is more, for this country, than 10,000 pesos for Peru. The truth is that one of Cerrato's brothers died, leaving 3,000 pesos yearly income to a daughter who survived him and only yesterday came from Castile. Your majesty may remember the time when Nuño de Guzmán presided in Mexico; he was empowered to grant Indians, but because he gave them to friends and dependents instead of conforming to your majesty's orders, the grants were revoked and annulled. It seems to me more just that your majesty should have what Cerrato has given revoked, since your majesty expressly ordered him not to do it, so that your royal justice and commands would be maintained and your royal name be feared, and others would not be so bold as to do such things in the future.

I declare this to your majesty as a loyal servant, the best I can, because for thirty-eight years I have served you. Therefore I implore your majesty to deign admit me among the number of the servants of the royal house, for I will take it as a great favor. And do not consider the lack of polish of these words, since as I am not a man of letters I do not know how to make more delicate propositions, but only to say most truthfully what happens. And I implore your majesty not to allow this letter to come back here into the hands of Cerrato, because other letters that the council of this city has written on matters of your royal service have been returned. May our Lord Jesus Christ guard your majesty, granting you many more years of life, and give his holy grace to the most illustrious [queen] and princes our lords, and through their royal persons and fortunate arms may our holy faith always be lifted up. From the city of Santiago de Guatemala, 22nd of February, 1552.

I kiss your Sacred Caesarean Catholic Majesty's sacred feet,

Bernal Díaz del Castillo

Bernal Díaz to King Philip, 1558

Catholic Royal Majesty:

I have been informed that a Francisco de Valle, your royal factor, is sending to request your Royal Council of the Indies to grant him some lands for farming in the jurisdiction of two Indian towns, called San Pedro and San Juan, in a place where the natives of those towns were accustomed to grow crops; and he is also writing to ask that he be given license to hire Indians from these towns to work other lands that he bought close to the towns. Your Royal Audiencia here will not give him as many as he asks, since your judges have seen that because they gave him some before, more than twenty households there have been vacated, and very recently too, since he has had possession of the lands I mentioned for only about ten months. The people to whom Francisco de Valle is entrusting this business there in Spain are Martín de Ramoín and Ochoa de Loyando. For your royal majesty's information, the factor, in partnership with a Balderrama, had bought certain lands from the chiefs of these towns I mentioned, without informing me of it as their encomendero, so that I would not disturb the sale. And since the chiefs believed the lands were of a size that around fifty bushels of wheat could be planted there, and no more, and did not know the extent of twelve *caballerías,* which is what they agreed to in the bill of sale, and since now enough land is being taken from them to make up the twelve caballerías, and more than twelve – lands that must be more than a league in length and another in width – they disapprove of the sale, and demand that it be annulled because of the great deceit in it. And here in your Royal Audiencia they are suing for justice and returning the money that was given them for the land, and also they say that they cleared and plowed the land and planted twelve bushels of maize there, and built houses, for such was the agreement. They say that if it is felt just, they will pay some expenses that were incurred in plowing the lands, provided that they be given what they harvested there this year, or at least half of it, or that they take it all and pay nothing for the plowing, whichever the factor should prefer.

The chiefs are doing this because truly they are very angry over the bad deeds they have received, such that the chiefs say that it is because of the factor that the houses I mentioned have been deserted, over twenty of them. If it hadn't been for me and the Dominican friars who reside in the town, more people would have left; but now they have stopped going. Catholic royal majesty, these towns are very fertile, given to good Christianity and holy doctrine, and they have very good churches and rich ornaments, with many singers and music of every kind, that is, musical instruments. In all these provinces there are no towns better treated nor which are called on for less tribute, and two Dominicans are among them continually; there are devout local Indian women who have a place of retreat to live apart, with income assigned for their maintenance. It is not right that such towns should receive harassment. I appeal to your royal majesty to deign, when you write to the Royal Audiencia here, to include a paragraph so that no Indians from these towns will be hired out to the factor, because the chiefs say that truly their hearts break when they see it; they say they will consent to being hired out to other Spaniards, but they will not work on lands belonging to the factor, for much pay or little. And I also ask your royal majesty to have the paragraph say that if they return the money they will be given their lands, and the factor will not involve himself with them directly or indirectly. Your judges know very well all that I say here, and they are already denying him Indians to hire for that reason, and because the friars of St Dominic defend them in what they see is just, especially those who reside there with them. And may your majesty also know that Licentiate Cerrato, former president of the Audiencia, gave the factor some caballerías of land by virtue of a royal decree of yours; he sold them as soon as they were given to him and now he asks for more land to the detriment of the poor Indians. And since I know that your majesty, most Christian as you are, will order them to be favored as you continually do, I will desist from further supplication.

I want to give account of who I am so that your majesty might deign to do me fuller favors. I am the son of Francisco Díaz the Gallant, God rest him, who was your councilman in Medina del Campo, and I myself am your councilman in this city. At present I am your *fiel ejecutor*, by order of the Royal Audiencia and by vote of the council. I am quite closely related to your former judge, God rest him, Licentiate Gutierre Velázquez, and I have served your majesty in these parts for the last forty years; I took part in the discovery and conquest of Mexico with the Marqués del Valle, which fact has been confirmed before now in your Royal Council of the Indies, and don fray Bartolomé de las Casas, former bishop of Chiapas, also knows it well. Now again I beg that you condescend to grant me the *fiel ejecutoría* of this land, that is, of this city, since I am such an old servant of yours and my father and relatives have always served you, and for this I will be most grateful. May our Lord Jesus Christ give your Catholic Royal Majesty many years of life with much health and augmentation of realms, as your royal majesty might desire and your loyal servant, in whom you may put your trust, would wish. From Guatemala, 20th of February, 1558.

I kiss your Catholic Majesty's royal feet,
Bernal Díaz del Castillo

[1] Published in Spanish in *Cartas de Indias*, pp. 38-47.

[2] See also Murdo J. MacLeod's treatment of Licentiate Cerrato in his *Spanish Central America: A Socioeconomic History, 1520-1720* (Berkeley and Los Angeles, 1973), pp. 108-16.

[3] An extensive illustration of encomenderos coexisting with a Spanish population in the area of their grants can be seen in Lockhart, 'Spaniards among Indians: Toluca in the Later Sixteenth Century,' *Creole Societies in Africa and the Americas*, ed. Franklin W. Knight (forthcoming).

13. The miner

Nicolás de Guevara, mining entrepreneur, in Potosí, to Simón Ruiz, merchant, in Medina del Campo, 1595[1]

> ...I soon came up here to the imperial town of Potosí, where I have lived the whole time, occupying myself in the business of extracting silver...

We have seen that encomiendas dominated the economy of much of the sixteenth-century Spanish American countryside, channeling labor and goods to the cities, as later other types of estates would do. To be complete, to be even tolerable for the Spaniards, the system had to include some way for them to buy iron, cloth, wine, and many other things obtainable only from Europe. Therefore the encomenderos showed a sharp interest in extracting precious metals (as in Letter 11). But placer gold soon ran out in most areas, while silver, though abundant in the central regions, proved to be concentrated in a few rich, long-lasting, mainly remotely located sites: in Mexico, at Zacatecas, Guanajuato, and some others; in Peru, at Potosí, the great Cerro Rico or Rich Mountain. There could not be a silver mine on every encomienda. Instead of everyone becoming a miner, the whole Spanish American economy oriented itself towards the mines as the ultimate source of currency. The mines did not become the greatest centers in themselves, being mainly in forbidding places and distant from the densest Indian populations (though Potosí was an impressive town for a time); but Spaniards in all walks of life flourished economically only to the extent that they could sell supplies and services to the mines, or profit from them through extensions of loans or credit, or participate indirectly, selling things in the Spanish cities to others who had closer contact. In some fashion they had to have access to the mine silver that alone would pay for European things.

The Mexican situation is complex because the greatest mines were altogether outside the area of dense sedentary Indian population; the encomienda could not be brought to bear directly. To take the example of Peru and Potosí (belonging to colonial greater Peru though in today's Bolivia), the encomenderos of the whole area from Cuzco south received tribute in silver because their Indians went to work in the mines, and they got yet more silver by selling in Potosí products as unusable by Europeans as *chuñu* and coca, to supply the Indian work force. Non-encomenderos entered the supply business too, and made fortunes; Potosí stimulated the rise of the Tucumán region in northwestern Argentina, which came to depend for its livelihood on sending livestock and livestock products to the mines. Merchants found Potosí an attractive market, and they also helped finance mining enterprises; the operations of the great international mercantile networks had two terminal points, Seville and Potosí. What the suppliers and miners earned was often spent in Lima, which continued to be the chief center for the Spanish population. The Lima market, full of Potosí silver, was the country's most lucrative, and the only recourse that existed for Spaniards in the central and northern part of the country.

Encomenderos and merchants seem to have been the first important miners, that is, mining entrepreneurs and investors (this was the sense the Spaniards gave to the word *minero*). But since both groups were heavily involved in undertakings of a very different nature, and silver mining was a specialized and intensive business, there soon came into being the special type of the miner. He might be an encomendero's relative, a former merchant, or a person with technical competence in mining. Or he might be none of these, for the rich mining sites sometimes saw enterprising people rise from nothing to great wealth in a short time. The successful miner was far less tied down than was the encomendero, and was very likely to return to Spain with his profits, or even more likely, to move to the capital, Lima or Mexico City, and begin to establish a position among the older families. Another possibility, of course, was the loss of everything. Mining was volatile.

While he continued his activity, the miner would aim for an integrated complex that was much like the encomendero's, and deserves the name of estate just as fully. In the present letter our Potosí miner speaks of some of its elements: mining sites, a refining mill, honorific municipal office (lucrative too, in this case). He must have also had Spanish technical supervisors, skilled refiners at the mill (black slaves and permanent Indian employees), and much temporary unskilled Indian help, as well as, if he could manage it, supportive enterprises farther away to provide food, animals, wood and other supplies.

The letter itself tells us a good deal of Nicolás de Guevara's origins. For one thing, he is a Basque. The Basques, with their iron deposits, were the miners of Spain, and were correspondingly prominent in the silver mines of the Indies, in both Mexico and Peru, to the point that in the early seventeenth century Potosí saw a serious anti-Basque reaction. Guevara does not come from nowhere: he has an uncle Licentiate Guevara in Madrid; he is distantly related through marriage to one of the greatest merchants of Spain; and prominent relatives have preceded him in Peru. We may presume that his way was smoothed by help and credit from his kinsmen and compatriots.

Potosí was many things, and spawned at least three genres of writing, namely controversy over its disruptive labor system, project-spinning concerning its technical difficulties, and praise of its wealth. This brief letter belongs to the last.

Very magnificent sir:

You will consider it something new to see a letter of mine from such remote parts, but recognizing the kinship there is between us, I wanted to take advantage of your favor on this occasion. I had a sister in the town of Belorado, married to an honorable man there named Andrés Ruiz, and my uncle Licentiate Pedro de Guevara has written me from Madrid that she died and left four children. To help bring them up, I thought I would send, through you, 350 gold pesos, to be delivered entire in Medina del Campo, the charges borne as appears in the authenticated bill of lading that accompanies this. A great friend of mine called Juan de Guesala is taking the money and will be very careful to deliver it when he arrives; he is going to live in Durango, Biscay, where I was born and raised. I beg you, when you receive this, to send the accompanying letter to Andrés

Ruiz, and tell him that when Juan de Guesala arrives the amount will be sent to him. Since that is a land of scarcity, they are doubtless in need.

Now that I am writing you, it seems proper to give you an account of my life. I came to Peru the year of '81 and soon came up here to the imperial town of Potosí, where I have lived the whole time, occupying myself in the business of extracting silver. I have many very good mining sites in the Rich Mountain, and a mill where I grind the ore. I also bought the office of municipal council secretary and notary public of this town, for 42,000 ducats in cash; it is the most profitable office having to do with papers that the king our lord offers in all his realms, and as to honor, it is the best thing here. I have or am gaining a great stock of ore to process, and if it yields well, with our Lord's aid, I mean to go back to Spain within three years. When I arrive, I will come to pay you my respects.

I married a second cousin of mine named doña Francisca de Lantadilla, from this land here, daughter of Martín de Ayales, with a dispensation brought from Rome. I wanted to give you such a long account of everything because it would not be right to neglect to give it to a person such as yourself. I beg you to do me the great favor of answering my letter and telling me in what way I might serve your grace, whose person I greatly desire that our Lord guard and increase.

Written in Potosí, 4th of April, 1595.

Nicolás de Guevara

[1] Published in Spanish, with comment, in Marie Helmer, 'Un tipo social: el "minero" de Potosi,' *Revista de Indias*, XVI (1956), 85-92.

14. Commerce across the Atlantic

Francisco de Escobar, merchant of Seville, to his
junior partner Diego de Ribera in Lima, 1553[1]

...I have written you with this fleet all about
everything going on...

The third great constituent of the life-support system of Spanish American cities, along with the encomiendas and the mines, was commerce. Since the reader has already been exposed to two merchants' letters of progressive difficulty (Letters 4 and 5), we now present him with the maximum challenge of a voluminous letter from the nerve center of one of the large trans-Atlantic companies, at a time when the trade had reached full maturity. The other two letters were written by junior partners in the Indies; this one is from a senior partner in Seville to the factor-partner in Lima. Francisco de Escobar, the merchant in Seville, is no novice to the Indies, however, for he had typically enough been active in Peru for years, accumulated capital during the first boom of Potosí, and advanced to head his own company based in Seville. On a several-year term, the company arrangement included two partners in Seville, a representative on the Isthmus to forward goods toward Peru, a partner in Lima seeing to distribution there, and underlings in Lima and other places in Peru.

The letter is written in stages, over a two-month period, and is really several letters in one. Certain leitmotifs run through the whole, one of the more charming being the advancing pregnancy of Escobar's wife Marcela de Carvajal. Not advancing, rather constantly being harped upon, are the 780 pesos that Juan López, the Panamá man, double-charged Escobar for transportation of goods. Escobar is unable to forget it for more than a couple of pages, and mentions it in every conceivable connection. The death of Juan López and the company reorganization made necessary thereby are the real occasion and substance of the letter. Escobar considers one type of company, then another, then yet another, with both organization and personnel changing constantly.

In the course of the discussion Escobar brings up some matters vital to an understanding of the evolution of trans-Atlantic commerce. He is quite uncertain whether to leave sale of goods in Panamá at the discretion of the representative there, which would take advantage of windfall high prices and allow quick reinvestment, or to use the more dependable, mechanical method of sending all goods on to the principal market in Lima. Everything turns on getting large and steady streams of silver back to Seville to pay debts and make investments; Escobar comes to this point again and again, and leaving nothing to the imagination, he admonishes his partner Ribera always to send whatever he has 'whenever ships leave Lima for Panamá in August, September, October, November, December or January.' The Seville merchants are against any local long-term investment in the Indies, as we see in Escobar's reports of arguments inside another firm (caused by the Lima representative's action in investing in local meat supply and transportation). Thus the large Seville firms at this time were still tending to keep direct control of trans-Atlantic trade all the way through to retail in the capitals of the Indies, and make any long-term, credit-stiffening investment in Spain. But divergent tendencies were being felt, tendencies which won out in the next century when most goods were sold wholesale at the ports to merchants who had taken firm root in Lima and Mexico City.

Another important aspect of commercial life coming through clearly in the letter is the extent to which the merchants manipulated and milked their own companies. All the partners took advantage of the expressed or tacit right to make separate investments and use company facilities to distribute the goods. Escobar maintains a whole store in Lima for the sale of his private merchandise. In order to help in setting up a new company, he in effect wants the Lima house belonging to the old company underevaluated. The apparent investments of the different partners actually represent prospective percentages of the profit, arrived at after much haggling.

The tone of the letter is mainly friendly, but we do see at times that it is the superior talking, chastising Ribera for neglect of remittances and for bad hiring practices, i.e., hiring someone other than Escobar's friends. At other times he wheedles a bit, since he very much wants Ribera to represent the company for some years more before being promoted to Seville – the ambition of practically all the merchants of this time.

As in the other merchant letters, here too names abound, and much of the color and interest lies hidden in them. Many belong, as is clear in the letter, to other merchants of Seville, competitors or possible partners of Escobar; what is not clear is that many of these people made their start in Peru as he did, so that in the commercial world a tight net of career patterns, friendships and rivalries held both sides of the Atlantic together. Even the Seville notary Juan Franco who prepares Escobar's papers was once chief notary of Lima, and Escobar knew him there. We have already mentioned three of the partners of Escobar's company; 'Mr Diego Núñez' is the fourth, in Seville with Escobar.

Some important patron—client relationships are glimpsed in the letter as well. Particularly small-scale merchants such as Escobar once was found it to their advantage sometimes to be the near-dependents of important encomenderos who favored them in various ways. In this letter we have Ana Suárez, who inherited a large encomienda of the Lima district, and was closely associated with Escobar when he was in Lima (Secretary Merlo is her second husband; he was secretary of Governor Vaca de Castro, writer of Letter 29, and married Ana Suárez through the latter's influence). The connection continues even though Escobar is now in Spain. Another relationship is that with Judge Altamirano of the Audiencia of Lima. Escobar is keeping tabs on a lawsuit in Granada concerning one of the judge's relatives. Also Escobar's wife is sending some special things for the judge's wife. One imagines that he and his firm received favors in return. Notice, by the way, that Escobar wavers on whether to call the judge's wife *doña* or not, something that could happen only in rather extreme cases. In fact she did not have the title, but this was such an anomaly in the wife of such a high official that Escobar uses the term once, then returns to the unadorned name. With Ana Suárez, long a camp follower and mistress of the first husband she married only on the day of his execution, there is no such wavering.

Another thread are Escobar's relatives. One is Alonso de Escobar, already in Peru when Francisco was, and now in Chile, not exactly part of the company, but still carrying out commissions for it in that most distant outpost. Escobar's sister and brother-in-law are now in Lima, and throughout the letter Escobar pushes their advancement. In Tierra Firme is a nephew, ready to start up the company ladder. This sending back of younger relatives was a basic mechanism long maintaining the strength of trans-Atlantic ties.

In addition to all these things, there is much in the letter on the debt-collection and courier service that was one part of mercantile affairs; on the Atlantic fleet system, by now quite fully developed; on profit levels; on conditions in Seville; on wars with the French, and even the most recent, if not most accurate news on English politics, so that Escobar could say with much justice that he had written 'all about everything going on here.'

Jesus   *Seville, 16th of October, 1553*
Sir:
     I have so much to write that I don't know where to begin, though I'll not write at length now. A caravel is leaving for Cape Verde; there being so many Frenchmen on the sea, we don't know whether it will meet with any or not, but on the chance that this might arrive, I will write. I'll say a few things that need to be said: first, a caravel that left Nombre de Dios on the 5th of February of this year and arrived here at the end of May, brought us letters from Gaspar Ramos and Alonso de Cazalla, in which they inform us of the death of Juan López, and though his death grieved me as a relation, as far as our property is concerned, God did us a great favor. He had handled business so badly and confusedly that I believe it was a great gain for our property to lose him. And as we had given power in Tierra Firme to Gaspar Ramos and Alonso de Cazalla to take over our affairs if he died, they did so, which was just the right thing. And being sure that as soon as you heard of his death you would hurry to come to Tierra Firme, we did not send a special person there for those matters, but in the fleet that is now ready to leave we are again sending you very full and explicit powers to take account of everything that has been done there, and I desire extremely that you should have come to Tierra Firme so you can intercept our messages there. For as I say,

considering it certain, we are not sending anyone, because we wish and desire that all of it should go through your hands, which would be better than through our own; and if perchance when this arrives you should not have gone to Tierra Firme, then by all means go and finish up matters there.

With the changing times we here may have an excess of merchandise, though you will not there. When you come to Tierra Firme you should in no way or manner sell the house in the city of Lima, because we want to make a new company and have you go back to reside there. Don't take it into your head to come to Castile now, because all Spain is so expensive and high priced that people need great means to be able to support themselves here. I would like you to be there another five or six years, whichever you think best, for the time that the company we are organizing should last, because in it would be only you and I and Mr Diego Núñez, without having this confusion in Nombre de Dios and Panamá, but only a man who would take care of the merchandise we would send from here, directing it on to you, and he would send here whatever you send him. All this is to be something very much among friends and brothers, because even if there were to be no one in the company but you and I, as long as I should live and you should want to stay there, I will not abandon the association nor stop sending you all my goods; though I don't want to get in debt to make shipments, just whatever I have, and you, and if Mr Diego Núñez wants to, whatever share he wants and no other volume, merely what we could ship without resorting to credit or exchange.

At the moment we are all in necessity because the fleet of which Carreño was general and which left on the 4th of November of last year has not been heard from to this day, nor has any ship come from New Spain or Santo Domingo, and so we are in great necessity, as is the whole kingdom, since almost the majority of the merchants have failed and there is not a penny to be borrowed in the whole city; if any bills of exchange are available, they are payable in Valencia or Lisbon, at something like 60 percent a year. Consider how many businesses could stand such a thing. Nor do we have silver pieces nor gold jewels;

everyone has had them melted down. The hardship and general necessity among all, rich and richest, just to get enough to eat, is such that you truly must see it to believe it. Every day we await the fleet of Carreño from New Spain and Santo Domingo. May our Lord see fit to bring them back safely, because truly the arrival of the fleet will revive this part of the country, and the whole kingdom as well. And as Juan López had done so badly in taking what you were sending us, we have suffered need. Still, praise the Lord, we came out of it better than most, because with properties and possessions that friends gave us to be leased out, we have taken care of almost all of the letters of credit; if it hadn't been for this help it seems to me we would have paid out more for loans than profited on the merchandise, but in the way I have said, we managed well enough, and weren't damaged as much as others have been.

I will come now to reviewing Juan López' accounts, and I think that just from the money he took from me there, there will be a deficit of 5,000 pesos. To amass money, in one account that he sent me he charges me with an item that reads as follows: 'Item, 780 pesos, the cost of 130 loads I transported for him in the packtrain and boats, being the merchandise that was appraised in the galleon for Chile and the one for Paita.' You also charge me with these 780 pesos in the current account you sent me, so that I am charged twice for the same amount, and may God pardon Juan López for it; a very fine fraud of his, to get paid there in Tierra Firme for my shipments and on the other hand send to you for payment. Search out this item that I mention and compare it with Juan López' account, because if you charge me with it, then Juan López shouldn't, so don't accept this item of his, so that I will not be charged more than once; and don't be neglectful in this matter.

At the time that Juan López died, there was a quantity of my wine in Panamá and Nombre de Dios, in jugs and casks, and also soap and other things of mine outside the company, all of which was sold at auction. I hope that Gaspar Ramos and Alonso de Cazalla sent me the money from it in the fleet that we expect, and didn't add it to the company assets or pay debts and other things that Juan López owed with it, because if they shouldn't have sent it to me and should have used it to pay the things I mentioned, they would be doing me a very bad turn, since it is all on my own account.

I feel sure that in this fleet we are now awaiting you will have sent me a quantity of money. At Sanlúcar there are now more than thirty ships, loaded and very well equipped, with bronze artillery and munitions. Each ship carries a double crew of sailors and 10 soldiers; the general of the fleet will be Cosme Rodríguez Farfán, named by the king, with two ships and an advice-boat carrying 500 soldiers. The two ships and boat carry no merchandise, but only artillery, munitions, provisions and fighting men; they are in very good order, and one goes as flagship. The fleet and convoy of Rodríguez Farfán will go straight to Nombre de Dios; in the latitude of San Germán the ships headed for New Spain and those headed for Santo Domingo will separate and each head its own way, while the two ships and advice-boat will continue with those going to Nombre de Dios, about fifteen ships at least, and as I say, all very good ones and well outfitted. The defense levy for the fleet is 2½ percent; lack of money has delayed the fleet's departure so much, because the shippers haven't a penny to pay the levies to the masters and the 2½ percent for the fleet. They say that when Carreño's fleet arrives there will be enough money to dispatch this one; if it doesn't come, we believe this fleet will not be able to leave until January, however much effort is put into it. May our Lord bring it in safety and bring also the others we await, so that we can emerge from the great need we are in, which is such that, by God, we are all weary and chastened.

In order, with the aid of God, to avoid finding ourselves in such straits again, we are sending plenty of merchandise in the fleet, though however much it is, it will hardly be enough, because no other fleet will depart for a year. There is great scarcity of merchandise in New Spain, Santo Domingo, and the other places, and we feel sure that great profits have been made in New Spain; in the last letters from there they write that merchandise was sold for 130 percent and more, and people think it will be much more now, since no ship has come from there for almost a year and a half, and we expect a great treasure of money here.

All Spain, praise our Lord, has had good weather. We have a very bitter war with France, the hardest fought that ever was seen. His majesty has taken two forts at a place called [Tebianrediun],[2] which is between Flanders and France, and his forces have entered the country there. The last letters we have from Flanders, from the 28th of August, report that his majesty was in good health and was going to his camp in person, and that the camp of his majesty and the French camp were only three leagues from each other. The general of his majesty's army is the prince of Piedmont, who is also the duke of Savoy. His majesty's forces are large, and so are those of the French. It is thought that the two camps met in battle this very day. May our Lord be pleased to give the victory to his majesty, since he is such a Christian prince. The Prince is in Valladolid now, since the court is there; he came from Acoca to El Pardo, which is the wood of Madrid, and now is back again in Valladolid, because don Diego de Acevedo came from his majesty's court with dispatches for him, and don Francisco de Mendoza came along. Up till now no viceroy has been appointed for Peru, except that they say that his majesty has left it up to the Prince whether to name don Francisco de Mendoza; we hope they will name him, although others claim the viceroy will be don Diego de Acevedo or the count of Palma. We all want it to be don Francisco de Mendoza, since he is such a good cavalier and deserves it.

In the month of February last, Anchueta's ship, of more than 300 tons, left Sanlúcar for Nombre de Dios, with permission to sail alone. It cost us dear, because within four days after it left Sanlúcar the French took it; it was very richly loaded, with a cargo worth 60,000 ducats or more. The loss did great damage among the merchants here, and cost me myself about 400 ducats; this was the greatest prize the French have taken on the Indies route.

On the feast of Magdalena a French fleet sacked La Palma, in the Canaries; it is said that what they took was worth over

200,000 ducats. And since, as I said, I don't consider this letter very sure to arrive because it is only going to Cape Verde, I will not write more news, though there is much to write.

The king of England died. He was still a boy, and they say a tutor of his killed him to seize the kingdom. There have been great arguments among them, but now the kingdom is peaceful under Madam María as queen, the dead king's sister; she is the emperor's cousin, and he was going to marry her before he married the empress. She is a woman of about forty; they say that the people of the kingdom are pressing her to marry, and with a native of England.

Our Prince's marriage is arranged with the Infanta of Portugal, the one they call the Rich.

Marcela de Carvajal is in good health and sends you her greetings. Our Lord has seen fit to grant us favors, and she is six months pregnant; she has had a very good pregnancy and is due in January. With the aid of God we will have a little Baltasar, or if it is a girl it will be Ana, please our Lord that it be for his service.

As I said, this fleet in which Cosme Rodríguez Farfán is going as general will be so good and so well equipped for the return trip that it will not fear all France; by all means strive to send us a great quantity of money in this fleet of Farfán because it will come in such security, and we will not insure a penny of it. For lack of money we are not sending merchandise in this fleet, except for four or five slaves, and some Avila pitch that is going on the ship of the Albos, of which Juan García is master. Francisco de Ampuero is going in this same ship, and the wife of Governor Balduña is also going in this fleet, in Buitrón's ship. Secretary Merlo has gone to Valladolid to confer with don Francisco de Mendoza; I don't believe he will go with this fleet, because he is trying to get permission to have milady Ana Suárez come here. I will report at length on everything with the fleet, and meanwhile hope that this reaches you.

In Tierra Firme try to obtain all the letters and papers I sent in the last fleet, Carreño's, that were directed to Juan López; they should all be in the hands of Mr Gaspar Ramos. Take care of the bills I sent to have collected in the city of San Miguel; I think the power to collect included Mr Gaspar Ramos. He would do me a favor by delegating the power to you so you could have the money collected.

Consider how well Juan López managed things; he never remitted the 800-odd pesos belonging to milady Ana Suárez that you sent him to be sent on to me. You will have to tell her to give you power to collect it; get a copy of the item in the register of the ship in which it was sent, and have it collected in Nombre de Dios. Another great cruelty of his was that he failed to send on the money belonging to Bartolomé de Jerez that you sent him, and its proper owner here is reduced to begging. We here need a copy from the register so it can be collected, and also copies of all the items that you sent him, so we will have clarity in everything.

There in Tierra Firme is a boy, my nephew, son of my sister; when you get there, look after him until, God willing, I will write with the fleet what should be done. Along with this letter will go one that Mr Núñez and I wrote, signed by both of us, and for what is lacking here I refer you to that one.

And if this should chance to reach your hands, tell Judge Altamirano that last December a decree was issued in Granada, ordering all of Mr Gonzalo de Torres' property returned to him. I was sending you an authorized copy of the order on the ship of Anchueta that the French took. The other party appealed, but I believe that with the aid of God I will be able to send news in the fleet that the judgment has been confirmed in review, because Mr Francisco González is in Granada and is certain they will confirm it. May it please the Lord that it turn out as you there desire.

Write me continuously, by way of Santo Domingo and by whatever other routes there should be, and tell about everything at length; as I say, I greatly wish that this might reach you at Nombre de Dios.

May our Lord give you, etc.

Seville, 25th of November, 1553

The above is a copy of a letter that went on the caravel for Cape Verde on the day that appears, and left from the bar at Sanlúcar on the 22nd of last month. Since then our Lord has seen fit to do us more favors than we deserve; on Wednesday, the 25th of last month, General Carreño and the fleet from Nombre de Dios and New Spain passed the bars at Sanlúcar, and I believe if all Spain arrived here the joy could not be greater. Blessed be the Lord. We did have a moment of suspense, which was that about a hundred leagues before reaching the Azores, the flagship got lost from the rest in a storm; it was richly loaded because in the Gulf, while the fleet was still all together, a ship of Bolaños' was leaking badly, and they took off all the money and passengers and put it all on the flagship I mentioned, which got separated from the fleet. We were greatly concerned because of all that came in it; a full half of what you were sending us came in that ship, because it was the best in the whole fleet. In the end our Lord saw fit to favor us, since within a week after Carreño arrived we had news that this flagship had reached Terceira, in the Azores and, because it was no longer navigable, unloaded all the money it carried and was beached there. In January, pleasing God, don Alonso will leave Sanlúcar with six heavily armed ships carrying almost 1,500 men and go straight to Terceira to bring back the money from this ship. He will come back along with a fleet from New Spain that is expected then; God willing, don Alonso will be here by March or April, because he is only going to Terceira with the fleet that guards this coast and gathers in ships coming from the Indies, to accompany and guard them as far as Sanlúcar; and this armada is at his majesty's expense.

With this fleet of Carreño I received your letters from the 12th of March and 12th of April of this year; our Lord knows the joy it gave me to know that you are well, which is the main thing I want to know, because I love and desire your health as my own. In the letter of March 12 you tell how last year you sent us a shipment of money. By now you will have found out what Juan López did with it, may God pardon him; he sent me only 4,000 pesos, and for the company he sent not a penny. It was a good thing he died, since he surely would have taken a good slice of what you just sent; may God pardon him everything, for truly he was the destroyer of our business and good name. And as to what you say of the pain you felt when you found out that Juan López had taken money, I readily believe that your pain equalled ours.

You say that you heard of Juan López' death through letters from Gaspar Ramos, and also that he and Alonso de Cazalla by power from us had taken over the property; you will also doubtless have heard how they sold the stocks of goods in Panamá and Nombre de Dios, and about the many debts that Juan López had left there, and what poor security he had maintained in everything. I will say no more about this except that truly our Lord did us a favor in taking Juan López and removing him from that post.

I had written you that we thought it would be well if you came to Nombre de Dios and Panamá to settle accounts on this affair, but now I tell you to stay at home without budging or leaving Lima, because we will send from here an adequate person to finish up matters, who will be stationed in Tierra Firme and be part of the new company that, God willing, we are going to make. As soon as you see this, we need for you to strive to close out everything having to do with the company so that we can finish up here; whatever you have to sell that belongs to the company, sell it now even if it be on credit, or in whatever way you think best, so that you can send us the conclusion of it and we can finish up here. Appraise the houses for the new company in such a way that you don't do it an injustice, but appraise them at what they could be sold for in cash. Do all this as quickly as you can, and also send us sufficient powers both to finish the old company and make the agreement on the new one. Let the power be made out to Luis Sánchez de Albo, Diego Díaz Becerril, Diego de Illescas, and Ruy Díaz de Gibraleón, or any one of them alone. Since this is a matter that must be arranged among us here, you need not worry that we will not do right by you; that you will see by the result.

In your letter of the 12th of April I see that you didn't want to come to Panamá, and am glad of it. Stay in Lima, and when you leave there, let it be when you are coming straight to this country to rest and take your pleasure from the company we will make, if it please God. I will invest at least 30,000 ducats in it, and Mr Diego Núñez 15,000 ducats, plus whatever you should put in. It will be a good company, and we will have no packtrains nor boats nor impediments in Panamá and Nombre de Dios, only a dwelling house, and we will not send there another person who will then or later cause us concern, because the person we send will understand perfectly that in everything he is to do what we and you tell him.

At the time when Carreño's fleet arrived, the other fleet of which Farfán is general was about to leave from Sanlúcar, but because of the arrival it has stayed on for some days; great demands for merchandise have come from all parts of the Indies. In New Spain shipments were sold for 150 percent, and in Nombre de Dios, at the time the fleet was ready to return, they say that merchandise was selling for even more than that. With this news from all parts of the Indies, there has been a great rush to ship things, and in twelve days I believe more than 500,000 ducats worth of merchandise have been bought; prices have all risen so quickly that in three days everything went up 25 percent. Since the ships were already loaded, what has risen most of all is freight; people have paid 30 ducats per ton to Nombre de Dios, cash down, and by God, this week I myself paid 30 ducats per ton, cash, from here to Nombre de Dios.

I have bought a little merchandise on my own account and am sending it in these ships, as you will see by the bills of lading; since it was bought within a week I couldn't sort things out very well, but just bought what I thought might be needed there, although we feel sure it will bring a large gain. Be so good as to send me the final accounting on all merchandise you have received for me that went through the hands of Juan López, and the goods he sent and in what ships, because I must finish up the account of the merchandise I sent Juan López and would like, since there has been enough time, that nothing of that account of mine be left unsettled, but that the final summary be sent. I sent some merchandise on my own account in the fleet of Carreño, and Gaspar Ramos received it in Nombre de Dios; he writes me that he sent it on to you as I had written him to; that is, Gaspar Ramos sent this merchandise from Carreño's fleet to you in my name. Keep a separate account of what I am sending in this fleet without getting it in any way mixed with the shipments that went through the hands of Juan López. As I say, everything that Juan López sent in my name from Nombre de Dios and Panamá is to be kept apart, and I am extremely desirous that when this arrives you should already have sent me the final accounting for it, but if by chance when this comes, there should be anything of mine left in that account, then sell it right away to close it out. Everyone tells us here that, praise our Lord, you have made a very great profit. May it be for His service and may it continue until today, but do be sure you keep selling the merchandise of mine that you should receive. I will not be sending more merchandise on my own account, though, until such time as we make the new company, and after it is made I intend to ship only on behalf of the company; I will have plenty just shipping for it.

As to what you sent in the ship of Juan de Areche, Gaspar Ramos and Alonso de Cazalla sent it all on, exactly as it came; half of it, praise God, is already here in the city, and the other half is at Terceira. As I said, it was coming in the flagship, and with the aid of God we will have it here by March or April. Though we have a bitter war with France, the enemy does us little damage, because the fleets are very secure, going and coming back with an armada, and besides that don Alonso sails between here and Terceira in the Azores with another very fine armada, awaiting the fleets, so that in addition to the convoy the fleet already has with it, on reaching the Azores don Alonso comes with his armada to guard it, and so all proceeds in very good order. The armada that goes to the Indies with the fleets is paid for by a defense levy of 2½ percent, and the one that don Alonso leads is at his majesty's expense.

It's amazing that the money you sent with Juan de Areche reached the fleet, it already being in Nombre de Dios ready to sail. Don't wait so late again to send money; rather whenever ships leave Lima for Panamá in August, September, October, November, December or January, always send whatever you should have. This will have two advantages: it will make sure that money reaches the fleets, and it will avoid running so much risk in only one ship. After all, what you have there is also the sea; sometimes ships sink between here and Sanlúcar, and the same thing could happen there.

As to what you say about the money belonging to Alonso de los Naranjos, I have a very satisfactory acknowledgment of the receipt of it all by his mother, made yesterday before Juan Franco, notary. He is getting a lot of papers ready for me for this fleet; I will do my best to see that they make it, but if not, they will go with the next one, and don't worry about any of it. The same will be done with the estate of Bachelor Ramos. As to what you say about the papers on the property that Gamboa owes and the black who has run away, we would be very grateful to have it collected, if possible, for Alonso de Naranjo's mother. She says that Valenzuela's son is obliged to pay the debt of 1,700 pesos by a new document Gamboa signed in Arequipa; although they had seized Gamboa's estate to pay Valenzuela's son, they gave him his property back and he issued new obligations. For this reason Valenzuela's son is obliged to pay, since the debt was secure, the property having been seized, and he returned it without being empowered to. I have informed Pedro López Urrea here of all this, and you look into it there. I received from Alonso de Carmona the 864 pesos, 6 tomines of the judicial order; some time ago I took the letter out of security to have the money paid to me here. All the letters you sent for people in this city were delivered, and those for elsewhere were sent on their way in good hands, and the same will be done with whatever you send. I was very glad to hear the news you sent about Charcas and the rest; please keep reporting on everything at length.

In matters of Chile, write to Alonso de Escobar entreating him to collect the estate of Juan Pinel as I already wrote him, as a work of charity, since those who are to receive it here are very poor people; and if it can't be collected, then let him send a statement to that effect, and I will have done my duty. Send him the letters I wrote him, and tell him to be sure to collect what is outstanding on the merchandise and what Bautista, the captain, owes me, and send it to me. If Alonso de Escobar should need something from you, then please send it to him, and you will be doing me a favor.

Milady Ana Suárez will be able to come here, God willing, because I am sending her his majesty's license to come to Spain for three years without giving bond, and God willing, when the three years have elapsed I believe she can get an extension. What she leaves there is to be in your hands, and you will be doing me a very great favor if you take care of it as though I were doing it myself. If a bond or some such thing is required, see to it, and I declare that whatever you do or any risk you should assume will be on my account and I will pay forthwith.

She will have to leave someone there with arms and a horse; I wish, since it has to be someone other than you, that it could be Lope de Salinas, my sister's husband, if he is in the city now. See if you can arrange it, since you will receive very ample powers for everything. If milady Ana Suárez should give you some money and not want it to come in her name, then so that I will know about it, put in the register that the money is mine and is coming on a separate account of mine for her, and that it goes at my risk; and I also wrote you at Nombre de Dios that it should come under this account I mean, without going into detail.

As to what you say of the great quantities of olives that have been sent, from now on I won't send any more. Whatever Captain Lope Martín should need and send to ask of you, please do it for him better than I would myself, and keep writing about it.

In the letter of April 12 I see the events in Charcas. May our Lord pardon the dead; they enjoyed little and have paid for it, and all those who should want to do anything in disservice of his majesty will pay the same. May our Lord maintain the kingdom in peace and quiet.

I was also glad to hear from you that Mr Rodrigo Niño arrived in Lima; give him greetings on my behalf if he is there.

As to what you say, that you consider it superfluous for you to come to Tierra Firme, or us either, we would have been sorry if you had come; stay there with the blessing of God in Lima, and when you come to Tierra Firme it will be not to stay there but to come straight on to this country, as I wrote before.

Please, in the matter of what Marcela de Carvajal sent in the trunk that was to be given to milady Ana Suárez, send me a memorandum of what arrived, because Juan López took two thirds of it or more, and see that what is missing is collected.

I already reported how Juan López charges me in his account 780 pesos for 130 loads of merchandise that he sent for me in the ships of Mafla to Chile and to Paita, and you charge me with the same item. Don't accept any of this in Juan López' account; I am not to pay it twice. I'm sending you an account of all the news here, and will continue to do so at length, and you must repay me in the same coin. I am writing in reply to the letters of doña María Martel and her sister. Rodrigo de Cantos is in Rome, having escaped from the jail where he was being held about his marriage here; they say he doesn't have a good case, and the woman here really is his wife. And please take care that all the letters I send you are given to the people they are intended for; the assets you have sent me go to the proper persons as you wish, and so I will keep doing with whatever you send.

Marcela de Carvajal, bless the Lord, is very well, and seven months pregnant now. She sends greetings and will write; little Melchor is well, and also sends greetings.

They are rushing us greatly to send off this fleet; for almost a month Francisco Tello has been in Sanlúcar inspecting the ships, pressing for departure, but we are not to know when they will leave; if there is any new development I will advise you.

I have had letters from Gabriel de la Cruz in Chile, who tells me of an obligation made out to me by Ulloa, lord of Caraballo, citizen of Charcas, for 200 pesos that he owed to this Gabriel de la Cruz. He had given that amount in gold to Ulloa in Chile to give to his wife here, because Ulloa was going to come to Spain, but he never did, and spent the money there. Later Gabriel de la

Cruz came from Chile to Lima to ask for it, and since Ulloa didn't have the means to pay then, he issued a written obligation to me, I believe Baltasar was the notary. This was in Lima in the year of '48, almost at the end of it, or the beginning of '49, and as I say, it is made out to me. Please have it looked up, and if Ulloa or assets of his should appear, have it collected, because it is to be given to Gabriel de la Cruz' wife, who needs it. It is a good deed and our Lord will repay it, so make an effort. This Ulloa also owes me a debt I would like to see collected; keep me posted on all this.

After the above was written, Diego Díaz Becerril and Mr Diego Núñez and I discussed what I will now tell you about. The company that existed between Alvaro de Illescas, Diego Díaz and Diego de Illescas, Gonzalo López and the rest, is being dissolved, because Diego Díaz and Diego de Illescas, saying that the agreement with them has not been fulfilled, have brought great suits against Alonso de Illescas, father of Alvaro de Illescas, and against Ruy Díaz de Gibraleón, and in short as I said, the company is being dissolved; and also Gonzalo López writes to Diego Díaz that he is very annoyed to see that Alvaro de Illescas had not remained. Diego Díaz has discussed our making a company with you residing there in the city of Lima, and Gonzalo López residing in Tierra Firme, and Mr Diego Núñez and I and Diego Díaz in this city; we think it should be considered a certainty and already arranged. Diego Díaz is writing with this fleet to Gonzalo López to send him power to put it into effect, and when this arrives, you send us your power for this too. I believe that with the aid of God it will be one of the best companies that have been formed in this land, and the best supplied. The investment in it will be 80,000 ducats or more, and it will be supplied as if it were 200,000 ducats. We don't want to have boats nor packtrains in Tierra Firme, but that Gonzalo López should send whole shipments on to you just as we send them from here. With this fleet we are sending Gonzalo López very full powers to take care of all our holdings there, and to examine the accounts of the executors and holders of the estate of Juan López. And in the first ship we need for you to send power to Gonzalo López for things there, approving the powers that we have sent him. You relax and have a good life, and God willing, we here will see to it that the principal trading house and business deals of Peru will be yours; and as I say, send powers for the new company. I think you can trust empowering me and Mr Diego Núñez and also Luis Sánchez de Albo, who is a very judicious and honest person, because although you will be absent at the time of agreement, be sure that you will be much more than present, because with Mr Diego Núñez and me here, and we are the ones who will decide things, you will see by the result whether you were missed; wait and see by how it comes out. I am very happy that we have been able to arrange this so that we can have a man as honest and prudent as Gonzalo López in Tierra Firme; and the main thing is having you, because you are the crucible into which all is poured. From today on, whatever you have to send us, whether to me or to Mr Diego Núñez, let it come to Tierra Firme consigned to Gonzalo López, and in all the ships that leave, write to him in a friendly way, since our friendship must be as a brotherhood of brothers.

When the fleet leaves, Mr Diego Núñez and I will start acquiring merchandise to ship on the account of this new company. All three of us here will invest whatever we have at the moment so that when the next fleet arrives you will get an abundance of merchandise, and it will be very easy for you because none of us three will send anything to you or to Gonzalo López on our own account, but all on the account of the company; I pray to our Lord that it all be for his service.

Send me two copies of all the shipments of merchandise that Juan López sent you on my individual account, and in what ships and when, because I must settle accounts with his brothers, and we must have complete clarity, since it is a matter of making final arrangements with heirs of the dead.

The merchandise I am sending in this fleet on my own account is already all consigned to Gonzalo López, for him to receive it and send on to you immediately; the merchandise was assembled in a rush and could not be properly assorted, because it was put together and loaded within a week, some of it freighted at 30 ducats a ton paid immediately in this city; but the demand for merchandise that has come from New Spain, that is, the high prices there, is something to wonder at.

Have no fear that the French will harm us, because the fleets go and come back in very good order, with many men and much artillery, and many strong ships. When this merchandise of mine that I'm now sending arrives, begin to sell it right away without waiting for more, because from now on we are going to do nothing but enjoy all seasons and go along selling every day; we will send a great quantity of merchandise so that you won't have to be always waiting. Send a memorandum of the merchandise you want shipped, and what prices things are selling for.

Gaspar Ramos writes me that he received the merchandise I sent him on my account in Carreño's fleet, and he sent it all on to you; I think, God willing, it will arrive in good time.

Along with this letter go some dispatches of Mr Pedro López so that you will send to Chile to collect some money owed him by Juan Ruiz, who used to make hats in Lima and has now become rich in Chile; have your power delegated to Alonso de Escobar, who will do this as well as myself, and also anything else that is necessary. Please do this, because it is our own affair.

I had written you to buy up some gold to send me because of the high price it was bringing, but now recently things have become very tight for the Genoese and others who buy gold in order to take it out of the kingdom, and the price has fallen greatly. The best gold that comes from Chile is sold in this city for 470 maravedís at most, and that which is not so good falls below that price, so send me no more gold, because I don't want to see us lose money with it, but send bars of silver even if they are bulkier, and let others send gold if they wish, unless it should be so cheap there that we can still make a profit here. And tell milady Ana Suárez the same, to care nothing for bringing along gold or any jewels, but to sell them there because here she can buy them for half as much, and much better and more to her taste.

After the above was written we were informed that there had arrived with this fleet a Diego Núñez Chaves, who was in Lima and had a company with Jaime Fajardo and Mesa, the citizen of Cuzco; he brought in the fleet more than 30,000 pesos of Fajardo's and more than 20,000 for Captain Lope Martín. As we have heard such good things about him, we sought to make company with him, and at last our Lord has permitted us to bring it about, as follows: we are investing 60,000 ducats in the company, I myself 35,000, Mr Diego Núñez 17,000, you 6,000 ducats, and Diego Núñez Chaves 2,000 ducats. You are to be in that city where you are, Diego Núñez Chaves is to be in Nombre de Dios, and we two in this city. And people who understand what a company is, Luis Sánchez de Albo and Ruy Díaz Gibraleón, say that the partner who is to be in Tierra Firme should earn 4,000 ducats for his industry, and finally we agreed to do ourselves this injustice. So the arrangement will be that you will invest 6,000 ducats and get a share of the profit as though you had invested 11,000; Diego Núñez Chaves invests 2,000 ducats, and his work will be counted for five, so he will share as though it were 7,000 ducats; Mr Diego Núñez and I will earn strictly according to our investments. Though you were absent, it seems that you did better than anyone else, for while Diego Núñez Chaves also earns 5,000 ducats for his person, yet it is more work and danger to be in Tierra Firme; you would do well to earn 4,000, which with the six you invest would make 10,000 ducats, but actually, as I say, we are counting you at 11,000. We have made this company in good time; the fleet is in Sanlúcar ready to leave, and we think it will depart before six days go by if the present weather holds. Diego Núñez Chaves is going in this fleet to Tierra Firme to conclude the business of the old company there. In the first fleet that should leave we will send a good shipment for the new company, with the aid of God; and then we will send the rest, to make up the 60,000 ducats, in the second fleet, so that within a year and a half, if two fleets go, we will have shipped all 60,000 ducats worth. I am sending a copy of the company agreement, and in the first ships that leave there you must send your approval of the company we have made, and also send the conclusion of the old company. Assess the houses for the new company, and send us word for how much, and also send the account of all the shipments that Juan López sent you on my account and in what ships, all very clear; and separately, aside from this, send me the account of what Gaspar Ramos or Alonso de Cazalla has sent, because we must finish up here with the heirs of Juan López, and we must pay whatever Juan López should owe in all the fleets, insofar as his share in the company is concerned. As I say, we need you to send proof of everything, because if we have a record of the affairs of Juan López and how much he destroyed and the bad accounts he kept, his principal and profit will vanish and there will be no reason for us to pay debts that should appear. God pardon him for it; amen.

I already told you that as to the item of the 780 pesos for loads of merchandise which Juan López sent on my account with Mafla and in the galleon for Chile, you are not to accept it, because as I already wrote, Juan López charges me with it in this account and I am only to pay it once, not twice.

Other times I have written you asking that Luis de Herrera, son of Dr Cabra, be given charge of the store, since he is an able boy, faithful and sufficient for the job. Now with this fleet people have brought good reports of him, especially Francisco Gutiérrez, citizen of this city, who stayed in the house of the Inspector of the Treasury and even, I believe, has some company with him. He tells me that Luis de Herrera is very able, much more so than someone else you have in the store, whom you put there to please Alvaro de Illescas. Also Martín Pérez, who was chief constable, and Mr Crespo, and many others who have come in this fleet, tell me what a good son Luis de Herrera is and how worthy of being trusted with affairs. It seems to me it would be more proper for you to favor my requests than to do what Alvaro de Illescas wants; I would be very gratified and pleased if, assuming you have not already put Luis Herrera in charge of the store when this arrives, that you do so right away, because it will please me extremely, and he takes the place of a brother for me, so I again entreat you to do me this favor.

I wrote earlier how the company of Alvaro de Illescas, Diego Díaz Becerril, Diego de Illescas, Gonzalo López and all the rest was dissolved and would not be continued. That still holds, and what they shipped to Nombre de Dios in this fleet on the company's account is to be sold in Nombre de Dios before being transported to Peru, and when it is sold, each of them is to get a share according to his investment. Besides this, Alonso de Illescas is very annoyed with his son Alvaro de Illescas for having invested there in the city of Lima in livestock, meat markets and other things, so that they are not going to send him merchandise or anything else; instead, according to our understanding, they are sending power to have someone examine his accounts, or have him come back to give account. And since I want to be and am his true friend, I am extremely desirous that Alvaro de Illescas should come here immediately to render an account of himself in person, because truly his reputation has suffered here. I think you should tell him this discreetly, without his seeing our letters, but just as something from friend to friend.

I already wrote you how milady Ana Suárez, God willing, will be coming here, and you, God willing, will receive ample power to manage her Indians and estate; I would like very much, since Lope de Salinas is there and is my sister's husband, for you to favor him so he can begin to make his fortune; he is honest and of good parts and I feel sure his deeds will reflect his origins. I will not go on about this, except to repeat that he is my sister's husband, and she herself is there with him, so do with him and his affairs as I would do with a brother of yours.

Sanlúcar, 12th of December, 1553

Two days ago I came to this port of Sanlúcar to see the fleet off and to help embark our partner Diego Núñez de Chaves; as the registers were already closed when we made company with him, it was necessary, in order to send him properly, for me to come here in person. God willing, I will return to Seville and my house within three days from now, leaving everything here ready for the journey, and the bundles of letters and dispatches distributed among the ships. If by chance the fleet should be delayed and there are new developments, I will advise you from Seville.

I am sending along some papers to collect a certain amount of money there in Lima from Nicolás de Ribera the Elder; please collect it, and when you have taken your commission, send it registered under the owner's name and at his risk, with provision for me to remove it from the House of Trade. Also be notified that all the collections we will send, even though they come at the risk of the owners, should carry instructions that either I or Mr Diego Núñez can take them from the House of Trade. And as to the letters of private individuals included with this, send them all on to the people they are meant for, and be especially careful with those going to Captain Lope Martín. I am also constantly sending papers to have money collected from people in Tierra Firme who owe me debts, and I write that if it cannot be collected there and the people should have gone to Peru, the papers should be sent on to you, and so it will be done; be advised from now on, that when these things come to you it should be understood that it is something of mine, so that I won't have to write about each special case.

Licentiate Francisco Martínez is going in this fleet to be prosecuting attorney of the Royal Audiencia there and of the kingdom of Peru. We lent him 200 ducats to outfit himself, the papers for which go along with this; have the collection made. The bishop of Charcas also goes in this fleet and owes me money I have lent him; an acknowledgment or formal obligation will accompany this, and you should have whatever that comes to collected also.

Mr alderman Pedro García de Jerez of this city, who is very much my patron and friend, is sending, for Mr Rodrigo de Contreras, former governor of Nicaragua, who is there in Lima, a barrel of soap, over 200 yards of Rouen cloth, and a copper barrel of rose water, which goes to Diego Núñez Chaves to be sent on to you; deliver it and collect whatever he should advise you the handling costs were. Also Marcela de Carvajal is sending, within the shipment that I am now sending, some nun's flounces of silk to trim kerchiefs, three netted bonnets, and seven ounces of gold fringe; all of it is to be shown to milady Leonor de Torres, wife of Judge Altamirano. And if you should care for part or all of it, take it, paying the cost plus only 5 percent, since here we pay 2½ percent for the defense levy and 2½ for sales tax, another 5 percent duty in Nombre de Dios, and 10 percent for insurance. This is all you need pay, and then you can take it. And since the fleet was already in such a rush when Marcela de Carvajal received the letters from milady doña Leonor to send her some things, no more could be sent. God willing, in the first fleet that leaves other things will be sent, for her grace to take what she pleases.

I know no more to say, and it seems to me I have gone on at very good length, as I wish you to do with me. May our Lord give you all the repose, happiness and prosperity that you desire and that I would wish for myself.

Also some other fringes of Portuguese thread in the shipment are to be given to milady Leonor de Torres; take what you care to of the little nun's flounces of silk and the gold fringes and the three bonnets of netting, and these fringes of Portuguese thread; in the first fleet Marcela de Carvajal will send other good things for the lady.

Once again I recommend to you my sister Juana de Escobar and her husband Lope de Salinas; since he has ability, favor him so he can make his way, and as I have written, I hope that when milady Ana Suárez comes, you will strive to see that the person who is in her house and encomienda should be Lope de Salinas. Do this as though it came from you, without anyone knowing that I am writing you about it; in everything do as I trust you will. From milady doña María Martel I have received no letter, except one from her brother; I am answering him about the affair of Rodrigo de Cantos, who should be in Rome at present. We don't know what will be negotiated there, except that people here affirm that the woman he had here is his wife. I intend to use what you just sent to buy merchandise to send with the first fleet; so far we haven't even taken the money out of the House of Trade, but when I get back to Seville I will try to get it out, and also the 50 pesos that are to be invested for you in feminine items. As to the 50 pesos you sent to be remitted to Trujillo, the day before leaving Seville I gave it to a Morales, muleteer of Trujillo, who was empowered by the person the money was intended for; and thus everything you send or send to order will be done.

Kissing your hand,
Francisco de Escobar

Sir:

I have written you with this fleet all about everything going on here, and how we have made a new company, and Diego Núñez Chaves will be residing in Tierra Firme; he just came from there, and is going back with this fleet. So that you will know him better, he is the one who brought the money of Alonso de Mesa, citizen of Cuzco, and of Captain Lope Martín. And you are to reside there in Lima for the term of the new company we have made, which is five years. The investment is 60,000 ducats; I invest 35,000 ducats, Mr Diego Núñez 17,000 ducats, you 6,000, and Diego Núñez Chaves 2,000. If by chance this should arrive before the large packets with the transcription of the company agreement, stay there in Lima, and if a ship should leave soon for Panamá, write to Diego Núñez Chaves, who has very ample powers from us, and also he will write to you when he gets there. I am also writing to Judge Altamirano, and if this should chance to arrive first, tell him I kiss his grace's hand a hundred thousand times, and tell him how the order was given in Granada in favor of Mr Gonzalo de Torres, and they are ordering all of his property returned. I came to this port of Sanlúcar six days ago to see this fleet off, and with the aid of God I'll be home again two days from now.

Marcela de Carvajal is well, and very advanced in pregnancy now at eight months; she sends greetings.

Our Lord give you all the contentment you desire. From Sanlúcar, 15th of December, 1553.

Along with this goes a copy of the shipments being sent in

this fleet. By Mr Diego Ruiz Cerrato I am sending you another very long letter of mine.

    Kissing your hand,

        Francisco de Escobar

[1] Archivo General de Indias (Seville), Justicia 402. A discussion of Escobar's career in the context of Peruvian commerce generally is in Lockhart, *Spanish Peru*, pp. 88-90, 95.

[2] Professor Geoffrey Symcox has suggested to us that Thérouanne may be what is intended by these garbled letters.

15. The professor of theology

Fray Juan de Mora, in Mexico City, to his brothers in Spain, 1574[1]

    ... And if one of my nephews knew Latin ...

Since there were many ecclesiastics and men of the law in the Indies, there was no lack of intellectuals to man the institutions of higher learning, both royal universities and academies or seminaries attached to the orders, that were soon established in the regional capitals. Except for some chairs of Indian languages, the content and form of instruction were the same as in Spain; the basic purpose of the schools was to train up members of the second and succeeding Spanish generations as lawyers, churchmen and physicians. The early Franciscans of Mexico, such great students of Indian language and culture, had little to do with the schools for Spaniards, and only rarely did these institutions attain the distinction seen in a few Jesuit professors of the latter sixteenth century, but at least they were there, giving some second sons of encomenderos or ambitious offspring of other Spaniards the qualifications to hold a church benefice or a post with one of the royal courts.

In the present letter our Augustinian friar and professor of theology tells us little about his teaching, though in his shameless preaching at his brothers he gives us a good sample of his pulpit style. Some interesting things emerge about the ecclesiastical world, which shows itself as a network of communications, not unlike the mercantile organizations, since the friar's letters to Spain often go through the sister of the Mexican archbishop. The church is even to some extent a business network, and fray Juan could see to the sale of some bibles now in demand in Mexico City. As a person who has made it, no less so than encomendero Andrés Chacón (Letter 11), fray Juan is, like him, prepared to send his relatives gifts and dowries, and would like to have a nephew or two around him. Family ties were an important constituent element in all Spanish organizations, including the intellectual and ecclesiastic.

Gentlemen and very beloved brothers:

May our good God ever dwell in your spirits and give you the health, grace and peace that I desire for you and all your families and households. Since for two years now I have not seen a letter from you in the ships and fleets that have come from Spain, I have felt some worry and care about your health and lives, so much so that I have begun to presume that there must be no one left there who remembers me. I would be greatly pleased to know that one of you is still alive, and so I am moved to write this letter, to make it known that the Lord is still pleased to grant me the health I have today. True, I am kept very busy, since I occupy a chair of holy scripture and preach constantly, but even with all this I am, glory to God, well, and I am established here in Mexico City. If one of my nephews were man enough to want to come here and see me, and had the spirit and strength to leave those little huts they have there, I would be very glad to have him, because I no longer believe the time will come when I can return home, unless God ordains something unforeseen. Let him who should want to come understand that he must be a man who can assert himself on his own, by his own good industry and diligence, as many others do here and make their fortunes. For my part I would do what I could to aid him and recommend him here, if he came as a man of good repute. And if he should want to bring some capital to begin with, let him invest it in some goods to be shipped with him, on the advice of some good merchant of Seville, or in some bibles that were recently printed in

Salamanca, called bibles of Ruperto Estephano, and others that they call bibles of Isidoro. Of course I will see that they find a market here, and the amount invested in them will be doubled. And if there is much linen available of the good homespun that is made there in that area, then a profit could be made from that too, and it would be a good beginning, because some who begin here later make fortunes, through their good industry. But those who come have to be men and not donkeys. I would want whoever comes at least to know reading, writing and counting, and be able to answer very faithfully for anything entrusted to him; a person like that will be greatly esteemed in this land, as anywhere.

I wish I were able to send you something at present, but I find myself without means to do so now; as time goes on I will do what I can. And if a good marriage presents itself for one or two of my nieces, then for that purpose I hereby set aside 100 pesos, and will send the money whenever I should be advised. But be sure they avoid allying themselves with people of low stock. And I declare that it is my will that the two who are to benefit are the eldest two among all those who are unmarried, and God will provide for the others who come after them, if He is pleased to give me health. They should pray for me, and try to be good women, honest, retired and God-fearing. God will favor them and remember them if they are as they should be, and busy themselves in serving Him and being very obedient to their parents. Understand that if I know that one of them so behaves I will favor her, and if any does not, then she can be dismissed as worthless and not consider me her uncle, because I will not have her for a niece. And let them not think that though I am here I lack persons who will report on them to me. And I say the same of my nephews, whom I also beg to strive to be very honest and very obedient and faithful servants wherever they go, because God cannot fail them if they are his servants and pride themselves on being good Christians and friends of the things of God, and very constant in their faith and obedient to all that the holy mother Roman church teaches. For the love of God, let them all strive for this and look that Satan does not deceive them. If they should be poor and find themselves in necessity, they should be very patient and give many thanks for it to the divine goodness, and understand that that is what best suits them for their salvation, if they know how to take advantage of it, enduring it all with much humility and patience, and adjusting themselves in all and through all to the divine will, which rules and governs everything as best suits our salvation and God's honor and glory.

And if one of my nephews knew Latin or wanted to be a friar, I would be glad if he would be in my order. Advise me, and I will send to recommend him to someone who will see after him. Or if not, then let him come here and I will see that he is given the habit so that he can serve God in it.

Nothing else occurs to me than to recommend to all the peace that as brothers and relatives we should have among ourselves. I earnestly charge you with this peace, and beg my God to give it to you, and with it grace, to serve and love Him as you are obliged. Amen.

From Mexico City, 29th of March, 1574. I greet all my sisters, relatives and friends.

Your least and true brother kisses your hands,
          Fray Juan de Mora

If you wished to write me with the bearer of this, who is from Torre Milano, and a relative of Mr Antón de Espejo who is now in this country, you can send the letter back with him, or with the bundle that a lady doña So-and-So de Moya, who lives in Pedroche, is sending; she is the sister of the archbishop here in this city, and with her letters those you write me will come in security. Be sure you write and advise me of all who are gone, and the number and names of those who are left of our brotherhood and kindred, and about the nephews and nieces, and which are married and which still to be married.

---

[1] Published in Spanish, with comment, in Otte, 'Die europäischen Siedler.'

16. The new arrival

Alonso Morales, tailor, in Puebla, Mexico, to his
cousin in Trujillo, Extremadura, 1576[1]

> ... Imagine that if back there in Spain we got 8
> reales for a coat and short cloak, here they give us
> 32 ...

On previous pages we have seen evidence of the fact that
private correspondence from the Indies to Spain consisted in
good part of propaganda inducing relatives to migration. The
appeals take many forms. One of the most characteristic is the
letter written by the settler just off the boat. Genuinely struck
by the differences between the new land and the old, though
not understanding the new things too deeply yet, still missing
home and kinfolk sharply, the new arrival perhaps more than
others was responsible for creating the image of a land of
opportunity, where everything is bigger and better, that same
half-truth, half-lie that has been told to people of the old
country since there has been migration.

Young Alonso Morales, probably still under twenty, has
recently arrived in Puebla in the company of his older cousin,
who paid his way from Spain, and he is now working off the
debt in his cousin's tailor shop. The picture he paints has
elements seen again and again in such letters. Food is good,
plentiful, and cheap. Everyone (every Spaniard, that is) has a
horse. There is plenty of work, and it is very well paid, three or
four times as well as in Spain. Spanish things are scarce and
expensive, but since one earns much, one can afford them. The
homeland is the reverse, 'that misery,' 'that wretched country,'
which is tolerable only for the rich. Such an image of the Indies,
enthusiastic but stopping a good deal short of streets paved with
gold, was perhaps all the more convincing in its relative solidity
and modesty. This particular letter did not fail of its effect,
since the recipient brought it to Seville to buttress his application for license to emigrate.

Dear cousin:

Since I know you'll be glad to hear from me, I will write, and by this letter I wish to announce that, bless the Lord, we had such good weather on the sea that you could think sea-voyaging a pleasant pastime; everything went so smoothly it couldn't have been better. But I can tell you that after we landed we underwent some hardships before reaching this city of Los Angeles; as soon as we arrived the climate attacked me and I was in serious condition, but our Lord saw fit to give me health to work. Your brother and I keep shop here and are doing well; there's enough to keep us and five or six helpers busy. And imagine that if back there in Spain we got 8 reales for a coat and short cloak, here they give us 32, and for a quilted doublet they give us 3 pesos, which is 24 reales, and one for a woman brings us 16 reales. If a helper does piecework, he earns 8 to 10 reales a day, and if he works for a daily wage they pay him 6 reales and his board. So you would give me great pleasure in leaving that misery there and coming here, because it would be greatly to your advantage, and it would give me great happiness to see you in this land. I swear to God that I am always thinking about you, and some days with much concern; it would rest my mind if you were here so I could give you account of my affairs. I work as much as I can, and will not be paid by your brother for this year because I owe it to him, as you know. (I have been paid often in blows, but in the end, he did it with good intentions.)

Do me the pleasure of coming here with the bearer of the letters, who is called Francisco Márquez and is your brother's *compadre*, because we have entreated him to bring you back. He says he will, if you want to come. You can be sure that if I had as much possibility as I have good will, I would send you some money, but I swear as a Christian that I don't take a penny for all the work I am doing now, because I see the good deed that your brother has done me. And also we arrived more than 100 ducats in debt. But in four months we have saved that much and more because, as I say, work is paid well here. And food is cheap. For a real they give you 16 pounds of beef, or 8 pounds of mutton and 8 loaves of bread; they harvest wheat twice a year, and a bushel and a half is worth 4 reales.

If you don't come, be sure that I will be very annoyed. Get my brother Pedro to come with you, and leave that wretched country, because it is only for people who have a lot of money, and here, no matter how poor a man may be, he never lacks a horse to ride and food to eat. Wine is expensive and costs 6 reales for half a gallon, but that doesn't make us stop drinking, because we think no more of a real than you do there of an ochavo. I won't persuade you further; you already see I have your welfare at heart.

I have nothing more to report, but do me the favor of giving my greetings to Francisco Hernández and Pedro Martín and Orellana the tailor, and Pedro González and all those who you know are my friends and yours, and first of all to our brothers and relatives. And with this I will cease, except to pray to our Lord to bring you to this land and give you the same health I desire for myself. From the city of Los Angeles, 20th of February, 1576.

Your brother who wishes you all good,
Alonso Morales

[1] Published in Spanish, with comment, in Otte, 'Cartas privadas de Puebla del siglo XVI,' *Jahrbuch für Geschichte von Staat, Wirtschaft und Gesellschaft Lateinamerikas,* III (1966), 10-87.

17. The tanner and his wife

Alonso Ortiz, in Mexico City, to his wife Leonor González, in Zafra, Extremadura, c. 1574–1575[1]

> ... I am pressed and hemmed in to earn a living for you and my children ...

The letter of tanner Alonso Ortiz illustrates two common phenomena. The first is one of the basic processes in the formation of Spanish American society. Artisans of all kinds came to settle in the Spanish cities, catering to the needs of a population which could pay in silver coming from the mines and encomiendas. Starting with nothing but their tools, Spanish craftsmen would at first perform most of the productive work themselves. If they had any success at all, they began to train helpers and expand, until they themselves graduated into supervision and marketing, while much of the shop work was done by blacks and Indians. Often, as here, the blacks, though slaves (or indeed because they were slaves and more permanent), were the foremen and most skilled workers, while the apprentices and less skilled were Indian. This sort of shop organization accomplished some things of vast cultural significance: it greatly increased the productivity of Spanish crafts, filling the larger cities with Spanish-style artifacts and services, and second, it was a prime factor in hastening the growth of a non-Spanish but Hispanized sector of the urban population. Skilled help was scarce and much in demand, so that Alonso Ortiz could find none at first. But now, after only a year, aided by a partner, he has trained or acquired a force of nine, and is showing a good profit.

Ortiz mentions the possible export of some cured hides to Spain. Let it be clear that his most important market is local, Mexico City itself. All Ortiz envisions is sending a hundred or so of the best hides from among the thousands he cures. His first attempt to do so came to nothing, and his plan for the future is most hypothetical. The export of hides to Europe was a quite marginal, unprofitable business until lower freight costs and higher demand finally made it really viable.

The second phenomenon is related to the fact that a certain number of immigrants to the Indies were married men unaccompanied by their wives. If the most numerous type of settler was a young unmarried male, there was certainly no lack of incentive for married men either, especially if things were not going well. Alonso Ortiz, it would appear, ran away from indebtedness in Zafra. Sometimes the whole family went together, but often the man would go ahead, meaning to send for wife and children when he was established, and this led to long separations that were frequent enough to strike Spaniards in the Indies as a social problem. Laws were on the books to the effect that a married man must have his wife come to live with him or himself be forcibly returned to Spain. The general unenforceability of this legislation is patent. It was there as a potential threat, however, and came into play on occasion, for various reasons. Authorities could deport troublemakers under this pretext. Or those interested in the person's departure could press the issue, whether business competitors (Ortiz mentions 'the other tanners') or personal enemies. Often enough creditors back in Spain brought action, or the wife herself might do so, as Ortiz' wife seems to have threatened to. In any case, Ortiz has now come under pressure of one of these types, and is sending his wife enough money to join him (nominally his partner is sending it, but he as good as says that this is merely a device so that the creditors in Zafra cannot claim it). If his wife should refuse to come for any reason, Ortiz could still stay on legally if she would give her permission and certify that his presence in America is necessary to support her — a position a little hard to justify in view of the fact that he has sent her nothing. Ortiz seriously expects his wife to come, but, less than sterling character that he seems to be, he could probably live with the other solution in equanimity. As to his real intentions concerning his debts in Zafra, they will not bear much scrutiny.

Milady:

This will be to give you an account of what is happening here and how I am doing up to the day this letter is dated. For about a year now I have been in good health and working at my trade, though I had few Indian helpers. I couldn't find any who were trained, since the other tanners had them, and it was not for me to take them away from them. In this year I must have made 500 pesos profit, and if I said 600 I wouldn't be lying; it's about the same as 500 ducats of Castile. But I no longer have to take off my shoes to work, because now I have eight Indians who work steadily, and a black belonging to my partner who aids me very well, and all I do is give instructions, buy, and sell. That is enough work, and indeed it is not little, though it seems little for me; actually I don't want to work at more than supervision so I won't get some sickness that would be the end of me, because great is my desire to see you again.

You can find out about all this from the messenger who is taking these letters, Juan Maya, citizen of Fregenal, who has been my neighbor for a year. He had a thousand kids slaughtered at my establishment, and the payment he gave me for it was very much to his advantage. And now here I am left in the tannery; but he has earned what he is taking with him, which must be about 10,000 pesos. He is an unpopular man, and didn't get along with any of his neighbors. If you chance to see him, keep an eye on him. He talks a lot; try to sit down and let him go, because he doesn't know how to stop talking. He is taking along a son of his; if perhaps you should see him, he has more sense than the father. Whatever he says will be neither more nor less than what is happening with me here. I thought I might send a hundred hides with him, and I asked him, but he said he was greatly burdened.

It doesn't matter at all, though, because my partner has decided to send for you, and is sending you 150 pesos just for your sustenance, and the rest can be paid when you get here. You will find this money in Seville in the possession of a councilman there who is the partner of Alonso Ramos, a merchant here in Mexico City. I won't say the name of the councilman here because I don't know it. I'll tell you in another letter when I have found out his name.[2] And for this I will send you a power of attorney, which you can delegate to anyone you wish to go and arrange things for you. I am also giving power to Melchor González and Alonso González, your brothers, so they can arrange it. Have them come along with you; I undertake to make their fortunes here, if they wish. My partner is sending this money, and it is his and goes as his, so that those gentlemen there to whom I owe money will not try to have it confiscated. And you can tell Mr Alonso Sánchez and Mr Francisco Pérez that in the next fleet I'll send them a hundred hides, worth 100,000 maravedís and more, because they will be chosen one by one from two thousand I will be curing. This year they will be paid what I owe them, if God wishes and I stay here, and what I owe and am obliged to pay to the rest will also be paid. Tell them to pray to God for my health as I pray for theirs, so that they can receive their payment.

And if perhaps you decide not to come, then send Francisco to me, because letters are going to this councilman who is to receive the money that he should arrange passage for him. And if you resolve not to come, send me your license, drawn up by a lawyer with as much legal force as possible, saying that you permit me to be in this city of Mexico for four years, because I am earning a living for you and for my children. And tell Melchor González and Alonso González that though I've sent them nothing from here and they have worked to support you, knowing that they give me pleasure thereby, then they should go ahead and do it, and if they do, they will please me greatly, and it will be a great debt which I will repay.

And milady, since in your letters you ask me to fulfil the promise I gave you in the letter I sent you from Santo Domingo, and you say you will expect me during the year of '75, now I say to you that as far as love of you and my children is concerned, I would have fulfilled it earlier, but I am pressed and hemmed in to earn a living for you and for my children, and it would be against you and my children to fulfill that promise, but rather I should go through this anguish to earn you a living. So make the decision and come quickly in this very fleet, and let no one hinder you from taking the voyage.

From Mexico City, district of San Pablo, tannery of Ronda, 8th of March.

Alonso Ortiz

[1] Published in Spanish, with comment, in Otte, 'Die europäischen Siedler.'

[2] He then did find out his name, and inserted it between the lines: García de León.

18. The troubadour

Sebastián de Pliego, in Puebla, to his wife Mari Díaz in Mecina-Bombarón, Granada, 1581.[1]

... I can't live without you ...

Not all husbands were like the Alonso Ortiz in the preceding letter. Others were solicitous, anxious to be with their families as quickly as possible, doing everything they could towards that end. In this letter, Sebastián de Pliego, who has been in Puebla only a short while, is already writing his wife for the second time, is sending her money, and in his great concern is giving her the most detailed instructions of what to sell, buy and bring for the trip. As he goes over everything, much of it twice, he brings the whole migration procedure, from the paperwork to the sea trip, to life for us. He also reaffirms the image seen in Letter 16, of the Indies as a land of plenty, in contrast to the lack of promise in old Spain. Pliego is unusually anxious about the question of proving lineage and identity, possibly because anyone from the Granada area, so recently won from the Moors, was somewhat suspect. His reference to the possible necessity of proving the family's antecedents in Brihuega betrays much. Textile workers from the central Castilian town of Brihuega were prominent in the development of early Puebla as the center of New Spain's textile production. The connection is confirmed in the fact that 'Juan de Brihuega' is sending the money for Pliego. Brihuega solidarity, then, operated despite the fact that Pliego's family had lived elsewhere for some time. Pliego was doubtless somehow involved in textile-making himself.

Of course the main thing we have here is the shining expression of unbreakable ties and love in Pliego's concern, his awkward jokes, and the wooden verses which we have attempted to translate.

Very desired and beloved wife:

The present letter is to let you know that, praise God, I am in good health, with much desire to see you. In the dispatch-boat I sent you a letter as soon as I arrived here in the city of Los Angeles, telling you what to do. First, with the aid of God and his blessed mother, when you see this, sell everything you have there, the property as well as what is in the house, except for usable linen, and buy all the linen you can to bring along, and some hanks of flax to be used for the house, God willing, and a bag of rosemary and lavender. Bring the paintings too, because here they have pictures of a different kind. Consider that you are to come with my brother and yours, and you will need everything.

When you get this, all of you should go to Madrid with the documents I am sending, which are a power of attorney to all three of you, and also a testimony, and also proof that I am a citizen of the city of Los Angeles and that my identity was established here. Do what you can to bring along convincing papers so that, with the papers from me, you will be given what I am sending; bring papers identifying each one of you, and also testimony that you are my wife. And by the love of God I entreat you to keep peace among yourselves and come as brother and sister, and even if he brings his wife, don't worry about it, there will be enough to provide for all, with God's help. Sell what you have, and your brother the same, and go to Tendilla and sell what is there too. Then come with what you have; buy some pack animals to bring you to Seville, and stay at the house of Juan Alvarez at the Arenas gate. Be sure to bring proof of the identity of your father and mother; if it can be established in Mecina, good, but if not then go to Brihuega; and get license for everyone. Always pray to God and his blessed mother that all will go well.

When you arrive in Seville go to the house of Francisco Gómez, or to the house of his brother-in-law Alonso Rodríguez de Valencia. Be sure that you have your identification as my wife and children, so that they will give you what you need when you get there. Don't take a cabin or a stateroom, but the common space like the rest, and remember that children in arms don't have to pay for passage. At sea they will give each one two pints of water, so take along twelve water jugs, or more if you want to. Take a hundredweight of hardtack for each person, and for everyone a hundredweight of raisins, three cured hams, almonds, sugar, twenty-five pounds of fish and the same of dogfish, and especially half a peck of chickpeas, and hazelnuts. Bring from home a good frying pan, a spit, a rolling pin and a ladle. In Seville buy a copper stewpot, plates and bowls, and also a kettle. Take two arrobas of wine, two more of vinegar, one of olive oil, and whatever else you should want. Buy two chests to hold what you are going to eat, or they will steal it all, and also for you to sleep on, and don't sleep alone, but with my brothers. There will be enough for all.

The first thing you have to do is go to the House of Trade to present your documents, and then pay for the passage. I have counted with my own hand the money that will be given to you, which is 100 pesos. Juan de Brihuega will take care of this and everything else. They will write to Granada saying that the money will be given only to you in person, and to no one else, because they will have a description of you and your children; if you don't come, they are to invest it for me. For the love of God come right away, because everything is well provided for. But if you don't come, I swear to God and the holy cross you will not see more money or letters from me as long as you live. So I have given them here what they will give you in Seville, knowing you will receive it.

Do buy yourself a good dress skirt of blue woolen of Baeza with its trimmings, and clogs for the girls, and buy for me a doublet of Dutch linen and some knitted stockings. Be sure to bring from Mecina your identification as my wife and daughters, so you can prove who you are.

> In the name of allpowerful God
> One and three, my treasure,
> I will serenade you now,
> To give you present pleasure.

> Mari Díaz is your name,
> For me there is no other such.
> I will give you a ring of gold,
> A metal worth very much.

> Lady for whom I long,
> Woman of my heart,
> How was this treason planned,
> That you should stay alone so long
> In such an unpromising land?

> My nights and days are spent

With but a single thought;
I know well you'll come for me
Where I by God was brought,
Because I pray with such intent.

This land I'm in is so
That no one lacks to eat,
And I don't lie, my sweet,
Because wherever I may go
At table I quickly take my seat.

The name of Juan de Brihuega's agent is Francisco Gómez, or in his absence Alonso Rodríguez, his brother-in-law, in the street where wine is sold in Seville. Take the letters to Seville, and also the papers I'm sending.

I can't live without you. So for the love of God, come, now that everything is so well arranged. Send me a letter in the dispatch-boat.

If your brother shouldn't want to come or were married, arrange a marriage for your daughter, and you will have more company. Tell Blas Mateo his brother says that if he will venture to come, he will pay his passage and whatever else he needs.

I say no more except to wish that God may preserve everyone there in Mecina generally, and may God give health to my *comadre*, Alonso Yáñez' wife. I would send some things, but there is no one going to Granada.

I will say no more than that I wish to see you with my eyes before I die. All that there is would not pay for the tears I have shed for you day after day. Say, I would like to see you count, to be sure you wouldn't say thirty is more than forty.

May God preserve all those in Ahudia. At your orders, as your husband who desires your wellbeing. From the city of Los Angeles, March, 1581.

      Sebastián de Pliego

[1] Published in Spanish, with comment, in Otte, 'Cartas privadas de Puebla.'

19. The nephew

Martín Fernández Cubero, cloth trader, in
Puebla, to his nephew Pedro Fernández Cubero
in Fuentelencina, New Castile, 1572[1]

> ... I could have arranged a marriage for you worth
> at least 15,000 pesos ...

> By God my only desire is to see people of mine in
> this land ...

The Spanish settlers were from every region in Spain and
from every walk of life. One thing that a great many of them
had in common was the quality of being nephews, nephews of
someone already in the Indies. It is not hard to imagine some of
the elements of the pattern. The original settler would probably
be a second son, leaving his older brother in Spain to inherit the
family fortune. Young and unmarried at the time of his departure, he would stay unmarried in the Indies until he had made a
good beginning (longer than that, in the case of Fernández Cubero). Having affairs to manage, needing aid and company, and
with no grown sons of his own, he would turn to the sons of his
older brother back home, who would be just coming of age.
However it may have worked in detail, the nephew was a key
figure. Nor was the importation of nephews an ephemeral phenomenon; David Brading has established its importance in maintaining the continuity of Spanish-Mexican merchant houses as
late as the latter eighteenth century.[2]

In this volume we have already seen two appeals for nephews,
and there will be more. To underline the importance of the
topic we include here this maximum appeal, which wheedles
and threatens, praises and taunts, using all the reasoning we
have seen before, plus the new factor that Fernández Cubero
wants to have someone to whom he can leave his considerable
wealth.

Nephew:

Many times I've written you telling of my life and the way in
which, since coming to this country, I have managed this busi-

ness and commerce and earned a living. Really, as this is a rich land and food is quite cheap, and I have continually lived alone, I have earned a great deal, as those gentlemen who have left here can very well tell you, having seen it with their own eyes, especially Mr Alonso Hernández and Mr Alonso de Rivas, the one from Brihuega. We used to go around together while they were here and were very great friends, all being from the same part of the country; at the time when each one of them left this land, it was hard for us all to part from one another. I wrote you another letter by Mr Alonso Rivas, and in the last fleet I received your answer to it, in which you reported that you had married, much to your liking, with Catalina, youngest daughter of Mr Alonso Gil, and that they gave you about 300 ducats with her. Nephew, may it be in the service of God and for your happiness, but I wish you had wanted to come here at the time when I sent you word through Alonso Hernández, from Pastrana, and through some others who left here; you would have been more able to then than now, being younger. If only you would have come at that time, either I am a man of little account, or with the aid of God I could have arranged a marriage for you worth at least 15,000 pesos, or more. Here men of your parts are not held in such small esteem as you have held yourself; though I, for having esteemed myself so much, am now old and still unmarried, as I have written you many times. Yet even so I live very much at my pleasure, without any of the annoyances of those who live with wife and children.

When Mr Alonso de Rivas left this land I would have liked to go with him if I could, and he wanted it even more than I did. But since I had most of my assets tied up in sales on credit, I couldn't pull away. Yet I would have come off much better if I had left because, as I am old and loaded down with years, one day coming along the road I fell while dismounting from my horse and broke a leg. That fall cost me twice as much as I would have spent if I had gone along with him; I would have considered well spent the half of my property that I would have left here, if I had known all that was going to happen. It must be my sins, but I'm not always able to get about now, and if a man doesn't have someone to take his affairs to heart and look after his property, everything goes badly. The time I was in bed cost me more in thefts and embezzlements than I will ever find out about, which would not have happened if I had had one of you to guard my property; I need a relative here, and I would make something of him. I have been so unhappy that not one of you cowards, even having the support here that you have in me, should have had the courage to risk coming here to see me and help me enjoy my estate. I have written about it many times, as you well know; I importuned your father, and he would never make the arrangements. Why, there are others who have the courage without having any support here, who make the fortunes they can without owing anyone anything, except the favor they get for being from that part of the country. So, nephew, I beg you for the love of God, since you didn't want to when you were young, then come here now with your wife and children (you say you have two), for by God my only desire is to see people of mine in this land, in order to favor and aid them with my assets and have someone to look after me now in my old age when I need consolation more than ever, and through the will of God I lack anyone else to give it to me. Though what I have in the business is worth more than 20,000 pesos, it gives me no happiness at all, since I have no children or heirs to leave it to. Therefore, nephew, you will give me the greatest happiness if you will come here with me; I have no one to give all this to but you, and if you do your part and come, I will do mine. As long as I live I will not leave you, because I desire nothing but to have you with me, and after the end of my days I will leave you what I have, since I have earned it for you, and if God gives you good fortune, that is what I want. But if you don't come now when there is opportunity, and if perhaps our Lord sees fit to take me, someday you will be sorry, and you will want to and not be able to. So I will say no more.

Advise me if my niece María, the daughter of my brother Francisco Fernández, got married, and if not, tell her I beg her to wait and I will send her something to get married with if she

will wait a year or two, so that she can make a reputable marriage. Our Lord keep you in his hand for his holy service. From
this city of Los Angeles, the 21st of March of 1572.

Give my greetings to Mr Martín Gómez and his wife and
children, and to Mr Francisco Sánchez del Moral and his brother
Alonso Sánchez, and to all the others who might ask about me.
And give your wife and children my greetings. The desire I have
to see you here is so great that I cannot exaggerate it, because I
know that when you taste this land you will not remember your
own.

He who wishes you all good,
Martín Fernández Cubero

[1] Published in Spanish, with comment, in Otte, 'Cartas privadas de Puebla.'

[2] *Miners and Merchants in Bourbon Mexico* (Cambridge, 1971).

20. The garden and the gate

Juan Prieto, in Potosí, to his wife in Valladolid,
Old Castile, 1551[1]

... so that they will build me a double door and a
stone arch into the garden ...

Spaniards were by no means immune to nostalgia. No people
were ever more insular, more attached to locality and lineage.
The original intention of a great many of the migrants was to
make money and return with it to Spain, and even those most
deeply entwined in the affairs of the Indies were often tempted
by the thought of returning, as several of these letters attest.
Here is the letter of a man absorbed by thoughts of home. Juan
Prieto is a small trader of some kind, perhaps one of those who
bought Indian products in the country and sold them in Potosí,
or one of the small independent merchants who brought shipments of goods from Arequipa. His business has gone quite well;
at the moment there is a lull. For weeks he has been dwelling on
what he will do when he gets home to Valladolid: improve
relations with the important people who were once his patrons;
have parties with compatriots who will go home at the same

time; retrieve his family from the in-laws with whom they are staying; start seeing about a good marriage for his daughter Sabina. At the center of his dreams is the vision of a sheltered garden, the garden of his own house, which is to be a green oasis, full of fruit trees, doves and rabbits, completely closed in from the outside ('there should be no aperture anywhere'). The crowning point is to be a double wooden door at the garden entry, framed in a cut stone portal, toward which Prieto is sending a good sum of money, and for which he gives lovingly detailed instructions.

Most Spaniards probably felt something like this at times. Surely no place was so conducive to nostalgia, though, as the mining towns: raw, unpleasant, and remote from the amenities of the capitals. Not one Spaniard in ten thought to stay in such a place longer than it would take him to amass a decent fortune. Meanwhile, thoughts of home were a morale builder and diversion, to which the only alternatives were the bullfights and tournaments Prieto mentions, or the gambling and fighting the mining camps were famous for.

The effect of this dreaming of home was not quite what it seems. Perhaps it slowed down identification with the new country but it also made being there more bearable, and may in the end have helped make it possible for people to stay away longer. Prieto left home for Peru around 1540. In this letter he says he would have come back long ago if it weren't for wanting to save money for the children. Here, in 1551, he says his departure is imminent. He wrote again from Potosí the next year, 1552, saying much the same; he was still there in 1554, the last we know.

Lady, sister and mother of my children:

For more than three years I haven't seen a letter from you; I don't know whether the reason is you or my bad luck, but I do beg you, if there has been any neglect in the past, let there be none in the future, because even though my departure is to be soon, I would really like to come upon letters from you and from my brothers and from Mr Hernando de Mucientes, since in deeds he is my brother. But it could be that when this arrives I might arrive with it, with the aid of God, because I am only waiting to know if they are bringing me some money they owe me in Chile, or to get some reply about it; all I'm doing now is eating up the profits.

I ask you please to put much effort into the collection of all I have sent, since you know it is the right thing to do. Last year I sent you 150 pesos in marked ingots through Servicial, who is from Valdunquillo, and a bar of silver worth 141 pesos, 2 tomines, through Esteban de Vivar, who is from Villa Baruz. I also wrote you that I was sending another bar with Luis de Soto; it didn't get there because he stayed in Lima and I took it back. Now I'm sending with a very great friend of mine called Bartolomé de Nava a bar assayed at 1,930 maravedís a mark, worth 210 pesos and a ducat since it weighs 49 marks and an ounce. He is from Huete; I think he will carry the money himself. If he comes there, please give him a good reception and don't neglect to get his advice, because he is an honest man.

I am also sending 50 pesos with Antonio de la Cuadra so that they will build me a double door and a stone arch into the garden, and have the door made too big rather than too little, so that the cart can enter, and at the height where its hubs pass, have them put a plate of iron on the doors all the way across, broad as a man's hand, so that when the cart comes in, even if the axle hits it won't damage the doors. And if it takes more than 50 pesos, don't let that be a hindrance, but go ahead and spend more, just so long as it's very well done. Antonio de la Cuadra is very much my patron and friend; he will look after this to do me a favor.

Lady, see to it that Mr Hernando de Mucientes takes part in all my affairs, because I am very pleased that he should. As to Mr Santalejos where you are now, lady, there is no necessity to write you about it since my departure will be so soon; I hope in God to spend part of what I bring with me on that house of his. I won't write that anything be done about it now because I intend to do it all from scratch.

I'm not writing to milady doña Isabel de Celada, but beg her to consider this letter hers, and tell her to keep the girl under her care for the love of God until I come, because if God permits I will go to serve her in whatever she should command me; and greet milady sister Ana Sánchez and tell her to look out for my daughter, and with the aid of God I will make it up to her when I come. Greet my sisters and yours and tell them to remember me in their prayers. I kiss the hands of my good friend Hernando de Uceda and his wife, and they should consider this letter theirs; I kiss the hands of all my lords and friends and ask that they pardon me for not writing them.

By your faith, lady, take special care with your children, especially my daughter Sabina; if possible I don't want the sun to see her, much less people, and in this way you will give me much peace of mind both there and here, because I give you my word if it weren't for the children I would have left here many years ago; and since you know, lady, how much reason there is to look after my honor, I will not be importunate, but remain begging God to hold us all in his hand and allow me to see you again in health as I desire. From this site of Potosí, the day of St John — and here you can see, lady, how much I love you and my children; the others are going to see the bullfights and the tournaments, while I don't spend time or lose sleep on anything but remembering you and them, and writing you. In the year of 1551,

At milady's command as your very own, liking and loving you more than himself,

　　Juan Prieto

Lady, see that the adobe walls they lay for the garden are even and very good and thick, and there should be no aperture anywhere, but all of it walled in, two rows high. And be sure that many grafts are started and trees planted, and if there aren't many rabbits in the rabbit hutch buy some and put them in, and the same with the doves, because many of my lords and friends are coming all together to that house when I arrive, who are the following: Pedro de Acevedo, who was receptor in the chancery, and Pedro de la Torre, son of Luis de la Torre the merchant, and Juan de León, son of the Vitoria woman in the street of the potters, and Francisco de la Serna, merchant, and Ruiz, the married one who lives without his wife in San Salvador, and Juan de Arcos, and many other gentlemen whom you, lady, don't know. Don't neglect to tell these gentlemen's relatives that they are coming.

[1] Archivo General de Indias, Justicia 1126, no. 3. A discussion of this letter in the broader context of transience is in Lockhart, *Spanish Peru*, p. 146.

21. The woman as settler

María de Carranza, wife of a textile-mill owner, in Puebla, to her brother Hernando de Soto in Seville, 1589[1]

... And buy four cured hams from Ronda ...

We include this letter less for its idiosyncrasies than for its lack of them, that is, to emphasize that there were indeed Spanish women settlers, part and parcel of the general migratory movement, and sharing the general characteristics. They came from the same towns and regions of Spain as the men, because they were their wives, sisters and nieces, and they went to the same parts of the Indies. This means that they were most numerous in Mexico and Peru, like most of the other hallmarks of development in the sixteenth century, whether Spanish artisans, silver mines or black slaves. Without making them into culture goddesses as the Spaniards themselves sometimes did (see Letter 3), we can see the crucial role of women settlers in placing households in the cities under entirely Spanish management. Not every last household, certainly; but by the time of this letter, Spaniards of all social types down to the artisan level were tending to marry Spanish women, whether new from Spain or born in the Indies.

If we search in the present letter for anything that might be special to a woman, we might say that the list of foods to buy is even more detailed than Sebastián de Pliego's in Letter 18 (though quite similar), or that María de Carranza does show a special concern for gathering together *all* relatives, much as the stereotypes of the time dictated. For the rest, this is a standard recruitment letter, with the usual images, inducements, plans and expressions of annoyance at the reluctance of the stay-at-homes. Most of it could have been written by any settler.

Desired and beloved brother of my heart:

I have never had a reply to the many letters I have written you, except one, and it gave me great joy to know of the health of yourself and my sister-in-law and my nephews, whom I hope our Lord someday lets me see, as I desire. My husband Diego Sánchez Guadalupe was no less happy than I, though for him as well as for me, after our having so desired it, and having put so much into sending to call you here, it would be a greater happiness to see you; yet you want to stay there in that poverty and need which people suffer in Spain. I ask you for the love of God to spare me such pain from your absence, and yourself such necessity, when I have the means to give you relief. Do be sure to come quickly now, and don't make your children endure hunger and necessity. I would have sent money for your trip, but since I have had no reply to my letters, I didn't dare. Go to Ronda and collect the rent from my houses, and if you wish to, mortgage them and take four or five years' income in advance; I leave it to your discretion. And invest all except what you need for travel in fine cloths, in Rouen and Dutch linens; be sure you do it yourself, and don't trust it to others.

Be aware that anyone who brings children must come very well prepared; six hundredweight of hardtack will be enough, but better have over that than under, and make it yourself, since you know how. And buy four cured hams from Ronda, and four cheeses; twelve pounds of rice; chickpeas and beans, rather too much than too little; all the spices; vinegar and olive oil, four jugs of each; jerked beef and mutton, plenty of it and well dressed; and as much linen and woolen clothing for you to wear as you can bring, because here it is very expensive.

Do everything in your power to bring along with you two masters of weaving coarse woolens and carding, for they will profit us greatly, and also a candlemaker, who should be an examined journeyman and good at his trade. Buy their provisions and make a contract with them from the day they sail, and I will fulfill whatever you agree to; I will pay their passage and any debts they have when they arrive. And you can do all this much better than I could. Your brother-in-law Diego Sánchez Guadalupe, to whom you owe more than to me, shares my desires; to make me happy he would have gone there himself, and I was tempted to let him for the sake of you and my sister-in-law and my nephews, but in order not to be left here alone and because he is an older man, I didn't let him go.

Tell the sister of my soul to consider this letter hers; how is it that her heart doesn't melt like mine for us to see each other? I understand that she is the reason you haven't come, yet she is the one who loses and has lost in not enjoying a land where food is plenteous and she can give me a good old age. I ask her, since it is in her own favor, to come quickly and make my old age happy with her arrival and that of my longed-for nephews.

Cristóbal de Velasco, my brother-in-law, was here, and I gave him hospitality which he enjoyed considerably, but then he went to Panamá and left me disconsolate in his absence, and I will not be satisfied until he comes back. Our Lord fulfill my desires, so that you can find relief, and I happiness.

I greet Aunt Ana de Ribera and Aunt Ana Ruiz, and when you come here, leave them where you can send them some presents, money and other things to help them, because we owe it to them, since they are sisters of our mother. Diego Sánchez Guadalupe is not writing because he is tired of sending letters and peevish that you don't answer, so he only gave permission for me to write. Maybe I will have more luck than he has had. I am sorry that so much is necessary for your own redemption.

I will send you power to collect on the property in Ronda or sell it, and I do not send it now because I am not sure it will reach your hands, for I think that if my letters had arrived, I would already have had some letter from you to enjoy. And if you decide not to come with this fleet because you aren't outfitted yet, write me, and give the letter to Francisco López de Olmos to be directed to the house of Alonso de Casas in Puebla.

Trusting our Lord will give me this happiness, I and mine continue in our hope, and we greet my sister-in-law and my beloved nephews. And as to my beloved daughter Mencía Gómez, I have reserved a very rich marriage for her. May God arrange it for his holy service as I wish. From Puebla, 2nd of October, 1589.

María de Carranza

[1] Published in Spanish, with comment, in Otte, 'Cartas privadas de Puebla.'

22. The farmer

Antonio Mateos, in Puebla, to his wife María Pérez in Spain, 1558[1]

... the valley of Atlixco, where they grow two crops of wheat a year...

The main areas of sixteenth-century Spanish settlement were the scene of an extraordinarily productive Indian agriculture, which would seem to have left little scope for Spanish farming. However, the Indians grew maize and other things that Spaniards would eat only from necessity. The conquerors in asking for rewards would sometimes list the eating of Indian foods among their great hardships. So from the earliest time there was a demand for meat from European livestock, as well as cereals, fruits, and vegetables of the European varieties.

At first most of this was procured through the encomienda, in a way of which we have seen an example in Letter 11. The encomendero would have one of his Spanish tribute collectors do the agricultural management, or he might hire someone especially for that purpose, usually a Spaniard on the humble side, newly arrived in the country, without many other possibilities. There would be a maintenance crew of a few blacks and permanent Indian employees, with the heavy labor of planting and harvesting done by Indians coming seasonally in fulfilment of their labor obligation to the encomendero. In the case of livestock, very little labor was required, and the small permanent crew was sufficient.

Since the Spanish cities in the central areas expanded so rapidly, in terms of both population and wealth, this system came under pressure almost immediately. Government officials, local entrepreneurs, younger relatives of encomenderos, and others who had some capital but no encomienda began to build up complexes just like those associated with the encomiendas, except for lack of rights to Indian tribute and labor. After a time of hiring seasonal labor from the encomenderos, they eventually succeeded in attaining an arrangement whereby Indian tribute labor was spread more evenly among the Spaniards and on a short-term basis, rather than being granted for a lifetime to one person in a whole area.

Even earlier and more pervasive than the large estate builders were the small fry, for food production was something susceptible of being carried out on a small scale and with little capital, and the market was increasingly good. These people, new and without connections, were of the same type as the employees of the encomenderos. Indeed, at first they were typically the very same people. Newcomers acquired experience and a little money by working for an encomendero, and then went off on their own. Their first ventures nearly everywhere were truck gardens on the edges of the cities. Supplying the mines was another early opportunity. As the small farmers became more established, raising the Spanish staple of wheat came to be one of their main activities; in Mexico the valley of Atlixco was before long dotted with small and medium-sized wheat farms belonging to *labradores* or non-encomendero farmers. Livestock required more capital, but as European livestock multiplied explosively, filling a vacant ecological niche, they became easier to acquire, and the marginal agriculturalists moved into this line as well.

The encomenderos put up stiff resistance to all this, but in the end acquiesced. In an area like Querétaro, with few Indians, but good farming and grazing land as well as access to markets in Mexico City and the mines, it could happen that there was only one encomendero among scores of farmer-settlers.[2] In a well-populated, centrally-located area such as Toluca, there would be several strong encomenderos, but the pressure was irresistible; in the end it was in the encomenderos' interests to let relatives and other potential allies have estates, and to allow their employees more independence. The encomendero actually sometimes found it profitable to sell a property to the very employee who had just been running it for him. He might also lease it to him, an intermediate solution with great advantages for both sides. In any case the encomendero usually maintained an informal social-economic dominance over the smallholders in his district, who needed his acquiescence and aid for full success. Often their enterprises failed, in which case they might come back to work for the encomendero.[3]

By the latter sixteenth century, in the countryside of the central areas, Indians still grew most of the maize, which did have market value as the main sustenance of the more Indian part of the urban and mining population, and therefore was an important, acceptable tribute item. Spanish estates were above all for livestock and wheat. The largest of them still belonged to encomenderos, followed by similar estates held by people who were socially and economically nearly their peers, and then smaller enterprises, of various degrees of marginality, held by humbler Spaniards. There was a continuum rather than two competing systems. The 'large' estates consisted of collections of small ones under one general management, each subunit run by people who were no different from the independent smallholders. Personnel passed back and forth between large and small estates constantly. There was a dialectic or cyclical process which might be expressed in simplest terms thus: where there was little or no market, smallholders might prevail; where the market was better, there would be a few large estates, with the small agriculturalists as their employees; if development became intensive, the smallholders would gain independence, and if successful they would tend to form large estates of their own.

The Antonio Mateos of this letter is clearly one of the smallholders we have been referring to. He is quite recently arrived, though not inordinately humble, given his literacy and concern for the education of his son. He has been in both the main branches of Spanish agriculture, livestock and wheat. He seems to feel that livestock is more profitable, wheat more stable and better as the economic basis for a family. He also shows us that the small agriculturalist had yet another incarnation, the muleteer, for it was a small step from transporting something to investing in it, and conditions sometimes forced farmers to do their own transporting, as happened with Mateos.

Very longed-for lady wife:

About a year and a half ago I wrote you greatly desiring to know about you and the health of yourself and my son Antón Mateos, and also about my sisters and your brother and mine Antón Pérez, but I have never had a letter or reply since you wrote when I sent you money by Juan de Ocampo. I don't know if you got the letter in which I told you that I sent you 50 ducats, and now again I tell you to collect the rest, since he gave you only 30; try to get the other 20 from him to make 50, as I say. In those letters I already wrote you things about this country; at present I will not say more of my life and business since Juan de Ocampo left, thinking that you will come with him if he comes back. With the desire to prepare for your arrival, I went to the valley of Atlixco, where they grow two crops of wheat a year, one irrigated and the other watered by rainfall; I thought that we could be there the rest of our lives. I was a farmer for a year in company with another farmer there; for the future I had found lands and bought four pair of oxen and everything necessary for our livelihood, since the land is the most luxuriant, and plenteous and abundant in grain, that there is in all New Spain. But after I got your letter saying you weren't coming, nor was it your intention to come here, I decided to sell the oxen and all the equipment.

This part of the country is, as I say, the richest in foodstuffs that there is anywhere, but poorer than other parts in money, and so, because of your not coming here and my needing money, I sold the oxen and the rest and bought a packtrain of horses to transport the wheat we had harvested there. My share was 300 bushels, but I couldn't find anyone to offer me a penny for it in the valley, so I bought the packtrain, as I say, and sold my wheat converted into flour in Mexico City, and also another lot that I bought after I had harvested my wheat. I was in this business for two years, but now I have sold the packtrain and am going back into livestock, where I expect to earn more profit from now on in a year than up till then in two. Truly, if I hadn't left livestock I would have had enough money to go home or would already be there, but I left raising animals, expecting your arrival, and was not able to return to it quickly. Now I have sold the packtrain and bought 1,500 muttons, with which I mean through God to make money, because from 500 ducats that I am investing now in cash I expect to earn more than 1,000 within two years, through the will of God our Lord.

Give Francisco Hernández Franco's wife a letter I am sending along with this one on behalf of her husband; I was so bold as to write her telling of him because the messenger was ready to leave, and there wasn't time to advise him so he could write himself. Greet the children of Juan Fernández Lucas for me, and tell them that when their brother Gonzalo Martín died, may God rest his soul, there remained here as his heir a son he had by an Indian woman, and they should pray to God for his soul.

I will not give a long account of the things of this land. Food provisions are cheap here, and things from Spain are expensive. I charge you not to take your son and mine Antonio Mateos out of school, but let him always learn and know more, and that way you will be doing the best thing for you and me. Give my greetings to my sisters and to your brother and mine and to my nephews, and also to all of your cousins and relatives and neighbors, and greet everyone who asks for me. I haven't heard from my cousins for four years and nine months; they left Mexico City and went I don't know where, nor do I know if they are alive or dead. No more, but may our Lord keep you in his hand for me. From this city of Los Angeles, day of St John, 1558, where I remain

Antonio Mateos

I have not heard from Leonor de la Cueva. About a month ago I saw Juan de Mesa, her husband, and he said she was well. Guiomar de la Cueva and all her daughters send you their greetings.

[1] Published in Spanish, with comment, in Otte, 'Cartas privadas de Puebla.'

[2] See John C. Super, 'Querétaro: Society and Economy in Early Provincial Mexico, 1590-1630.' UCLA doctoral dissertation, 1973.

[3] See Lockhart, 'Spaniards among Indians,' for a detailed treatment of the labradores of the Toluca valley in the late sixteenth century.

23. The petty dealer

Andrés García, in Mexico City, to his nephew Pedro Guiñón in Colmenar Viejo, New Castile, 1571[1]

> ... I deal in Campeche wood and cotton blankets and wax, and I also have a certain business in cacao ...

The petty trader was first cousin of the petty agriculturalist. The activities of both were attractive to penniless newcomers because they could be undertaken without great capital or connections. Often called *tratante* or dealer, as distinct from the *mercader*, who was usually an import merchant, the small trader was rather lower on the scale than the small farmer. Ex-seamen, the lowest of the low, often became tratantes on land. Immigrants of foreign origin (especially Italians, for some reason) tended to gravitate to local small trade, whereas among the farmers the only non-Spaniards, in any numbers, were the nearly Spanish Portuguese. The tratantes dealt in anything that could be bought cheaply in the local economy and resold for silver. They were taverners, peddlers, traders of nags and used clothing. Their most characteristic operation was selling to the Indian population of the cities and mines, people who, if not as rich as the Spaniards, were able to pay money for the *ropa de la tierra* ('native cloth'), and other products of the traditional Indian economy which they still desired and which the dealers gladly supplied them at a profit.

Andrés García is the very epitome of a tratante. We can surmise this good industrious man's social status among Spaniards by the fact that he is great friends with a mulatto woman, and married to an Indian. His trade is exclusively in Indian products, sold at the *tiánguiz* of San Juan in the southwest district of Mexico City, the most important Indian market in the city proper. (*Tianquiztli*, Nahuatl for 'market,' was picked up by the Spaniards and applied to Indian markets specifically; in this sense the word was even carried to other parts of the Indies.) The products García sells are Indian, but not from the region of the capital. They come a long distance, from the southern lowlands of Yucatán, Chiapas and the Guatemalan coast of Soconusco. (When García says he has a cacao business 'in Soconusco,' he means he is involved in production or buying there; the cacao would be sold in Mexico City.) Trade in these products between highland and lowland long antedates the conquest, of course. Marginal Spaniards are here following in the steps of the Aztec *pochteca*. In this way the tratante becomes to an extent a long-distance merchant and importer after all. Also, with time, some of the Indian products gain entry into the Spanish market. García's clientele would be predominantly Indian, but some of the cacao and much of the Campeche wood would be bought by Spaniards. García seems well on his way to lasting wealth. In Spanish social ranking the achievement is not comparable, though in another generation it could be. Note the ambivalence of what he says about his marriage. It is true that for various reasons Spaniards even in the central areas did marry Indians and lived happily on that basis; almost all of such Spaniards were out of the same social stratum as García.

In other aspects this is, as the reader will quickly see, a typical 'nephew letter.'

Dear nephew:

In other letters I have written you, telling you where I am and how things are going with me, and I will keep doing the same until I should see a letter from you, as I greatly desire. After leaving you and our kinfolk, I went through many different hardships. As you saw, I came in the ship of Felipe Boquín, and in Veracruz, which is the port of this land of New Spain, he sold off everything I owned to get forty ducats that I owed him. I arrived on the point of dying, and might well have died in fact, if it weren't for a woman called Inés Núñez, who is of dark skin; she made me very comfortable, and I owe her more than my very mother. If God should bring you here safely, try to go to her house, because I have already told her about you.

Nephew, I live in Mexico City in the tiánguiz of San Juan, among the shops of Tegada. I deal in Campeche wood and cotton blankets and wax, and I also have a certain business in cacao in Soconusco. But now, nephew, I am advanced in years and can no longer take care of all this. I wish, if it please God, that you would come to this land, as I have written you in other letters, so that I could rest and you would remain in the business.

I am married here to a woman very much to my taste. And though there in Spain it might shock you that I have married an Indian woman, here one loses nothing of his honor, because the Indians are a nation held in much esteem. And besides, I can tell you that in the ten years that we have been married we have had no children, praised be our Lord. And she is after me more every day, ever since I told her that I have a nephew whom I raised from infancy and love as if he were my son; she is of the opinion that if God our Lord brings you to this land, we should leave you our property, what we have, as to a legitimate son and heir, because after the end of our days we want to have someone here to do good for our souls. And if you could, bring along your cousin Pedro López, son of Catalina López, our kinswoman, because he could earn as much here from his trade as he wants, and anyway he wouldn't have to, because I have enough for myself and for others, praised be our Lord.

Nephew, I entreat you again to come, because it is a matter of great importance to you; don't imagine remote regions far from your native land, or the hardships that are usually met on the way, but rather the ease you will have here. And if you do make this change, the merchant Alonso Moreno in Seville will provide well for you, if it is for the purpose of coming here, because I spoke to him when he left here, and I've written him about it too, and I know he will outfit you very well. And if you can, come in the ship of Mr Antón Sánchez, a person to whom I have done favors, and knowing the kinship between us, he will treat you well.

Greet everyone from me, and they should consider this letter theirs, and let them know that if one of them should reach this country, he would not be in need, with the aid of our Lord.

My wife Mari Hernández sends you many greetings and entreats you the same as I, because we greatly desire to see you in this land. May our Lord guard you and let me see you again as I wish. Written the 10th day of the month of February of the year of the Lord 1571, from Mexico City.

Ready to serve you in all, your true uncle, who loves you more than himself,

Andrés García

[1] Published in Spanish, with comment, in Otte, 'Die europäischen Siedler.'

24. The Flemish tailors

Pedro de Anver to a compatriot in Cuzco, 1547[1]

. . . Jos del Miere says you should be sure to come
to his house . . .

'Foreigners,' that is, non-Spanish Europeans, were a minority in the Spanish Indies, held in low esteem and often drifting towards marginal areas and occupations, but they were a standard phenomenon nonetheless, appearing everywhere, quite essential to the Spaniards as mariners and in certain specialized trades. Over time, they melted into the lower and middle reaches of the Spanish population, losing their distinctiveness. But in the first generation, precisely because they were in such a minority position, lines of common ethnicity and craft structured their lives, even more than with the Spaniards. The Greek gunners were one world, the Genoese sailors another, the Flemish silversmiths another; inside that framework each group had its principal friends, enemies, and business connections. Those little worlds had great cohesion and independence, and were not easily disturbed by even cataclysmic events outside.

Here, our world is that of Flemish clothing makers in Peru. The writer, 'Peter of Antwerp,' is a tailor, and so is the Maestre

Diego Flamenco (Master Jacob Fleming) who is mentioned. Jos del Miere (Joos van der Meer) is a hosier, while the recipient of the letter seems to be more of a producer of leather items. They write and visit each other; they give each other news on prices and demand; they use each other as a business network to collect debts from Spaniards around the country for whom they have done work; and they come into conflict with each other, since we see that Maestre Diego has had the man in Cuzco thrown into jail for a debt. At this time, 1547, Peru was under the rebel government of Gonzalo Pizarro and was approaching the climax of its most shattering civil war. There is some mention of this in the letter, along with some rather poorly informed gossip, that 'Dr,' actually Licentiate, Gasca had arrived in the north with 'a few' men, actually plenty to attract the whole of Spanish Peru to the royal side in quite short order. And indeed, Maestre Diego was quite heavily involved in the rebellion itself. But the emphasis is on visits, prices, loans, and family news: Jos del Miere's wife has had a baby.

Sir:

Two days ago I received a letter from you in which you tell me that Maestre Diego has you in jail. I am amazed that you should want to tell me such a thing, because I know very well that they wouldn't throw you in jail for so little.

In another letter I wrote you of the efforts I made to collect from Captain Juan de Acosta and from Marchena; I haven't been able to do more.

I believe you will be coming here very soon; Antonio de Robles is going there to bring our friends back, because Dr de la Gasca is in Trujillo with a few men. Juan de Acosta has gone to scout the countryside with Maestre Diego and Gálvez, and other cavaliers.

I also wrote you how everything is very expensive, and that you should supply yourself with everything you might need, and if you thought best you should bring your wife along, because here a leather jacket is worth 100 pesos, and a pair of boots 20.

If you should not be able to satisfy Maestre Diego, when you come here you will not want for a hundred pesos, and because the messenger is leaving I will say no more now, except may our Lord give you what you desire. I beg you to bring a leather jacket and some boots and a blanket, because people are eager for them here.

Jos del Miere salutes you; his wife bore a son.

From Lima, 21st of May. Jos del Miere says you should be sure to come to his house.

At your service,
Pedro de Anver

[1] Published in Spanish in Juan Pérez de Tudela, ed., *Documentos relativos a don Pedro de la Gasca y a Gonzalo Pizarro*, II, p. 548.

25. The nobleman

Don Alonso Enríquez de Guzmán, with Alma-gro's forces at Guaytará, Peru, to fray Francisco de Bobadilla, provincial head of the Mercedarian order, with Pizarro's forces at Lima y Caxca, 1538[1]

... I will come there over the objections of wretches, knowing it will anger the devil; and I would be no bad acquisition for hell ...

Since it had people of all types and estates, the Spanish In-dies also had some high noblemen, bearing the title 'don' by birthright, related to counts and dukes, habitués of the Spanish royal court or the courtly circles of Seville. Not much in evi-dence in the conquest itself, the courtly nobles began to be attracted to the Indies after the wealth of Peru and Mexico had made itself felt. Some set out alone, more went in the entourage of governors and viceroys of the central regions, until there came to be a good contingent of them in the great capitals, frequenting the viceregal courts. Having experienced the court of Spain and learned its manners, they were little impressed with what they saw in the Indies, and were not inclined to make adjustments. A large proportion of them returned to Castile, with or without the fortune they needed to mend their positions there.

Don Alonso Enríquez de Guzmán was an early representative of this group (though his brother preceded him, as can be seen in Letter 31). When he arrived in Peru in 1535 both Governor Pizarro and the Spanish populace made much of him, and he might have had almost any position. But before long he was on the other side of the Pizarro–Almagro conflict, and by 1539 he was on his way back to Spain.

The present letter illustrates the extent to which the high nobles in America continued to act as though they were at court. The situation here is serious; Almagro has returned disappointed from Chile, seized Cuzco, and advanced far north towards Lima with an armed camp. Pizarro has come out from Lima to face him, and fighting seems imminent. In the event, the decisive battle will not occur for four months yet. (See Letters 9 and 10.) Don Alonso, with the Almagrists, addresses himself to an influential ecclesiastic on the other side, fray Francisco de Bobadilla, head of the Mercedarian order in Tierra Firme and Peru. But what is don Alonso at? The basic message would seem to be a timely and appropriate one: Try to persuade your people not to fight, because of the great damage it will do both sides, but be sure that if you try to take Cuzco back we will resist fiercely, and the Pizarros will lose everything. Parts of the letter, the fifth paragraph for example, seem to ring of high sincerity and an eloquence flowing from true emotion. But in other parts there is rhetoric for display, along with jokes in good and bad taste. Among other things don Alonso offers to arrange this sober friar's marriage. At times he indulges in camp gossip and nose-thumbing, and he ends wishing that fray Francisco be 'a father in this world and a saint in the other,' i.e., that he have many children and die soon. This is the court intriguer at work, taking every side of every question, reveling in talk, allusions, gossip and taunts. Fray Francisco, not knowing what to make of it, answered briefly, perhaps with some irony of his own, asking don Alonso's pardon 'if I have somehow annoyed you.'

Very reverend and magnificent sir:

I fear that though I wish to serve and please your paternity and be reputed in your good judgment as a peaceful man dedicated to the service of God and the king and the good name of Governor don Francisco Pizarro, because of my argumentative nature you and others there may believe that I am eager for the battle to begin. The truth is that in my own praise I can assure your paternity that if it had not been for me and the royal officials and Licentiate Prado, we would already have returned to Lima y Caxca, or even gone to Lima without stopping in Caxca. But he who attacks first is the guilty one, and I remember that when the emperor our lord sent me to Ibiza as captain general against Barbarossa, who was coming to attack it, he included in my instructions, among many other paragraphs, one that read thus: 'Also we order and charge you that if the Moors, enemies of our holy faith, should come against the said city or island and you should come to blows with them, strive, without considering the advantage they have from having started hostilities, to take as many as you can alive, killing as few as possible, since they are our relations, and in order not to hinder any whom the Holy Spirit should illumine in our holy Catholic faith.' Yet I must also say that now I do not fail to advise that we die and kill for our law and our king, and for the former especially, seeing that those against us show that they follow not reason and the law of God, but the law of Mohammad, since they rely more on force than on the merits, and the judge is at the door who can give what is rightful; yet for them, muskets are the law more than the orders of their king and lord and what he very clearly shows and says and commands, and it is evangelical law that no one should seek satisfaction on his own authority. And since his majesty wanted us to give life to the Moors, should we not do as much for Christians?

I assure your paternity, since you are the soul and body of Governor don Francisco Pizarro, and I myself am no less his servant than his most faithful follower, and I swear, as God is truth, and by the most holy trinity, and by this habit of Santiago in which I will be condemned or saved, that according to all I know or feel, there are 400 men here as unanimous and agreed, as determined to die, as eager to fight to gain a decision, as sure of victory as they are certain of their belief in God. And so in truth it will no longer avail our antagonists to think that through agreements or threat of force they can enter here into paradise without performing deeds that merit it. If his majesty should send a specific order for what we hold to be given up, it will be given, not with trumpets and kettledrums, but with the tears of men, since Governor don Diego de Almagro has helped so much to win it with his property and life and his eye.

I am shocked when Juan de Vallejo assures us that your paternity desires peace, and that Governor don Francisco Pizarro does not wish war and is a very good Christian and your servant. By my sins, if you two are with us, who is against us? If it is the anger of Hernando Pizarro, then restrain him; if it is the importunity of the citizens of Cuzco, I well know how the wise philosopher says that the man who is angry or has an interest in the matter is not to be admitted to council. Consider that Hernando Pizarro is a putrid monster, and the citizens of Cuzco are covetous and rebellious and more jealous of their encomienda Indians than of their Indian women, because they are afraid their encomiendas will be taken away and given to the men of Chile. This, so much the worse for them, is the loyalty they have, and for this they want to risk the fame and honor in this world, and the glory of heaven in the other, that God has seen fit to give to this good old man their governor. If it is for covetousness of black gold, let them consider the fate of the rich miser, and with how much less they would have been content ten years ago, and how little time is left for the governor to enjoy what he has wanted and what he now has. I said that Hernando Pizarro is putrid because he is a man so rotted by anger and sense of honor that this black honor puts men's souls in hell and their bodies in much necessity in this world, especially as to inordinate greed.

You, sir, have become more annoyed than is right, considering not what could come of it in the future, but only the blinding anger that has you in its grip, when there is no question of honor at stake for you, and you have lost none, so you should be content to refrain from regaining it in the face of God and king and at the risk of so many Christians. If those there are made of good stuff and there are a thousand of us on both sides together, not a hundred will be left alive; and if of bad stuff, why should they want to tempt fortune again? I promise and assure that if Hernando Pizarro is taken again they will not let him loose this time. And since you have such a suitable, reasonable and secure position, gained so honorably, and you are of marriageable age, your reputation and estate are enough to get you the daughter of some great lord; don't grasp for the sky with your hands; don't leave eating capons for spiritless sheep. And since I have promised to arrange your marriage, let me warn you that the way you are exercising your office is a hindrance to my purpose; let it not be that the devil should have raised you up in order to pull you down. Hold yourself close to the cross on which God suffered for us sinners; adhere to the love that I know you have always had for our emperor. Take an example from his majesty: let us conquer infidels; if Christians are guilty, let us not want to be kings or confessors, and let us not usurp the king's justice nor make ourselves judges of our own causes.

Consider that very surely he who is losing the game is the one who interrupts it; consider that the part of Christian men, fearful of God and king, brave, valiant and hardy, is to be patient, to win heaven and credit with their prince especially through their obeisance, to conquer their enemies leaving room for time, justice and reason, to bear up under the load to the point of bursting; and then, all these efforts made, comes the time for a man's force and anger and wildness, which are then not only to the purpose, but help remove defects, for when the man comes to be tested in the crucible he is more inflamed, free of all dross and lead, and if any should remain, the smoke will bear it away.

Truly, sir, I desire all peace and concord; my concern for it makes this letter lengthy, and also my being so much your paternity's servant, though recent, and since I cannot speak in your presence I take joy in speaking through this letter. From

Juan de Vallejo as well as from other sources I have come to know your paternity's goodness and the good will you have in these matters, so I beg you to consider me your very great friend and servant, and as such I extol myself to you and will never repent of it, for I am a much better and more constant friend than an enemy, though I make a very reasonable enemy too, for that matter. And so I implore you always to be at the side of the governor, and let the devil not be able to do more than you, because we here consider you a good angel that God sent to guard us. Contrive that the evil one, whose identity I do not know, and if I did do not want to say, should not be more powerful. As to the reverend father Vice-provincial fray Juan de Olías, to what other purpose should he want his life than to spend it where he can serve God and his majesty, and die for the faith of Jesus Christ, so that he be repaid in the same coin? And since he has shown such good will up to now, I ask him for the love of God to persevere in it together with your paternity. And if we are in the wrong, then come here and preach to us, and we will hear and obey you, because I do not want to be so presumptuous as not to listen to you, and so I challenge you both, in the name of God, once, twice, and three times, to come, and thus relieve my conscience, and no notary is required, because it is known to all that if we are in darkness you must illumine us, and if we are, then so are you over there, and we are all Christians.

May the devil take my soul if I do not fear as much and even more the perdition of don Francisco Pizarro and his people than that of Governor don Diego de Almagro and his, to judge by reason and the forces of the land and the spirit of these men, each thinking he will be what he is in fact, a governor, and trying to avoid being an outcast or worse, for which they will die like rabid wolves. I consider our victory certain, but the anger of God and the king, and the loss of souls, grieves me, and also that most of what will be lost is what Governor don Francisco Pizarro won with such effort, especially since I believe he has justice on his side; but if it is so, he will have what is his, and if not, why should he want it? Even if he should take it by force and maintain it in this black world, in the clarity of judgment and in perpetual life he would pay for it. In this I think I do your paternity a service, and I swear to God and the holy cross that I will come there over the objections of wretches, knowing it will anger the devil; and I would be no bad acquisition for hell.

If I did want to come there, it would be to see royal factor Illán Suárez with his grave deportment among those firebrands, and the lieutenant governor giving judgments against benefactors. I don't know what they found wrong with royal accountant Juan de Guzmán, who was going to report to his majesty as his officer. It would have been better to give him supplies in sign of wishing him a good journey, since he shows himself so faithful to his king, and they shouldn't have hidden anything from him or tried to stop him from asking anything; he whose piss is clear thumbs his nose at the physician. They say that Captain Francisco de Godoy walks about sad-faced, and goes to Licentiate de la Gama as St John to the Mother of God when he permitted her to be badly treated. We were enlightened about this by two innocents whom we captured and then let go. They also said that your paternity said to them 'Little sinners, do you think you can go to fight against Christians?'

And so I cease, praying that our Lord guard and augment your paternity's very reverend and magnificent person, making you a father in this world and a saint in the other. From this site of Guaytará, today, 1st of January, 1538.

At your paternity's service,
Don Alonso Enríquez de Guzmán

Fray Francisco de Bobadilla's reply

Very magnificent sir:

May the grace of the Holy Spirit be with you. I received your letter, so long and so wise, and have no other recourse than to abbreviate my reply, informing you that with your letter or without it I cannot placate the anger and interests of these gentlemen. May God remedy it; I am unable to. And so I cease, asking your pardon if I have somehow annoyed you, and assuring you that I will serve you better in the future. I continue to pray to our Lord for your life and estate. From Lima y Caxca, January 4th, 1538.

From your servant,
Fray Francisco de Bobadilla
Provincial superior of Our Lady of Mercy

[1] Published in Spanish in Porras, *Cartas del Perú*, pp. 274-7, among other places.

26. The Hispanized Indian

Don Martín, Indian nobleman, interpreter and encomendero, to rebel governor Gonzalo Pizarro in Lima, 1547[1]

> ... I have my hair cut, by which I would be very easily recognized ...

The Indians of the whole vast reach of South and Central America were affected by the sixteenth-century European presence: by epidemic disease, demands for new kinds of tribute and labor, reduction of their own interregional trade, addition of new techniques, plants and animals, reorganization of local political and religious life, and much more. The majority of the population, however, long continued to live in the same provincial and local units as before, within a functioning Indian society which retained its vitality and viability. These people had little direct contact with the Spanish life of the cities, to which they were tied only through encomienda obligations and the relatively few secular and ecclesiastic encomienda representatives who came out into the countryside.

Two types of Indians did come into direct and frequent contact with Spaniards. The first, and the more important for the growth and transformation of Spanish American society, were the Spaniards' permanent servants, employees and dependents. The tribute and temporary labor provided by the encomienda were not enough. The Spaniards needed auxiliaries, people on a permanent basis who would learn something of their skills and their language, and who could then be their trusted retainers, or work at skilled crafts, or help with maintenance and supervision in their enterprises. The most prominent such auxiliaries were the ubiquitous blacks, whether as slaves or freedmen. From the beginning there were Indians in this role as well, who came to outnumber the blacks by far, and before the end of the colonial period had supplanted them in many areas.

Indian societies of many parts of America already knew not only nobles and commoners, but a third type: the person, often an outsider, who was the direct dependent of a nobleman, rather than sharing in general community obligations and rights. It was easy for the Spaniards to utilize such people, simply transferring the allegiance from an Indian nobleman to a Spaniard; even when the persons employed or commandeered were not of the dependent class, the existence of the type and function in preconquest society gave a framework of expectations. In the Caribbean the Spaniards found the word *naboría* for this type, and they carried it from there to Central America; in Peru, where the institution was particularly strong and idiosyncratic, they adopted the local word *yanacona* (actually a plural form, interpreted by the Spaniards as singular). Always on the increase numerically, the Spanish-speaking, partly Hispanized Indian, more outside Indian society than in it, came to represent a large proportion of the population of Spanish cities, mining towns and estates.

The second category of Indian dealing with Spaniards on a regular basis was the personage they called the *cacique* or 'chief,' another word they heard first in the Caribbean and spread everywhere. At times they even tried to create caciques where there were none. But generally one may equate the caciques with the traditional rulers of provincial units, vital to the Spaniards because it was only through their inherent powers in the Indian communities that the encomiendas could be made to deliver tribute and labor. The entries in a great Nahuatl tribute book of the 1530s for the Cuernavaca region of Mexico, that area being under Cortés as Marqués del Valle, tell us the whole story: 'Francisco Yaotl gives his tribute to Martín Huitznauatl, and Martín gives it to the cacique, and the cacique gives it to the Marqués.' Where such an arrangement was not built into Indian society, there could be no encomiendas in the usual sense. So the Spaniards, though they did manipulate the caciques, also relied on them greatly, gave them various kinds of support, and even sometimes courted them. But since the cacique's power base was in Indian society, he was typically less deeply and quickly affected by European culture than the Spaniards' servants and employees.

Don Martín, the writer of our present letter, is somewhere between yanacona and cacique. He seems to have been connected with Andean nobility, but he came among Spaniards as one of the interpreters who were so important in the early years of the conquest. On an exploratory voyage to Peru, in the Piura region, Francisco Pizarro requested a boy to learn the language. He was given don Martín, who was thus among Spanish speakers for years, even in Spain itself, before Peru was ever conquered. He learned beautiful Spanish, did the interpreting at critical junctures of the conquest, and much like doña Marina in Mexico, was given handsome rewards within Spanish society itself. He became chief interpreter of the realm and received an encomienda in the Lima district, on the basis of which, like any other encomendero, he set up an establishment in Lima, married a Spanish wife, hired Spanish stewards, and so on.

In this letter of 1547 we see don Martín well on his way to downfall, adhering to his patrons the Pizarros unconditionally; at the defeat of Gonzalo Pizarro in 1548 don Martín will be punished, deprived of his property, and exiled, shortly thereafter to die in Spain. At the moment the letter is written, Gonzalo Pizarro is in Lima, acting as governor in defiance of the crown, while Licentiate Gasca has landed in northern Trujillo with forces raised in the king's name. Pizarro has stationed don Martín at the latter's encomienda up the coast towards Trujillo to watch the roads and the sea. Just recently he has sent don Martín orders to go in disguise and spy out the enemy's strength in Trujillo, probably conferring with some Spaniards there who can be trusted. Don Martín declines, because he has not only adopted Spanish dress completely, but has had his hair cut Spanish style, so that he could no longer pass for an ordinary Indian. But don Martín does not lack someone to send, since he heads a whole crew of Spanish-speaking yanaconas. Don Martín, his men, and others like them are mediating between the two worlds, able to communicate with the Spaniards but also continuing to bring Andean status, techniques and institutions into play; in the letter we see this symbolized in the Andean words used, not only *yana*, but *quipu* or colored-string accounting device, and *tambo*, the Andean way-station and storage place.

The Alcántara mentioned was an encomendero of Trujillo who was then in the hills hiding from the Pizarrists. 'Fray Pedro' was fray Pedro Muñoz, a Mercedarian friar in Trujillo who was an inflamed Pizarrist partisan. As a final detail, note how don Martín when speaking Spanish uses Spanish categories, including that of 'Indian,' which was a concept foreign to the alleged Indians, and which they practically never used in their own languages, preferring to think of themselves as many distinct peoples.

Very illustrious sir:

The moment I saw your lordship's letter I would have fulfilled what your lordship commanded me therein and considered it a very great favor to be able to serve your lordship in something, since my desire is none other. But because I have my hair cut, by which I would be very easily recognized, I decided not to do it myself, but immediately sent a yanacona of mine who speaks very good Spanish, with two other Indians from this valley, to Trujillo, to find out what your lordship ordered me to. He will do it as well as I could myself because, as I said, he speaks very good Spanish and I gave him full instructions. As soon as he finds out, your lordship can be certain that he will bring back a true account on his quipu of the men, ships and captains. When he comes, I will go with what news he brings to give your lordship account of everything, and kiss your feet and serve you in what your lordship should wish to command me.

As soon as Captain Martín de Olmos arrived here, I sent

another Spanish-speaking yanacona of mine to Tarma to see if
there were any Spaniards at the tambo; when he got there he
found no Spaniards, but near the tambo on a hill he found an
Indian of Tarma with a letter that Alcántara's wife was sending
to her husband, as your lordship can see from it. My yanacona
said that the Indian who gave it to him was not the one who
brought it from Trujillo, but another Indian; the one who had
the letter came with my yanacona as far as four leagues from
here, where he remained exhausted. I then sent another Indian
to bring him here so I could ask him who gave him the letter, or
if he knew anything about Trujillo. If he comes, I will question
him on everything and report what I find out.

Captain Martín de Olmos is returning to Lima because he
thinks he is no longer needed here.

I am very careful to maintain Indians on the roads to know
who comes or goes, and I will continue to do so always, even if
I go up the valley as I intend to do, to be more secure.

What my Indians saw in the sea were four ships, of which I
sent your lordship a drawing on paper. They saw them between
this tambo and that of Tarma. They also say that five Spaniards
were going by the head of this valley toward where your lordship is, and another time, two others on horseback and one on
foot. I told fray Pedro to tell your lordship this. There is nothing else to report to your lordship. When there is, I will be the
messenger, as I said.

Our Lord guard your lordship's very illustrious person and
augment your estate as your lordship desires. From this tambo
of Guarmey, Wednesday, 13th of May, 1547.

Your lordship's least servant and follower who kisses your
very illustrious hands and feet,
    Don Martín

[1]Published in Spanish in Pérez de Tudela, *Documentos relativos a don
Pedro de la Gasca*, I, pp. 154-5. Don Martín's life is treated in detail in
Lockhart, *The Men of Cajamarca*, pp. 447-55, and also, in the context of
Spanish–Indian contact, in *Spanish Peru*, pp. 213-15.

27. Indian high society

Don Pedro Enrique Moctezuma, in Mexico City,
to his relatives doña Magdalena Axayaca, doña
Petronila Pimentel, and doña Bárbola de la Con-
cepción, in nearby Iztapalapa, 1587[1]

> ... Ma yehuatzin S̄p̄ū Sancto ytlan moyetztie yn
> cenca mahuiztic amotlacoanimantzin tlacocihuapi-
> piltine ...
>
> May the Holy Spirit dwell in your very honored
> precious souls, dear ladies ...

If all Indian rulers were 'caciques,' still there were some distinctions recognized by the Spaniards. Encomiendas, pensions
and honorific titles went to a few direct descendants of Moctezuma in Mexico, and of Atahuallpa and Huascar in Peru. And
aside from the question of Spanish recognition, a corps of high
nobility maintained itself in and around each of the former
imperial centers, Mexico City and Cuzco, even after decimation
in the conquest. For a century or more these groups continued
to exist in important Spanish cities, quite well received by the
Spaniards, sometimes marrying into Spanish society at a high
level, yet long retaining a self-awareness and distinct life style.
In Peru, since Quechua was rarely written down, the nobles
tended to do their writing in Spanish. But the nobles of Mexico,
where after the conquest literacy in Nahuatl was widespread,
have left us chronicles and correspondence in their own tongue.

Our main purpose here is to give the reader some rough notion of the refined, elegant, hyperflorid tone of these people's
discourse, still very much that of the preconquest Aztec nobility despite the integration of Spanish terms and concepts – a
rough notion, we say, because the English is a pale reflection of
the parallelisms, circumlocutions and multiple reverentials
which the richness of the Nahuatl allows without artificiality or
coyness.

Some dynastic background will be necessary for understanding. The only son of Emperor Moctezuma to live on into the

Spanish period, at least the only one enjoying recognition, was
don Pedro Moctezuma. He received the encomienda of Tultengo
in the Tula district and owned considerable property, including
a large house on the square of San Sebastián, the northeastern
district of Mexico City. A series of royal decrees confirmed his
rights and gave him a large pension besides. On his death, his
legitimate son don Martín Moctezuma succeeded. As this letter
is written, don Martín has also died, and there is great controversy over the succession. The writer of the letter, don Pedro
Enrique, is a grandson of don Pedro and nephew of don Martín,
and lives in their house in San Sebastián. That he is an actual
claimant is not clear, but he surely is opposed to the claims of a
certain don Francisco; this latter is the son of doña Inés, don
Pedro's widow, but not of don Pedro himself, so that he is
making his claim through the maternal line alone. The three
ladies who are recipients of the letter are also descended from
Aztec emperors. At the moment they are in physical possession
of the originals of some of the royal decrees relating to the
Moctezumas. This is what don Pedro Enrique is writing about;
he wants to have the decrees to present to the Royal Audiencia
and demolish don Francisco's case. In the end, a son of don
Pedro's who was then in Spain, don Diego Luis, succeeded to
both encomienda and property.

May the Holy Spirit dwell in your very honored precious
souls, dear ladies. Know that I have heard and received your
message, and very great joy and consolation it gave me that the
Lord of the earth, Lord God, grants you health. May it be his
wish that you always fare as I desire for you, dear ladies. Now
in some measure I kiss your hands and feet, and as to the
governorship of the sir ruler señor don Alonso Axayacatzin, my
late grandfather, I greet and in every way salute what he there
bequeathed you; may you exercise it fully.

Dear ladies, may I not at such a time upset you, and if so
please forgive me, by our Lord God. And in this let me not give
you pain, my dear ladies, since I have already informed you and
you are already aware of how the son of the lady my grand-

mother doña Inés, don Francisco, wishes and desires our house here in Mexico City: the house where both my late grandfather the esteemed sir don Pedro Moctezuma, and my uncle who died here, the late señor don Martín Moctezuma, lived out their lives, and which they bequeathed to us. Don Francisco considers himself the holder of the lord rulers' grants, concessions and decrees, and, as you have heard, he is taking my late sir grandfather señor don Pedro as his father, saying that he is his youngest son. As to this, I will investigate the matter and he will surely come to shame.

Now here is something with which I will content your hearts as much as what the lord rulers left us spreads discord. For know that I am sending there to you your uncles the nobles who are here at our house in Mexico City, don Martín de Aguilar and don Martín Cortés, to kiss your hands and feet. And as to why I am sending them to you, know that I am requesting the royal concession and decrees; may you concede this and send them to us. May everyone yet be content; here we will make a statement to the Royal Audiencia so that everyone will be satisfied. Dear ladies, may you grant this, because I am sending your uncles to bring the papers back, so that they will not be lost somewhere. Surely you will not reject us, dear ladies. And may I in some way attain your message; if my illness were not still a little heavy on me, I would go myself to give you satisfaction. May your hearts not be troubled by all this, and you will hear what happens when it is divulged. My ladies, this is all with which I importune you and which you are to hear. May our Lord give you his grace in his holy service. Done in Mexico City on the 9th of October, year of 1587.

Your younger brother who salutes you from afar,

Don Pedro Enrique Moctezuma

[1] Published in Nahuatl and English in Arthur J. O. Anderson, Frances Berdan, and James Lockhart, trans. and eds., *Beyond the Codices* (University of California Press, forthcoming). The translation there is slightly more literal, and several difficult points in the interpretation of the original are discussed.

28. An Indian town addresses the king

The city council of Huejotzingo, Mexico, to King Philip, 1560[1]

> ... But as to those Tlaxcalans, in many places they ran away, and often fought badly ...

As fully pre-Columbian in tone as the previous letter, this text is representative of public rather than private discourse. With its length and full development, the language has breathing room; the rhetoric rolls on to establish an atmosphere, leading inexorably to the main point, a new high tribute assessment, which by the time it arrives seems the climax and crowning disaster of the history of Huejotzingo. This is oratory, an art as well developed among the Aztecs as among the Greeks. Such speeches as this were addressed by nobles to the emperor or other high dignitaries, and examples of the genre may be seen in Book VI of Sahagún's *Florentine Codex*.[2] Of course here the subject matter is postconquest, and a considerable amount of Spanish and Christian terminology has crept into the text. Yet the stylistic devices and most of the vocabulary are retained from earlier oratorical practice. So is the structure, consisting of large paragraph-sized units, each introduced by the invocation *totecuiyoe totlatocatzine* ('O our lord, O our king'), and each an extensive elaboration of a single basic idea. In a way, it is small wonder that when Nahuatl speakers gave their petitions to Spaniards to translate, the result was often a text less than half the length of the original.

The message is approximately as follows: We salute you, high king. From a distant land we appeal for your mercy. When the Spaniards first came here, we greeted them as friends and helped them in all their wars, far more than the people of Tlaxcala. We accepted Christianity gladly and peacefully, whereas the Tlaxcalans resisted. Now your officials have assessed us a burdensome tribute. All the governors who went before treated us well, and we served them faithfully. What crime have we committed to deserve this? We humbly protest, and dutifully inform you that with such a tribute the city of Huejotzingo will soon cease to exist. The friar who bears this letter can tell you more.

The transparency of this is likely to bring a smile, in view of the contrast with the rhetorical grandeur built upon it. But this was the way of Nahuatl oratory. The elaboration was no attempt to disguise, nor exactly to construct a logically convincing argument. Rather one took joy in repeating the idea in slightly varying forms until a magnificent fabric came into being, a verbal tapestry spread out in the panels of the great paragraphs.

The letter asserts, and correctly so, that Huejotzingo was an independent province before the arrival of the Spaniards, not paying tribute to the Aztec empire. In this, as in its internal structure of four subprovinces and in much else, Huejotzingo greatly resembled its northern neighbor Tlaxcala. As soon as the Spanish invaders had proved their power, both provinces joined them against the enemy of all, the Mexica. Tlaxcala, being the larger, received the lion's share of the credit, leaving those of Huejotzingo resentful of both the Tlaxcalans and their special privileges, as their letter shows. The feeling and the situation also demonstrate something very basic and general about the self-perceptions of Indians almost everywhere. To them the local province or city-state was the primary unit of existence, a people in and of itself. The relation between a given province and its neighbors was ordinarily one of strong rivalry in every aspect of life. In fact there were usually smaller units inside the province with their own myths and ambitions of separateness. The existence of empires in preconquest times hardly affected this phenomenon, which also survived the Spanish conquest and continued strong for centuries. Notice that the writer of this letter, unlike Spanish-speaking don Martín in Peru, never once uses the word 'Indian,' coming no closer than the phrase 'we people here.' There is a unitary perception of Spaniards as a group, but Indians are referred to by the individual provincial names.

One other important constituent of the Indians' conceptual

organization of their world appears here: the nobleman–commoner distinction. This must, indeed, be given close second place to provincial separatism in the definition of Indian self-awareness, far ahead of any perception of Indianness. Underneath the rigid ethos was mobility and complexity, as always in human societies, but still a strong insistence on the different status, rights and character of noblemen had come into being in the main centers of population, the central Andes as well as Mesoamerica. Like small-unit awareness, this distinction, and the noble group itself, survived the conquest handily. Within less than a generation all the important Indian towns in the central areas were reorganized, in principle, as municipalities in the Spanish fashion, with a presiding officer, two or more alcaldes, and a corps of councilmen, but this did not much affect the social scheme. With few exceptions the presiding officer was the cacique or a close relative, and the alcaldes and councilmen were noblemen. Notice that in the Huejotzingo letter it is taken for granted that all the council members are nobles. And as usual in municipal petitions, they represent the noblemen's interests, here complaining that they have been reduced to the status of commoners, a far cry from the literal truth, seeing that during these very years the nobles of Tlaxcala and Huejotzingo were converting their often amorphous privileges into full ownership of land and legally recognized rights to goods and services from tenants.

Catholic Royal Majesty:

Our lord sovereign, you the king don Felipe our lord, we bow low in great reverence to your high dignity, we prostrate and humble ourselves before you, very high and feared king through omnipotent God, giver of life. We do not deserve to kiss your feet, only from afar we bow down to you, you who are most high and Christian and very pleasing to God our Lord, for you are his true representative here on earth, and you govern us and lead us in Christianity. All of us, creatures and subjects of life-giving God, we vassals and servants of your majesty, we people here, we who dwell here in New Spain, all together we look to you, our eyes and hearts go out toward you; we have confidence in you in the eyes of our Lord God, for he put us in your hand to guard, and he assigned us to you for us to be your servants and your helpers. By our Lord God and by your very honored and very high majesty, remember us, have compassion with us, for very great is the poverty and affliction visited on us who dwell here in New Spain.

Our lord sovereign, king don Felipe our lord, with our words we appear and stand before you, we of Huejotzingo who guard for you your city – we citizens, I the governor and we the alcaldes and councilmen and we the lords and nobles, your men and your servants – very humbly we address you: Oh unfortunate are we, very great and heavy sadness and affliction lie upon us. Your pity and compassion do not reach us; we do not deserve, we do not attain your rulership. And all the while since your subjects the Spaniards arrived, all the while we have been looking toward you, we have been confidently expecting that sometime your pity would reach us, as we also had confidence in and were awaiting the mercy of your very revered dear father the ruler of the world, don Carlos the late emperor. Therefore now, our lord sovereign, we bow humbly before you; may we deserve your pity, may the very greatly compassionate and merciful God enlighten you so that your pity is exercised on us. For we hear, and so it is said to us, that you are very merciful and humane towards all your vassals; and when there appears before you a vassal of yours in poverty, so it is said, then you have pity on him in your very revered majesty, and in God omnipotent you help him. May we now also deserve and attain the same, for every day such poverty and affliction reaches us and is visited on us that we weep and mourn. Oh unfortunate are we, what will come of us, we your poor vassals of Huejotzingo, we who live in your city? If you were not so far away, many times we would appear before you. Though we greatly wish and desire to reach you and appear before you, we are unable, because we are very poor and do not have what is needed for the journey on the boat, nor things to eat, nor anything to pay people in order to be able to reach you. Therefore now we appear before you only in our words; we set before you our poor prayer. May you only in your very great Christianity and very revered high majesty attend well to this our prayer.

Our lord sovereign, before anyone told us or made us acquainted with your fame and your story, most high and feared universal king who rules all, and before we were told or taught the glory and name of our Lord God, before the faith reached us, and before we were Christians, when your servants the Spaniards came to us and your Captain General don Hernando Cortés arrived, although we were not yet acquainted with the omnipotent, very compassionate holy Trinity, yet our Lord God the ruler of heaven and possessor of earth caused us to deserve that in his mercy he enlightened us so that we took you as our king, to belong to you and become your people and your subjects; not a single town here in New Spain surpassed us, in that first and earliest we cast ourselves toward you, we gave ourselves to you. And furthermore, no one intimidated us, no one forced us, but truly God caused us to deserve that voluntarily we adhered to you, so that we gladly received the newly arrived Spaniards who reached us here in New Spain. For we left our homes behind to go a great distance to meet them; we went twenty leagues to greet Captain General don Hernando Cortés and the others whom he led. We received them gladly, we embraced them, we saluted them with many tears, though we were not acquainted with them, and our fathers and grandfathers also did not know them; but by the mercy of our Lord God we truly came to know them. Since they are our neighbors, therefore we loved them; nowhere did we attack them. Truly we fed them and served them; some arrived sick so that we carried them in our arms and on our backs, and we served them in many other ways which we are not able to say here. Although the people who are called and named Tlaxcalans indeed helped, yet we strongly pressed them to give aid, and we counseled them not to make war; but though we so admonished them they fought and made war for two weeks. But we, when a Spaniard was afflicted, at once we would manage to reach him, like no one else. We do not lie in this, for all the conquerors know it well, those who have died and those now living.

And when they began their conquest and warmaking, then also we well prepared ourselves to aid them, for out came all of our war gear, our arms and provisions and all our equipment, and we not merely named someone, we went in person, we who rule, and we brought all our nobles and all of our vassals to aid the Spaniards. We helped not only in warfare, but also we gave them everything they needed; we fed and clothed them, and we would carry in our arms and on our backs those whom they wounded in war or who were very ill, and we did all the tasks in preparing for war. And so that they could fight the Mexica with boats, we worked hard; we gave the Spaniards the wood and pitch with which they built the boats. And when they conquered the Mexica and all their adherents, we never abandoned them or left them. And as they went to conquer Michoacan, Jalisco, and Colhuacan, and at Pánuco and Oaxaca and Tehuantepec and Guatemala, we were the only ones who went along while they conquered and made war here in New Spain until they had finished the conquest; we never abandoned them, in no way did we hold back their warmaking, though some of us were destroyed in it, nor were any of our subjects left, for we did our duty very well. But as to those Tlaxcalans, several of their nobles were hanged for making war poorly; in many places they ran away, and often fought badly. In this we do not lie, for the conquerors know it well.

Our lord sovereign, we also say and declare before you that your fathers the twelve sons of St Francis, whom the very high priestly ruler the Holy Father sent and whom you sent, both of you taking pity on us so that they would teach us the gospel, came to us to teach us the holy Catholic faith and belief, to make us acquainted with the single deity God our Lord. And then likewise God favored and enlightened us of Huejotzingo, who dwell in your city, so that we gladly received them. When they entered the city of Huejotzingo, of our own free will we honored them and showed them much esteem. When they advised us to abandon the wicked belief in many gods, we forthwith voluntarily left it. Likewise they did us the good deed of telling us to destroy and burn the stones and wood that we worshiped as gods, and we did it; very willingly we destroyed, demolished and burned the temples. Also when they imparted to us the holy gospel, the holy Catholic faith, with very good will and desire we received and grasped it. No one frightened us into it, no one forced us, but very willingly we seized it, quietly and peacefully we arranged and ordered it among ourselves; no one, neither nobleman nor commoner, was ever tortured or burned for this, as was done on all sides here in New Spain. The people of many towns were forced and tortured, were hanged and burned because they did not want to leave idolatry, and unwillingly they received the gospel and faith. Especially those Tlaxcalans pushed out and rejected the fathers, and would not receive the faith, for many of the high nobles were burned, and some hanged, for combating the advocacy and service of our Lord God. But we of Huejotzingo, we your poor vassals, we never did anything in your harm, always we served you in every command you sent or what at your command we were ordered. Very quietly, peacefully we took and grasped it all, though only through the mercy of God did we do it, since it was not within our personal power. Therefore now, in and through God, may you hear these our words, all that we say and declare before you, so that you will take pity on us, so that you will exercise your rulership on us to console us and aid us in this trouble with which we daily weep and are sad. We are afflicted and sore pressed, and your town and city of Huejotzingo is as if it is about to disappear and be destroyed. Here is what is being done to us: now your stewards the royal officials and the prosecuting attorney Dr Maldonado are assessing us a very great tribute to belong to you. The tribute we are to give is 14,800 pesos in money, and also all the bushels of maize.

Our lord sovereign, never has such a thing happened to us in all the time since your servants and vassals the Spaniards came to us, for your servant don Hernando Cortés, late captain general, the Marqués del Valle, in all the time he lived here with us, always greatly cherished us and kept us happy; he never disturbed nor agitated us. Although we gave him tribute, he assigned it to us only with moderation; even though we gave him gold, it was only very little – no matter how much, or in what way, or if it was not very pure, he just received it gladly. He never reprimanded us or afflicted us, because it was evident to him and he understood well how very greatly we served and aided him. Also he told us many times that he would speak in our favor before you, that he would help us and inform you of all the ways in which we have aided and served you. And when he went before you, you confirmed him and were merciful to him, you honored and rewarded him for the way he had served you here in New Spain. But perhaps when before you he forgot us. How then shall we speak? We did not reach you, we were not given audience before you. Who then will speak for us? Unfortunate are we. Therefore now we place ourselves before you, our sovereign lord. And when you sent your representatives the President and Bishop don Sebastián Ramírez and the judges Licentiate Salmerón and Licentiates Ceinos, Quiroga, and Maldonado, they well affirmed and sustained the orders you gave for us people here, us who live in New Spain. In many things they aided us and lightened the very great tribute we had, and from many things that were our tasks they delivered us, they pardoned us all of it. And we your poor vassals, we of Huejotzingo who dwell in your city, when Licentiate Salmerón came to us and entered the city of Huejotzingo, he saw how troubled the town was with our tribute in gold, 60 pieces that we gave each year, and that it troubled us because gold does not appear here and is not to be found in our province, though we searched for it everywhere. Then at once Licentiate Salmerón pardoned it on your behalf, so that he made a replacement and substitution of the money, setting our tribute in money at 2,050 pesos. And in all the time we were thus assessed, we kept doing it, we hastened to give it to you, since we are your subjects and belong to you; we never neglected it, we never did poorly, we made it all up. But now we are taken aback and very afraid and we ask, have we done something wrong, have we somehow behaved badly and ill toward you, our sovereign lord, or have we committed some sin against almighty God? Perhaps you have heard something of our wickedness and for that reason now this very great tribute has fallen upon us, seven times exceeding all we had paid before, the 2,000 pesos. And we declare to you that it will not be long before your city of Huejotzingo completely disappears and perishes, because our fathers, grandfathers and ancestors knew no tribute and gave tribute to no one, but were independent, and we nobles who guard your subjects are now truly very poor. Nobility is seen among us no longer; now we resemble the commoners. As they eat and dress, so do we; we have been very greatly afflicted, and our poverty has reached its culmination. Of prosperity and honor such as our fathers and grandfathers and forebears enjoyed, there is no longer the slightest trace among us.

Oh our lord sovereign king, we rely on you as on God the one deity who dwells in heaven, we trust in you as our father. Take pity on us, have compassion with us. May you especially remember those who live and subsist in the wilds, those who move us to tears and pity; truly we share just such poverty as theirs, wherefore we speak out before you, so that afterwards you will not become angry with us when your subjects have disappeared or perished. Here ends this our poor prayer.

We cannot write here for you the very many ways in which your city of Huejotzingo is poor and stricken; we are leaving that to our dear father fray Alonso de Buendía, son of St Francis, if God the one deity wills that he should arrive safely before you. He will be able to tell you much more about our anguish and poverty, since he learned and saw it well while he was prior here in the city of Huejotzingo for two years. We hope that he will tell and read this to you, for we have much confidence in him and have placed ourselves completely in his hands. This is all with which we come and appear before you; this letter was done in the city of Huejotzingo on the 30th day of the month of July, in the year of the birth of our Lord Jesus Christ 1560.

Your poor vassals who bow down humbly to you from afar.

Don Leonardo Ramírez, governor. Don Mateo de la Corona, alcalde. Diego Alameda, alcalde. Don Felipe de Mendoza, alcalde. Hernando de Meneses. Miguel de Alvarado. Alonso Pimentel. Agustín Osorio. Don Francisco Vázquez. Don Diego de Chaves. Juan de Almo[a]. Diego de Niza. Agustín de Santo Tomás. Diego Suárez. Toribio de San Cristóbal Motolinia.

[1] Published in Nahuatl and English in Anderson, Berdan, and Lockhart, *Beyond the Codices*. As with Letter 27, some obscure points of the translation are discussed there.

[2] Charles E. Dibble and Arthur J. O. Anderson, trans., *Florentine Codex. Book 6: Rhetoric and Moral Philosophy* (Santa Fe, New Mexico, 1969).

PART III: OFFICIALS AND CLERICS

Oh sacred majesty, how just and good are the
royal orders you send to this province, and how
officials mold them here and do what they wish!

Bernal Díaz del Castillo, Guatemala, 1552

Letters from governors and prominent ecclesiastics fill the great
Archive of the Indies. They were, for reasons not unrelated to
the relative legibility of their script, among the first documents
to interest Spanish American historians; consequently they
dominate the documentary collections of the nineteenth century, and are second only to the chronicles of the conquest in
familiarity.

Despite this popularity, the governors' letters, directed usually to the king and royal council, are among the least informative
writings of man. They magnify small problems and hide large
ones; they denigrate the actions of predecessors and represent
routine procedures as important policy innovations; they give
the weight of official truth to uninformed gossip, malicious
stereotypes, and superficial observations. Letters from judges,
treasury officials, bishops and friars share many of the same
characteristics, with the addition of constant highly colored
criticism of the governor and of each other, as almost institu-
tionalized rivals.

We include some examples of this type of public official
correspondence because it was a part of the cultural life of the
time. If one gets a notion of the conventions of such writing
and the types of motivation underlying it, one can gain from it
considerable knowledge concerning the correspondents' mental-
ity and stance, and learn at least something about general conditions. However, in these letters one learns very little indeed
about officials and clerics' manner of operation, a phenomenon
of an altogether different level. Affected very strongly by con-

173

siderations of region, family, social position, economic necessity and group rivalry, officials in real situations perforce acted differently than might seem to be dictated by royal decrees or their own public pronouncements. To give some sense of this, we also include several private letters from the holders of various types of office. When talking to relatives and friends rather than to the king, they touch a different subject matter, are much franker, and reveal profound similarities to other settlers. The institutions use the same methods as the society in which they are immersed, and they reflect it perhaps more than they shape it.

29. How a governor operates

Licenciate Cristóbal Vaca de Castro, governor of Peru, to his wife doña María de Quiñones in Valladolid, Old Castile, 1542[1]

> ... In everything seek the aid of the president of the Royal Council, because since I have given his brother a very good encomienda of Indians here ...

> So I have made this small profit from the goods I brought with me ...

Already in other sections (Letters 9 and 12) we have seen how, through necessity and inclination, governors tended to treat their offices and jurisdictions as a private, familial domain. However upright a governor was or meant to be, if he was to be effective he must have support at home in Spain, faithful followers in the Indies, and economic sinews beyond meager salaries. Thus certain procedures were almost universal for Spanish American viceroys and governors. Owing their initial appointment and continued term in office to court figures high in the king's favor or on the Council of the Indies, they showed gratitude and curried favor by sending letters and gifts, giving plums of patronage to the courtiers' relatives, etc. Any governor setting out for America would have to go into debt to outfit himself for the trip; his prospective position, however, gave him abundant credit, which he would generally use not only for his immediate needs, but also for investment, direct or indirect, in goods destined to be sold in his district. He took with him an entourage of relatives and compatriots that made up an embryo government, including people who could be trusted to perform tasks for him at all levels, as executives, secretaries, constables and henchmen; in the district of his authority he would find yet other compatriots, and he would use them too, trading favors for the extra loyalty assured by the regional tie. Success as governor might lead to yet higher posts in Spain, noble titles and distinctions, the founding or augmentation of a family entail, splendid marriages for the governor's children, and related advantages. Such possibilities were of course in the governor's mind from the beginning, and he steered things accordingly.

These then were the core mechanisms of government, its anatomy and system of reward, the nature of which shaped governmental action decisively. Where the governor had strong backers at court, a large regional following, and wealth and patronage at his command, he could assert himself mightily. Without them he ordinarily could not. In either case, in the absence of strong hierarchies or a truly activist state, quasi-personal characteristics were the determinant. Even the strong governor was more an adjudicator of disputes and allocator of resources than an instigator of 'policies.'

Since selective patronage was so basic, there was little flavor of immorality or corruption associated with it. Yet only rarely do we find it mentioned in public correspondence, except in a hostile way by the governors' enemies; it was after all a phenomenon of the roots rather than of the surface. In the present letter we tap the level of the confidential, as a governor gives his wife at home a frank account of his actions and use of patronage, and advises her how best to please the figures at court and solicit rewards for him.

The governor, Licentiate Vaca de Castro, has appeared before in these pages as the judge expected in Peru to investigate the Pizarrists' execution of Almagro and to divide the jurisdictions (see Letters 9, 10 and 25). On his arrival he found Pizarro assassinated and Almagro the Younger having seized power. As he rather vaingloriously but not inaccurately asserts, he put down the rebellion and reestablished royal authority with nothing but the king's name, latent Pizarrist strength and his own initiative, and in this letter he is thinking primarily of his rewards for doing so.

Lady:

I know how troubled you will be, now that a Dominican friar named fray Francisco Martínez and an Alonso de Villalobos from Castroverde have arrived there, as I hope by our Lord God they have done in safety, and doubtless you have seen the letters they carried, written the 18th of August of this year of '42, in which I wrote you how I was going to give battle to the traitors don Diego de Almagro and his captains and men, who had usurped the realm from his majesty and killed the Marqués its governor, and you still must not know how it turned out. So I decided to send my man Francisco Becerra, bearer of this, to relieve you, lady, of the worry and let you know that I did battle with them, the most cruel and hard fought that ever was seen, the two sides being as equally divided as they were, and it pleased our Lord and his glorious mother to grant me that day, Saturday September 16, the most glorious victory ever given to any captain general in the world. Although I entered the fighting at the time of danger, for three of the forty who entered with me were killed and others wounded, I came off free, though my sword, clothing and armor were not free of the blood of the enemy. Since the messenger will give you a long account of everything, and I believe Páez is writing of all that has happened to me since I left there, I will say no more here, than beg you to give thanks for it to God our Lord and the glorious virgin our Lady, his mother.

Lady, I have done his majesty a great service in winning him back this realm from such rebels, so many and so well armed, mounted, and gunned, who had the country occupied and intimidated with such and so many desecrations against his majesty, since they publicly killed his governor and sacked houses and killed many others and seized the country and all the royal revenues, and took over everything, so that when I entered the realm the only town I found on his majesty's side was Quito, 300 leagues from the city of Lima, where those traitors had decided to defend this realm against his majesty, and even take Panamá and Nombre de Dios from him, and they had very good means to do it, me being without a penny (because his majesty had nothing in this realm) and without men, and there were no weapons or horses, since the enemies had stolen everything. Despite all this, and more that the messenger will tell you, I managed things so well and diligently that I found money, men, arms and horses, and what else was needed to conquer and win, as I say, this realm. And since it was thought that the Marqués don Francisco Pizarro had done such a great service in winning this realm from Indians, which was winning it from lambs, that they gave him a marquisate here, and afterwards he lost it all by his own fault and I won it back after it had been lost, and from people of our nation, and such as I have described, I would like to see if we can have his majesty favor me in the things in a memorandum going inside this letter (the messenger carries another like it). For such services and good news it would be nothing to give me all this I ask; it would be more proper for his majesty to give me more than I ask, since I gave him this realm, and for similar things and of less service others have been given principalities. And in these things to be asked that are noted in the memo, do much or little according to how you see that my services here are being received there, and as the opportunities allow; and if you think it suiting to take the trouble of speaking about it to the Comendador Mayor and Secretary Sámano and the Cardinal and the Count of Osorno and the members of the Council of the Indies, then do it, because it will be to our advantage; and in everything seek the aid of the president of the Royal Council, because since I have given his brother a very good encomienda of Indians here, with a very rich silver mine, having found him starving in that poor country of Cali, he has an obligation to do good in what concerns me. And also seek the aid of doña María de Mendoza, the Comendador Mayor's wife. Since I have taken care to serve them all, it is right that in this way they should reward and pay me; and since I, lady, have exerted myself here and am deserving, it would be well that an effort should be made there to obtain some advantage and that you should insist with them, because when cavaliers perform services like these, it is customary for them to found entails and noble houses.

And though, lady, I am sending along the memorandum of what is to be asked, you must consider, as I said, how people there are viewing my services and things here, and try out what it is possible to get, extending or cutting back according to what you see and what seems best to you and Francisco Becerra and Dr Pero López and perhaps Almaguer; they will say what we would do best to ask for, especially Almaguer. But I, who have seen things here and have served and striven and know that I gave his majesty this realm with my own hand, I know very well that it is little to ask. Dr Pero López may see this letter as far as it touches on these matters, and say what he thinks it best to do.

And when you should go to the house of one of those whom I have mentioned, go in style, on your mule, well accompanied, with a squire and an old and venerable chaplain, and servant boys and pages. It would be well to stay on speaking terms with doña María de Mendoza, and visit her and give her some things, and that way she will do as we wish; and the Countess of Rivadavia, her mother, will help us, because I have served her. All this is understood to be for when the court is in Valladolid; when it's elsewhere, it will be enough for you to write to them all.

Though only a few days ago I saw in a letter that came from Seville, that Diego de Aller and Alonso de Argüello, whom I had sent from here last year and who embarked in Nombre de Dios on the first of April with dispatches for his majesty and for you, had arrived safely in Seville (and may it please our Lord that it is true, for nothing in the world could give me greater pleasure), still I will mention here the substance of what I wrote and sent by them, and also what I wrote by the friar and Alonso de Villalobos; until I am sure that you have received the letters and what they carried I will not stop mentioning briefly in all the letters I should write what I wrote and sent, as I say.

By Diego de Aller I wrote to his majesty and all the court, and also gave him a memorandum instructing him what he was to do; the father and Alonso de Villalobos carried the same, though fuller and with additions; and Becerra is carrying the same, with what is to be requested now. With all of them I wrote telling of things here and my health, and because, God willing, Becerra will tell you, I will not write it here. I wrote to you by Diego de Aller how I had sent 2,500 ducats from Santo Domingo to pay Juan Navarro, and as I have seen since, by your letters and his and from Francisco de Reloba, that the money arrived safely and was paid, and a little of what Francisco carried was left over, there is no more to say here than to give thanks to God for it.

Also, lady, I wrote you how Diego de Aller was instructed, and after him the friar and Villalobos if he should not have done it, to collect from some merchants in Seville what was lost on the sea in the ship of Pero de Aburto, since they insured it for me; I feel sure that if Diego de Aller arrived, as they say, it will have been done. If not, Villalobos or the father will collect it, and if not, then let Francisco go do it. The bill of insurance remained in the hands of Juan Navarro when I left from San-lúcar. In Seville Diego de Aller was also to collect 33,000-odd maravedís owed me by a Juan de la Puebla from several hundredweight of hardtack that Carranza sold him in Sanlúcar. Lady, find out what he has done in this matter and collect anything still owing.

Lady, I also wrote you with Diego de Aller how I was sending you by him 5,550 pesos, besides what I gave him and Argüello for themselves, 800 ducats to Diego de Aller and 400 to Argüello for travel, trouble and expense. And I wrote that of the 5,550 pesos, there were to be paid to Hernando Romano 1,500 ducats that he lent me, as you know, when I left there, and also 300 that I wanted him to be given as interest. From the rest that was left over I said that you should give doña Catalina 1 million maravedís for her marriage, and you should buy a house there. Diego de Aller took the money in bars of a kind of gold that will be worth more there, because it has silver mixed in. Some other trifles that he took beyond this are listed in a memo inside this letter, and the friar and Alonso de Villalobos took the receipts that he made out for all he took, so that they could collect it in case of necessity.

Lady, I also wrote you with Diego de Aller to watch over the studies of our boys and take good care of the things of your house, since you know that without that there is no wellbeing, and to arrange the marriage of doña Catalina, if something of the right nature should present itself, and thus I again beg you to try to attain it. I wrote you almost the same thing with father fray Francisco Martínez and Alonso de Villalobos as with Diego de Aller and therefore there is no reason to repeat it, except that with this letter there is a memo of all they took and that I sent you with them and what Becerra carried, signed with his name. Take strict account of all of them and collect everything and see to its security as I will say farther on in this letter, and also keep the memos safe. So I have made this small profit from the goods I brought with me, because since I took so much with me, thinking it would be necessary here, there was enough left to be sold by a man of mine, and the money comes from that. What you must thank me for are the things of gold alloy, the finest that have been made here; and for doña Catalina I am sending eight pairs of tweezers that are much esteemed, because the ones in Spain are worth nothing compared to these. They are also to be sent to the Countess of Miranda and whoever else you might think best, because I already know that you, lady, don't need them; with them, they say here, the Indian women remove all their body hair, however downy it might be, and the men remove their beards if any grow, because they consider it elegant to have none. Four of them are of gold, not very fine, so that they will be strong, and four of silver.

I trust to our Lord God that all I have sent and now am sending has reached or will reach you safely; may it please him in his mercy and goodness that it be so, as you and our children there need it, since it suited him that I endure such travail and danger to earn it, with his aid.

In one matter you must take great care and exercise much diligence, and that is that you receive very secretly everything that has come there and should now arrive, so that even those at the house don't know about it, and you keep it secretly outside the house, deposited in some monastery, or where Doctor Pero López should think best; confide in him, because I do believe his grace is to be trusted, or still, if it could be, I would want no one to know about it but you and Jerónimo Vaca, if you think that he will keep quiet. You must pretend poverty, and say that I have sent you nothing but certain monies to pay Hernando Romano and Juan Navarro 4,000 pesos that I borrowed for my voyage, and with that all the rest can be hidden. But you are only to talk of this in case of necessity, if something should be suspected or discovered and it be necessary to give answers and explanations, and for no other reason. This is best because though all put together it is very little, the less the king and his favorites see, the more favors they will do me, and when you answer me about what arrived, it will be enough to say that you received my letters and all that was mentioned in the memos, and the same with the messengers.

When I came here I was empowered by the Comendador Mayor of León to collect his revenues in Peru. Now I am sending him 4,000 pesos; the money is to remain in Panamá to be sent along with his majesty's gold. I was also empowered by Secretary Sámano to collect some debts owed him here; I am sending him 1,000 pesos. It seems good that you should know this and what is being done with it. The rest that I say Becerra is taking is listed in the memorandum going with this, and when you answer about what arrived, it will be enough to say that you received the letter and all that was mentioned in the memorandum, and the same with the messengers.

The wife of a secretary of mine sent along with fray Francisco Martínez and Villalobos some little things, like a hat and a medal, for doña Catalina; she wrote to her and also to you, but the letters were lost. Answer her as if you received them, and it will be the same.

I've not received letters from you since the one you wrote in July of 1541. Now they tell me that letters are coming from Castile; may it please God that some come from you, and with the good news I desire.

Lady, I am still in good health, though sated with the hardships that this land and war have given me. For eight months I never had my armor off my back, sleeping in it most of the time, because it was necessary in order not to give opportunity to some wretches among my followers, as well as to guard me against the enemies, especially for two weeks before the battle. Even now I can't live carelessly; but all of it is nothing, compared to the pain of your absence. All this of my health and the good success that God has given me and gives me in matters here, I attribute to your prayers and doña Catalina's and the nuns'. God keep it thus, and let us see each other again in health, as we desire. Amen.

If you should think proper to give some of the gold alloy things to doña María de Mendoza, do it, for I'll send plenty, or to the wife of a Councilor of the Indies or to someone else when you see it is necessary and advantageous; do there as you see fit, since it is good to please people.

After this was written I decided to send Carranza along with Francisco Becerra, pardoning the past annoyances, for the greater security of what I am sending, so that if one should fall ill the other would arrive, with the aid of God, and also for the security of the dispatches Becerra is carrying, and so what they take is the responsibility of both; also with this arrangement you will be able to hear of the things here in a more familiar way. And lady, treat Becerra with respect, since he is to manage negotiations at court and all the important matters, though Carranza can help too where needed. I ordered 8 ducats to be given to the nuns; have it done, and if after the other letters you still have not given 50 ducats to Juan de Reloba's father, send it now, since it is owed him for things of his that were sold here after he died.

I am writing to Mr Antonio de Fonseca that if he knows of some good cavalier with a good entail who should be available for marriage, he should write of it to you, so that, if you should think best, proposals could be made.

I will not write what I wrote in another letter, that a cavalier of Sahagún called Per Ansúrez had asked me to write you to do him the favor of having his wife, who is in Sahagún, come to your house to be in your company, and so I wrote to you about it, because besides being from our part of the country and the relative of relatives, he is now captain of my guard and my great servant and a person who loves me faithfully, of whom there are few or none here. If it is not done by the time he arrives, it will not be necessary, but if he should want it to be done, or anything else that suits him, do it. He will have charge of all my affairs; he knows them well and will know how to negotiate them well, and has favor there to do it. Confide everything to him and Becerra; he has been told about keeping everything secret as I wrote above, including what he is taking to give you, which is also listed in another memo with this letter, signed by his name. In matters of security do as he thinks best, for he will act skilfully in this.

I also charged him, if some good purchase should present itself there, to negotiate for it, in his own name. It will be done as seems best to you; he carries a memorandum of things that it seemed to me might be bought now. I say in his name and as if for him, because not so much as a straw should be bought for me and in my name; rather it should be understood that you and I don't have a penny.

I had here a servant, from Villabrajima near Medina de Rioseco, who was in charge of the house and served me well and faithfully; he died, to my great sorrow, leaving a daughter, still a girl, in Villabrajima. I am writing a letter, which goes with this one, to his relatives to take her to our house to serve you, and later I would arrange her marriage, because he entrusted me with it in his will and had served me well. Lady, I beg you to send the letter to the relatives, and if they send her, take charge of her.

If perchance his majesty and those masters and friends of mine there should ordain that I be here longer, which after all, lady, you see would not be bad for us, in order to be able to buy property for a good entail so that memory would remain of our parents and of us, and if you want to send here Pedro de Quiñones or Antonio, do as seems best to you, for if they come with Captain Per Ansúrez, I know that they will be well treated; and if not, do as you think best, because I don't want you to blame me if some other opportunity should present itself.

Nothing else comes to mind to write, except to beg our Lord to guard you and all our sons and daughters, to free us all from evil and let us see each other again in health, as we desire. Cuzco, 28th of November, 1542.

> Licentiate Vaca de Castro

Memorandum of what Diego de Aller took to give to doña María de Quiñones, my wife, in Valladolid.

He received and is responsible for 5,550 pesos of 450 maravedís each, in bars of gold of that quality; part of it was worth more because the gold was with silver and assayed by carats.

He also took four emeralds, one in the form of a button set in gold, weighing, with the gold, 2½ pesos, 9 grains.

Another, set in a ring with the gold broken in the middle, in the thin part opposite the setting, all weighing 1½ pesos.

Two other small emeralds of equal size with two golden signs in the middle of the emeralds.

Also two vases, one of silver and gold, weighing 52 pesos, and the other of silver with colored stones on top, weighing 72 pesos.

A two-handled cup of gold without a lid, of fine gold, made by Indians, weighing 73 pesos.

A thread of gold alloy, weighing 18 pesos.

Another thread of gold alloy, dark purple, weighing 5 pesos.

Another small thread of alloy, with turquoise.

A saltshaker, divided into two halves, of fine gold, weighing 15 pesos.

A small chain of fine gold, with a small golden ring having an emerald and a turquoise stone set in it together, weighing 14 pesos.

Diego de Aller took 200 pesos to deliver to Enao, who works for the Comendador Mayor, given him by the royal treasurer of Quito, named Rodrigo Núñez.

He also took another 93 pesos for Enao that a Diego de Torres, citizen of Quito, was sending him.

He also took 80 pesos that the city of Quito was sending to be given to a lawyer at court to aid them in their affairs; he was to give it to Licentiate Hernando Díaz, attorney at court, or if he should be absent or dead, to a Dr Avalos, son-in-law of Licentiate Villa, attorney for accountants at court.

For the above-mentioned things that he took, Diego de Aller left receipts in my possession, signed with his name, which receipts father fray Francisco Martínez and Villalobos took with them; and Becerra and Carranza took another copy.

[1] Published in Spanish in Porras, *Cartas del Perú*, pp. 510-16.

30. Alarm and drastic remedies: A viceroy's view of New Spain

Don Luis de Velasco, viceroy of New Spain, to the emperor, 1553[1]

> ... There are some measures I will mention here that are necessary and almost forced upon us if this land is not to be lost ...

If the previous letter was unusually private talk from a governor, in this one we have pronouncedly public correspondence. The general tone of official letters from governors to the crown is simply described: hysteria. Eternal emergency reigns. In don Luis de Velasco's picture, Spaniards may not be able to maintain a presence in Mexico; all elements of the population are on the verge of rebellion; the mines will soon be abandoned for lack of labor; the food supply situation is likened to a state of siege. Can this be the most peaceful and populous Spanish

American colony at the time when discoveries of great silver mines are revolutionizing its economy, a land so plentiful in food and supplies that never an immigrant fails to comment on it? Don Luis is merely using the rhetoric of the genre, which had become so high pitched that only screams were worthy of attention. Both writers and recipients of such letters were perfectly capable of translating the shrieks into exclamation marks, and today's readers must also learn the art. The best way would be to read ten examples of governors' letters from ten different times and places, observing how little the tone, vocabulary and content vary. For that we lack space, but it would be easy to find numerous letters in the best-known documentary collections which are close to this one in substance.

Other standard items here are the crude social stereotypes. Everyone is always idle, Spaniards as well as Indians, and the worst are always the blacks, mulattoes and mestizos. The solution proposed is always the same, mass deportation. (Needless to say, this was never carried out anywhere, nor immigration restricted meaningfully, though it is true that in the very early days expeditions into unpromising areas served as a safety valve with considerable effect.) The viceroy always feels that the Audiencia is insolent, that is, he would rather see it fully subordinated to him than have it act as a countervailing force, as it was meant to. Complaints about salaries, though in fact in a certain sense highly justified, are also endemic in this literature, as are pro forma requests for quick retirement, uttered mainly to reinforce the point.

Governor-correspondents thus generally took the position that impending disaster could be averted only by giving them a free hand (this was the real message, and vast quixotic measures such as deportations, reorganizations of cities, huge fortifications, etc., were usually window dressing). In one matter they changed their tune. When it came to revenue remittances, so important to the crown and to gubernatorial reputations, the governors became optimists. They reported in detail what they were sending and promised much more soon, very much like the merchant-factors of the commercial world when writing to their seniors in Seville. The closer one comes to matters of routine administration and staffing, the more realistic and knowledgeable one finds the governors. Velasco's proposal of adding criminal judges to the Audiencia is well made. In the matter of collecting the deficit of the deceased royal factor, he is sober reason itself, against the doctrinaire and unrealistic position of the officials in Spain.

The 'distribution' that Velasco refers to as being suggested by the conquerors was their petition for perpetual hereditary rights to their encomiendas, a last-ditch, less than successful effort to maintain the early total encomendero dominance.

Sacred Catholic Caesarean Majesty:

In every ship that has left New Spain I have written to your majesty, giving a long and detailed account of the state of things in the country and what has been done since my arrival, in fulfilment of your majesty's order and instruction, and I have had no reply from your majesty, nor even evidence that my letters have been summarized for you. It is two years and a half since I wrote the first of them; I suspect that the great concerns and wars that have presented themselves have been the reason why your majesty has not had answers sent. May it please God our Lord that it all have as favorable an outcome as we servants of your majesty desire.

Carrying out the new laws and provisions that were given me and that have been sent since has put the land in great trouble and necessity, which every day grows greater because their execution came all at once. Among the Spaniards there is great discontent and much poverty, and among the Indians more laxity and ease than their little constancy will suffer. I am afraid that troubles very hard to remedy are going to come from one side or the other, because the country is so full of blacks and mestizos, who greatly outnumber the Spaniards, and all of whom wish to purchase their liberty with the lives of their masters; this bad breed will join anyone who rebels, whether Spaniards or Indians. In order to preserve this land in the service of our Lord and obedience to your majesty, there are some measures I will mention here that are necessary and almost forced upon us if this land is not to be lost. May your majesty order these things to be considered and make what provision you see fit; in advising you what I feel and serving faithfully to death I will do my duty. What I would regret more than death would be that the land should be lost while it was my responsibility.

The principal thing your majesty should order to be proclaimed is the distribution that has been suggested by the conquerors and settlers, provided only that the grants your majesty should make them would not give any of them jurisdiction, and provided the tributes were very moderate, of which the encomenderos would give a sixth or a seventh for the support of the churches and monasteries. The friars and priests would be in charge of the administration of the sacraments and the religious instruction of the natives, giving the principal responsibility for this to the prelates and taking it away from the encomenderos. In this way you will discharge your royal conscience, do right by those who have served you, and keep the Spaniards in the country and make it secure. Those who inform your majesty that the land can be held by friars alone, without being defended by Spaniards who have the means with which to serve and something to lose if they don't do their duty, in my view deceive themselves and do not know the natives well, because they are not so firm in our holy faith, nor have they so forgotten the evil beliefs they had in the time of their infidelity, that such great matters should be trusted to their virtue.

Next, your majesty should order that part of the Spanish people, mestizos, and blacks be culled out and sent on some conquest, since there are too many in the land; and if this is not to be done, then order the door shut to Spaniards of any kind, so they will not enter New Spain, and deport the mestizos who could be sent in the ships that go back to Spain, because they are very harmful for the Indians; those who remained would take heed, seeing that some of them were being ejected from the country. Your majesty should order that not so many licenses be given to import blacks, because here in New Spain there are more than twenty thousand, and they are increasing greatly; there could come to be so many of them that they would put the land in disorder.

Next, your majesty should grant the habit of the Order of Santiago to some cavaliers and gentlemen who have property here in New Spain, those few of them who have merits, because it would be obliging them anew to be faithful vassals, live a virtuous Christian life, and remain firm in your majesty's service; because if the important people remain firm, it will go far toward keeping those who are lower from becoming restless.

Next, let your majesty order that, in addition to the eight Spanish towns that have been settled, four or five more be founded in suitable places, since there are such places where they can be given suitable lands for their sustenance; but this cannot be done unless the Indians help with the buildings and some bits of land are taken from them; there is enough and more than enough for all if they would adapt to each other.

Let your majesty order that all those who have encomiendas live and reside in the bishopric where their Indians are, and have their households in the main cities and towns where the principal churches are established and the prelates reside, so that there can be some proper accounting for them; the way they now live is confused. Mexico City and its surroundings are so loaded with people that food is scarce. The provinces of Michoacan, Colima and Zacatula are very difficult to supply; and the Villa de la Purificación and Pánuco, which are Spanish towns, are being depopulated because part of the land is hot and there are few Indians, and the Spaniards have been forbidden to use even their services, and the tributes have been lowered. I see no other way to keep these Spanish places from being completely emptied of people than that your majesty order that encomenderos live and reside, as I said, in the provinces where they have encomiendas, in the chief towns of the bishoprics, and not in the places of their encomiendas, among the Indians.

In matters of good government and the administration of justice, if the small experience I have does not mislead me, it is

very important that there be three or four criminal judges in the
Royal Audiencia here, trained men of the law and persons of
confidence, with the same income as the civil judges, and with
the powers that the judges in Valladolid and Granada have,
among Spaniards as well as among Indians, and between Indians
and Spaniards. This would have a great effect, because justice
would be done with speed and rigor, which is most necessary to
bring calm to the country; the civil judges have so many duties
that they cannot attend to criminal cases promptly, and thus
crimes are forgotten, or the prisoners die in jail before the judgment reaches them, as sometimes happens.

Next, the civil judges who are appointed should understand
from the beginning that they will not hold office for more than
five or six years, so that they will not take root in the land nor
carry on secret commerce, which is more harmful to the commonwealth than public trading; not that I know that those
presently serving have such dealings, but they can have them
without it being known, because they do business through intermediaries.

Next, whoever governs here should have fuller powers than
your majesty has given to me, because every time I give orders
in matters of general administration, they appeal to the Audiencia, and most times the order never takes effect, which is very
harmful and gives rise to effrontery from which serious trouble
could result. The greatest service I have done your majesty in
this office has been to put up with some of these Audiencia
judges, who have certainly exceeded the bounds in some things,
claiming that they are superior, and if I had not used great
moderation and patience, there could not have failed to be great
division and confusion in the land. I beg your majesty to
remedy this by quickly ordering a review of the Audiencia, so it
will be understood how we live and serve, and let more serious
persons, of greater experience and conscience, be appointed to
the court than some of the ones appointed in the past.

Your majesty would do me a great favor in giving me license,
after I am reviewed, to return to die in Spain, where, in order to
come and serve as your majesty ordered me, I left wife and

children in much necessity, because I have no enterprises or revenues in this land; truly the salary lacks 3,000 ducats and more of covering what I am forced to spend each year, and so the little property I have is mortgaged and I am in debt; I hope not to have to pay it off posthumously. I beg your majesty to deign grant me a sufficient salary or the license that I ask, before I reach utter ruin, since your majesty always does favors to those who have served and now serve you, and I think I am one of the deserving ones, for the fidelity and care with which I have served for more than thirty years. I find myself old and poor and two thousand leagues from my home and relatives and friends, where I cannot assert myself except through favors your majesty should do me; and since I ask it in order better to serve, it does not seem insolent to ask. Your majesty granted me, when you ordered me to leave the office in Navarre, 200,000 maravedís for life, until such time as something else equivalent should be done for me; I have the habit of Santiago and have professed in the order, and if your majesty were so pleased, you could favor me there.

In the ships of the present fleet I am sending 100,000 pesos from the royal treasury, distributed among ships as your majesty has ordered; they will also carry the equivalent of 1,300,000 ducats belonging to individuals; another fleet will depart in September or October of this year, and another good shipment will be sent.

The mines and all the properties of value here in New Spain are diminishing greatly on account of the abolition of personal services and Indian porters, because without that it is impossible to work mines or supply them with provisions. What horses and other beasts of burden can transport is little, and let no one depend on the Spaniards and blacks and mestizos to make up for the Indians, because they can neither dig ore nor smelt. Let no one make your majesty believe that the mines can be worked without Indians; rather the moment they raise their hands from labor the mines will be finished, unless the Spaniards work them personally, and I doubt that they would do that though they die of hunger. And even if they wanted to do it, they are few compared to the many people occupied, some in digging the ore underneath the ground, others in washing and separating, others in grinding ore and smelting, others in making charcoal, which are all different trades. May your majesty order consideration of what can be decreed so that the mines will not be abandoned totally, because when the freeing of Indian slaves is finished, which will be soon, there will be great losses in the royal treasury and in individual fortunes, since there is no mine so rich that it can stand being worked by people on daily wages without having twice as much cost as profit.

If the tithes and the fifths continue in future years at the same value as in the past, your majesty will profit in the agreement you ordered made with doña María de Mendoza and with her son the Comendador Mayor in the office of smelter and marker of precious metals, since you gave them 3 million maravedis each year from the House of Trade in Seville, instead of 15,000–20,000 ducats yearly, and however great the diminution might be, there will be no loss.

The late royal factor Hernando de Salazar was found to owe 200,000 ducats or a little less, as I wrote your majesty; seeing that the property he left was not enough to pay 10,000, I thought best to take bondsmen for the deficit, though at long term, which was seven years, of which three have already elapsed. The regent wrote me that your majesty was being consulted as to the collection of the deficit and the acceptance of the bond, that I would be informed of your royal will, and that meanwhile I should collect the deficit. So I would, if there were any estate or any persons against whom to have recourse; but since there are not, I made the agreement and accepted the bond and understood that I had done your majesty a good service in insuring such a good sum of money when it had been lost. It would not be well to touch the small estate that the factor left, which is a house and some other property of little value, because, as it was a condition of the bond that it would be valid only if your majesty should accept it, if the estate of the factor were seized, the bondsmen would be freed of responsibility, and they would give 20,000 ducats to see that done, so that they could be out of it. May your majesty order that the bonds and the agreement be approved, because otherwise there is no way to collect 10,000 ducats. This is what appears to me to be in your royal service, and I will make no change until I receive further orders.

The regent in conjunction with the Council of the Indies has sent to order me to carry out everything decreed and ordered in the many laws and other new provisions, which is being done, with great resentment among the Spaniards, since it touches all of them in general. Among other things, the Council has declared that it is personal service to have Indians carry tributes belonging to the royal treasury to this city; since the greater part of this tribute is provisions, and carrying them has been forbidden, there is great need in this city, and we can find no means to remedy it. If the Indians do not supply it, no industry or effort of mine nor of the Spaniards will suffice to supply the city even with bread, water, firewood, and fodder for horses, which are our strength in this land. Counting the number of people who generally reside in the city, I find that between Spaniards and Indians, mestizos, blacks and strangers who come on business, there are usually two hundred thousand mouths to feed. Consider how they are to be maintained, when there are not a thousand farmers among them, and the city is surrounded by a lake, if provisions are not brought from outside. Carts and beasts of burden are not enough to do it; it is much that they provide firewood and charcoal, since the Indians were relieved from having to carry that because they considered it a great hardship. As to other provisions, wheat and maize, if it is not done with Indians, this city and the other Spanish cities here cannot be supplied, and let it be understood that at present, as the personal services continue to be removed, there is necessity as great as what people usually suffer in a siege. I do my best to see to the supply, but even so, if the law is to be kept, the Spanish commonwealth will be gravely risked. Let your majesty consider whether it is best to maintain Spaniards here; if so, there is no choice but to give them a land in which they can live and maintain themselves. If this is not to be conceded them, let your majesty order that they go back to Spain if they can, and not return again. Until I have a reply from your majesty I will temporize with the members of both commonwealths as best I can; I beg your majesty to send me orders promptly as to your pleasure.

May our Lord guard the imperial person of your majesty and increase your realms and principalities. From Mexico City, 4th of May, 1553.

Your Sacred Catholic Caesarean Majesty's faithful servant who kisses your majesty's imperial feet,

Don Luis de Velasco

[1] Published in Spanish in *Cartas de Indias*, pp. 263-9.

31. The concerns of a judge

Licenciate Diego Delgadillo, judge of the Royal Audiencia of New Spain, in Mexico City, to Juan de la Torre, merchant, in Seville, 1529[1]

> ...I know you will be glad I do things for my relatives and friends...

The First Audiencia of New Spain, headed by Nuño de Guzmán as President, was dismissed in disgrace not long after its creation for various impolitic actions, but above all for dispensing patronage with too little regard for the rights of the conquerors. Ever since, the First Audiencia has had a consistently bad press with historians. The present personal letter from one of its members indeed demonstrates blatant awarding of office to relatives for profit, as well as the judge's large-scale economic ventures on his own behalf. But in truth, Audiencia members in later times acted quite similarly, though more under wraps and with greater limitations on them, as competing interests grew more numerous and more watchful. When viceroys came to rule in Mexico and Peru, Audiencias there lost some of their patronage (in areas such as Guatemala and Quito, however, the Audiencia under its president was still the governing body and retained full appointive power). Judges of later years tended to limit their visible participation in the economy to real estate and indirect investment; their favorite means of public penetration into society was the marriage of their children into locally prominent families. Even in the later period high court judges may have continued active business enterprise privately, as don Luis de Velasco (Letter 30) suspected.

Licenciate Delgadillo goes into some detail here about the entourage which judges as well as governors brought with them to the Indies. In doing so he illustrates the toll that disease sometimes took of new arrivals from Spain. And though he singlemindedly takes his judgeship as a business operation, throughout the letter he evinces a liveliness of mind as well as, in the second part, a tangible homesickness for Seville, his friends there, and even his mule, to whom he sends greetings. Delgadillo was no monster, but a complex human being whose ambitions and activities were like those of other government officials of his time. If his outspokenness seems a little unusual, his thoroughness in pursuing his ends was less so, and his manner of using the family tie not at all.

Sir:

From Santo Domingo I wrote to you at length what had happened on my journey until that time, and quite a few adventures there were. If I were to try to tell the details of everything up to today, I believe it would be impossible, because so many misfortunes have come upon me and my little following, that it is a piteous thing. But since God has been so good as to grant health to me and my brother at present, I give Him infinite thanks for everything, and especially for this outstanding favor. You must believe that God greatly blesses those to whom he gives health in this land, because many die the moment they take a fever, as has happened to many who came in this last fleet, and it is the greatest pity in the world to think about.

From Santo Domingo to this country we had the best weather in the world, better than we had had until then, but I never got up from my bed until I saw land. When we reached the port, on the morning of the 6th of November, we put my brother Berrio and Alcalde Lope de Samaniego ashore, and they went on foot for five leagues, as far as the city of Veracruz, where people were astonished to see them appear on a hill overlooking a river next to the city. When they realized they were people from Castile, whom they were not at all expecting to see then, there was great pleasure and rejoicing, and all the city came out. That night they returned to the ships to sleep, then the next day we disembarked and came into the city, to the great pleasure of his majesty's servants and to the sorrow of others who would not wish to see his name nor officers of justice in the land. We were there twenty days having our gear unloaded and awaiting a reply from our President Nuño de Guzmán, as his majesty had ordered us.

After four days we decided to go hunting for deer, which are plentiful in that area and are caught with greyhounds, like hares back in Spain. There are days when they catch four to six of them with two hounds, not that the deer are small, because they are larger than those back there, nor that they run less, but because there are ten or twenty leagues of plain as flat as a floorboard, and in some places forty to eighty leagues, with grass as high as your knee or higher. And, as I say, while I was going on this hunt half a league from the city, a deer sprang out and, eager as I have always been known to be to distinguish myself and my hounds, and because it appeared near at hand, I ran after the deer until it was tiring, when to avoid trampling the hound my dappled horse fell; I caught a leg underneath and almost broke it. To this day I have a bruised thigh, and I broke a bone in my left arm; I was like dead and thought I was already in the other world, much worse than that time with my wife, God rest her. And so they brought me back and took all the measures that could have been taken in Seville, for there was good provision for everything. They purged me, and I was very ill, but it pleased our Lord God and his blessed mother to give me health. Then when I got better, my companions in office decided that we should come here to Mexico City to join the President at an appointed place. The day that we left we went five leagues, and that night all three of my companions fell ill; Licentiate Matienzo and Maldonado could go no farther except in litters on the shoulders of Indians. And so we set forth and continued on our way, but they were so ill that we decided to leave them along the way, and Licentiate Parada and I went ahead so that the President would not be waiting for us. When we reached the place where we were to wait, we were there for several days awaiting the President, who was in Texcoco, eight leagues from this city; then the day after my companions arrived, half dead, we decided that we would all four set out for this city. That night Licentiate Parada, who had been very well and strong, fell ill. And so the next day we entered Mexico City to a great reception they prepared for us, and triumphal arches saying *Benedictus qui venit in nomine domini*, but all three of my companions were in litters on the point of death, and even I, the only one on horseback, had my arm in a sling, a picture of grief. Within a week Licentiate Maldonado and Licentiate Parada died, without being heard or seen, and Matienzo and I were left with the work of all, which is surely insupportable.

Besides these misfortunes, my brother Berrio fell ill half way here, and I thought he would die on me, he was so weak, and I no longer expected anything of him. I sent him to Mexico City buried in a litter, as if I had given him up for lost, with Luis de Berrio, my cousin, who came out forty leagues from the city to meet me, and in another litter I sent Velasquito, who died as soon as he reached Mexico City. And in another litter I sent Francisquito, who is emaciated and unhealthy to this day. And in another litter I sent Baltasar de Gallegos, brother of Licentiate Gallegos, who was dying on me along the way; I had found him in Veracruz and brought him with me. My greetings to his brother the licentiate, and tell him Baltasar de Gallegos is well now and has gone, as I strongly urged him to do, to Yucatán with Francisco de Montejo, who is governor there. I brought Santisteban along in a hammock, since he had fallen ill on me in Veracruz, and on arrival here he died. Lope and Rojas got sick on me too, and after I had treated them and spent more than you can believe, they abandoned me. The only ones I have left are my Francisco and Juan the Red, who is the best and most loyal servant I have ever seen, though he too cost me plenty of money to bring here, for passage and for illnesses. Each blood-letting cost me a gold peso, and a purge ten, and so on.

But all this, and the 280-odd thousand maravedís I paid for freight and loans, is no more to me than a penny, as long as I have my health, because with health you can achieve every-thing, and all the more so in this country. I have bought one of two slaves that Francisco de Alcázar sent here, at a cost of 165 gold pesos; I could have brought two slaves from back there if I had known they were worth such a price here. And I could have brought my mule along and not had to buy another that I paid 150 pesos for, which is a man's fortune back in Spain. But to remedy all this I have sent four hundred slaves to mine gold, and pleasing God I believe there will be a very good return, and it will lead somewhere, because you know I want it all to ar-range marriages for my daughter and your sister. And you may believe that since I have exposed myself so to fortune and strange lands, I will eat mud or do whatever I have to to attain my purpose. I also want you to know that this is the best land warmed by the sun. There is nothing wrong with it but being so far from the Guadalquivir and San Martín and San Andrés, though there is no lack of saints here either, even if they are not to be honored, nor do I intend to observe their feast days nor to fast in their vigils.

Since I know you will be glad to see that I have become a farmer, I will tell you that I have bought sixty cows expected to calve, which is a great property for a man here, and the cows cost 105 pesos a head; from that you can see whether I am a man of deeds or not. I think that God will aid me so that I will profit soon. Pray to God for it, because it will all be for your service.

My brother Berrio has been given the office of alcalde mayor and captain of the town and province of Oaxaca, which is a very good thing and very profitable and honorific, and I believe that with his diligence and the aid of God we will profit greatly there. He kisses your hands a thousand times and will write you. You can read his letter, and listen to Alonso de Herrera, who will give you a very long account of this and of anything else you should want to know about me. Don Juan Enríquez, brother of don Alonso Enríquez, has been given the office of captain and alcalde mayor of the town of Villarreal and the province of Chiapas, which is a kingdom in itself. Tell milord don Alonso about it, if he is there, and tell him that being as I am Sevillian and his servant and friend, I have done and will do all I can in his service and that of milord don Juan, to favor the increase of his life and honor. They have made my cousin Luis de Berrio captain and alcalde in the province of the Zapotecas, which is a very good thing. As I say, every one of these is a kingdom, and in this one and in my brother's there are great mines of gold and silver. Alderman Barrios is to inspect the province of Oaxaca where Berrio is going, which is a commission of great responsibility and profit. He is to be treated the same as my brother Berrio, because he deserves everything, and I consider him in the same light as a brother. I kiss the hands of his grace Licentiate Infante, and tell him that all three of his brothers who are here are well, and I will do what I can for them, as for my brother Berrio.

I have given you such a long account of these things because I promised you to and I know you will be glad that I do things for my relatives and friends, and also because I am like lovers who don't want to stop writing, and because I know my letters will not give you displeasure. And so that you will think the more of it, I want you to know that every double sheet of paper costs a real. You already know that Almerío borrowed some money from Luis Hernández de Alfaro, with me as his guarantor, and on the sea he was so generous and helpful that my own brother wouldn't have done as much, so we were too careless of him in Santo Domingo. I did for him all I would for a brother; he was cleared of the death of his wife, and he was left much in my debt. And then God ordained that an illness came on him which immediately took away his speech, and the next day he died without confession, the most pitiful death that ever was seen. I took his goods for what he owed for freight and the loans of which I was the guarantor, and I had them auctioned off, which paid the debts, and I believe there will be

some money left over. But since this is written before the
verification of the accounts, I will not affirm that anything will
be left. He had in his chests here a skirt of black damask, and
another of black woolen, and a mantle of serge with silk, which
I believe belonged to the lady Mencía de Aguilar. Find out from
her, and give her this letter I am writing. And if these skirts are
hers, bring proof of it before a deputy there, or before the
judges of the House of Trade, and send a power of attorney
here to my brother Berrio, or to Alderman Cristóbal de Barrios
or Andrés de Barrios his brother, so that it can be collected
from me and sent back, which I will do very gladly. I am writing
to her to do the same. See to it there that it is done. Or the
power could be made out to Rodrigo de Zamora, merchant and
citizen of this city; when you see him express my regards and
ask him to tell me if there is any way I can serve him, since he
knows that I will do it with all good will.

I kiss the hands of his grace the precentor of the cathedral. I
am writing him a letter, not as long as I would wish, because I
lack the time, and also in order not to fatigue his grace. Always
show him my letters, because he will write to Granada to my
mother, since they always write back and forth, and inform him
of all you know that is done here, because I consider him my
patron, and he takes the place of a father for me. Nor am I
writing at length to Prebendary Alonso Alvarez; show him this
letter. Let all that he should order be done, and tell him I would
like to be part of his household, if I could, and that he can find
out from Alonso de Herrera about all the things of here. I kiss
milady Isabel Ramírez' hands a thousand times and am writing
her a letter now. Give it to her, and ask her to read it and
answer me. I will also send her something from here, if I can, so
that when she sees it she will remember me; if I can send
anything, Alonso de Herrera will take it. And tell her that if she
stays in my lodging I relinquish it to her, because it comes to
her by inheritance and belongs to her by many just titles.

In the letter I wrote to you from Santo Domingo I asked you
to send me some books of Erasmus. Send them to me in the
first ship for here, and I will pay for everything. I don't want to

send greetings to milady Juana Benítez, because I know she won't receive them. And in order not to fall into shame I leave it aside, to give you news of her husband and spouse, who is well and quite a gentleman and rich; things have gone well for him since we came to this country. I wish him wealth because it will all be for her service. I believe he is writing with these ships.

Give Beatriz Hernández my greetings, even though she should not wish to receive them, and also milady Constanza Hernández, and Espinosa; I know they will be glad to have them, and to such people give as many greetings as they want to hear, and put it down to my account. Give my greetings to Canon Ojeda and kiss his hands; I gave his letter to Juan Ramos, who is very well. At present he doesn't want to go home, because of the signs that he is in the best country there is in the world. He's not in this city, but in the city of Veracruz, the port where blood-letting is so profitable, since they charge a peso for each time, and the people who come there fall over like birds in the daytime. I do beg you to tell me if there is any way I can serve you here; you well know I will do it most willingly.

To our friend the wife of Damián, who lives in the little square of Luis de Saavedra, you must give my greetings, and tell her her husband is very well and a gentleman, and is suing Pedro de Alvarado for 4,000 pesos he owes him. And I believe his suit is just.

I have such desire to see you that I don't want to stop writing, and I go searching around the suburbs toward the lake and running over old memoranda to have something to say, and you must pay me in the same coin.

I kiss the hands of milady doña Violante and Hernando de Baeza and milady Juana de Trejo. I also say hello to my mule, if she is there, and I will never lose my sorrow for not having brought her with me. When we arrived I bought one of the ones that came with us, and it cost me 160 pesos, though mine is worth sixty times more. God knows how glad I would be if she were here; send her to me though it should cost 100 ducats, and if there are few mules being sent maybe the freight will cost less.

Milady María de los Angeles is very well and very beautiful and rich, for women who come here have all that, and property, and much else besides. She sends you a thousand greetings, being here as I write this paragraph. She wants to marry, and will marry very well. So if you are to send any merchandise, let it be women, which is the best business now in this country, and don't worry about her.

Assure the merchants at the cathedral steps that all the women are still alive, except doña Francisca, Alvarado's wife, who died, they say of thirst, because since Alvarado didn't stop over at La Gomera, they ran out of water, and she drank orange-flower water; they say it affected her liver, and she died on reaching the city of Veracruz here in New Spain.

I won't prolong this, because I am tired of writing so much. In the ship of Juan Alvarez, your friend, which is ready to leave after this present one, I will write again, and send something, if there is anything to send. For the rest, my brother Berrio is writing you at length, and I refer you to his letter, because he speaks of matters outside my profession and which I do not understand, so I don't want to meddle in them. I will take anything that is done for him as a favor to me, and anything that I can do to benefit you here I will gladly do.

May our Lord make you as great a lord as you might wish. From this great City of Mexico of New Spain, today, Palm Sunday, the 21st of March, 1529.

At your service,

Licentiate Delgadillo

[1] Published in Spanish, with comment, in Otte, 'La Nueva España en 1529,' pp. 95-111.

32. The bishop and the governor

Fray Francisco de Toral, bishop of Yucatán, to
the king, 1567[1]

> ... Your majesty saw fit to place me here in this
> land as investigator and look-out (for that is the
> function of the bishop) ...

The obligatory rivals of colonial Spanish America were the
governor and the bishop (or viceroy and archbishop, or in a
lesser Spanish city the corregidor and whoever the locality's
senior ecclesiastic might be). As fray Francisco de Toral inti-
mates, the crown, which appointed the bishops, expected them
to observe and report on the activities of government officials.
Often a newly arriving prelate carried the mission of formally
reviewing the governor's management of affairs; bishops and
archbishops also served as interim governors and viceroys on
occasion. All this, aside from long having been the practice, was
based on the fact that bishops were highly placed members of a
hierarchy as much within the crown's appointive domain as was
the secular government, but quite separate from it. Spanish
settlers perceived the situation in the same way. Whenever there
was a conflict among them, if one party got the governor's ear,
the other would run to the bishop. Disaffected government
officials sought alliance with the bishop; dissident ecclesiastical
groups (here the Franciscans) with the governor. The constant
jockeying between ecclesiastical and secular courts over jurisdic-
tional matters often led to governor–bishop confrontations.
Everything tended to play the two off against each other as
institutional opposite poles, from which beginning they not
infrequently became cordial enemies as well. Inexperienced
practitioners of Spanish American history often ascribe conflict
of this kind to the irascibility of the individuals, but it was so
standard that governors thought nothing of being excommunicated and excoriated from the pulpit.

For all these reasons, criticism of governors takes up much
space in the correspondence of bishops with the crown. The

present letter is an unusually pure example, launching after the briefest courtesy formulas into a detailed enumeration of the governor's faults. Though this particular battle seems a bit more entrenched than usual, the complaints registered are among the commonplaces of the literature.

Sacred Catholic Majesty:

I have no attorney or solicitor in your majesty's royal court, because I know your majesty's most Christian disposition, and also because I have nothing to solicit or ask for myself; and thus I say in this letter what I have written in many others, that your majesty's royal conscience is very burdened and aggrieved by don Luis de Céspedes, the governor, so much so that I cannot exaggerate, nor express enough in persuading your majesty to have pity on yourself and us, and take from this land a man so beyond all reason.

And in summary, I say that he has this whole land at the point of death by spreading discord among your majesty's vassals, telling different ones things that have not happened; his intention in this is that they should not be united in love and charity, so that they will not overthrow him. Particularly he has shown this by working to have the cathedral chapter against me, as it has been since he came, and the reason is what I have said. And he has done the same thing with the friars, telling them I want to destroy them, though I work to serve them as much as I possibly can, and he does it all to gain advantage with all of them, to have them on his side, knowing that I will be writing to your majesty the truth, and to obscure and remove my credibility in your majesty's eyes, and so that he will be believed, since they are all united, sending reports and gossip. Since the whole field is his, he does and informs as he pleases.

He has found ways, because I denounced the things the friars did against the natives, to make them bear me great hate for it, and because I wrote to your majesty the facts of the case, and also the case of the Spaniards, whom I asked for tithes to support the ministers of the church. For as I indicated to your majesty, they are dying of hunger, and the divine office is not held in the mother church, because there is no one to say it. And though I brought your majesty's order of execution and presented it, the governor would not obey it, but convinced the citizens to appeal; and even though that was against all justice and law and in disrespect of your majesty, he got away with it. Since the Spaniards receive these and other similar favors from him, they endorse him, and say and write what he wishes, and the friars do the same, and they even make the natives write things they do not understand. They give them letters already written and make them sign them, and the poor people don't understand them, as natives who have signed without understanding have come to tell me, and I believe the chiefs will be writing to your majesty about it.

The bad personal example that don Luis gives cannot be written down; it will appear when there is a review. One must greatly regret and lament that the person who is in your majesty's place should scandalize simple people with his bad example; he has taught the people here to have dancing parties and masquerades, and lewdness in them; he doesn't go to mass except Sundays and holy days, and even then he often comes late; he goes at night and at suspicious times to lewd houses, and favors the dissolute, and so I cannot do justice in punishing concubinage or other public sins.

He has accustomed the Spaniards to lose their reverence for the prelate and the church, to the point of saying that laymen shall not swear before an ecclesiastical judge without his license, and that the prelate cannot compel them to; and thus many have shown contempt. And to avoid proceeding against him, I let this pass as well as other most important matters, considering that he carries your majesty's staff and is in your place. Your majesty should remedy it quickly.

He will not hear or cooperate with anything that is against what he does. Though one shows him laws, conciliar decrees and even orders of your majesty, he does as he will against all law, without respecting prelate or ecclesiastic, saying he is above all; and thus he has proceeded against ecclesiastics and taken information against them, and this without bringing charges, but to avenge himself for their having said something against what he wanted. Everything he does is with great anger and fury, not with zeal for justice.

He has done great injuries to many Spaniards and to the natives, oppressing them with personal services to content the Spaniards. It is a great weight on the conscience to see the hapless natives so vexed; I have seen a daughter taken from her mother to serve blacks and mestizos, and even a wife from her husband, and other hardships with the tributes, so that the natives are at the point of despair.

Since your majesty saw fit to place me here in this land as investigator and look-out (for that is the function of the bishop), I advise your majesty what happens, so that you will send the remedy, which should be the proper person, and not letters or royal orders, and let it be soon, for Christianity is being lost, and the temporal order too.

If your majesty thought it best and deigned to entrust the government of this land to Adelantado Pero Menéndez, I believe he could remedy some of the aberrations with his good Christianity and his substance. Not only for spiritual things, but also for the relief of Florida it appears to me that it would be well if it were all under one government, because this land here could supply Florida with provisions and would be guarded and safe from enemies, knowing that it was the Adelantado's responsibility, and thus the citizens would feel secure and the benefit would be general. And let it not be argued that it is too far, because this land has always been governed from even farther away, from Mexico City and from Guatemala, and the soldiers of Florida could rest assured that they would be provided with the necessary from this land until they can grow food there.

Evangelical ministers are needed here to teach the natives the law of God, for there is no one to instruct them. There are about fourteen friars for 150 leagues of inhabited land, and of these there are only three who can preach, and two other beginners; there is need for fifty friars, and some should be well read, for it is a great shame that there are only two who know how to preach to the Spaniards; and it would be well if some persons of letters and religion came to head the order.

Priests are also needed, persons for benefices, of letters and conscience; yet the tithes are small, and if your majesty does not favor them as you always have with new churches, a church cannot be established in this land. By the love of our Lord, may your majesty provide and remedy it.

I do little good in this country, since I do not know the language, and I am in the worst of health; may it suit your majesty to transfer me to some place where I could be of use. Here I am hated by the Spaniards and the friars; your majesty will know why from whoever comes here to carry out the review. For twenty-five years I have been serving your majesty in the Indies, and have always been loved by all, except since don Luis came. Our Lord be praised for everything. If your majesty delays in sending help, I will come myself to supplicate, even if I have to come as a beggar, for I lack the money to come as a bishop.

May our Lord illumine your majesty and guard you for us with increase of realms and principalities, for the extension of the patrimony of Jesus Christ and of your royal crown. From Mérida in Yucatán, 20th of April, 1567.

Your royal majesty's unworthy chaplain,

    Frater Franciscus

    episcopus yucatanensis

[1] Published in Spanish in *Cartas de Indias*, pp. 242-5.

33. A bishop's affairs

Fray Juan de Zumárraga, first bishop of Mexico City, to his nephew Francisco de Urquiaga, in Durango, Biscay, 1548[1]

> ...My concern is to carry out my old desire for that hostelry...

Bishops shared with all Spanish settlers the attribute of coming from a certain region in Spain. Like governors, they surrounded themselves with a retinue of trusted people, often their compatriots or relatives, to whom they gave posts of special responsibility and whom they helped in various ways. Our present example is all the more indicative of the trend because Bishop Zumárraga had the reputation of not favoring relatives, which he doubtless did not, unduly, but only within the universally accepted framework of preferring relatives when they were qualified.

An interesting case seen in the letter is that of Sancho García. Zumárraga, at the instance of his nephew (always the nephew) in his home town of Durango, brought García to Mexico, and it was through his favor, he implies, that García became wealthy. With the wealth he returned to Durango and married a relative of Zumárraga's. Now he has become uppity, and the crusty bishop resents it. Zumárraga also mentions a relative now in Mexico, Martín de Urquiaga, apparently a younger brother of the Francisco to whom the letter is addressed, and therefore also the bishop's nephew. Martín is a recently ordained priest. Zumárraga has not given him any great plum in the curacy of the remote mining camp of Sultepec; on the other hand, not every beginning priest already has a chaplaincy in addition to a curacy. Zumárraga is watching Martín, and would be prepared to favor him further, but only, apparently, if he fulfills his promise: 'we will see what can be done.' A grand-nephew, son of the recipient of the letter, was also on his way to Mexico, but died in a shipwreck – something so much in the ordinary run of events that it fails to get prominent mention, and a sentence later when the bishop speaks of consolation, he is no longer thinking of the death of Francisco's son, but of the bad marriage of their relative to Sancho García.

The closest thing to Zumárraga's heart, as his career reaches its end, is an endowment in Durango, a sort of symbolic coming home and perpetuation of his name, much like an entail for non-ecclesiastics. It is a worthy charity, but there would be other charities as worthy as a hostelry in one's home town devoted to receiving weary traveling friars such as one once was oneself. Here, as in the whole letter, Zumárraga shows the depth of his regional roots.

Beloved nephew:

Our Lord be with you. Urtuño de Avendaño, who is always
your advocate and intercessor, wrote me from there in Durango
always to remember you and your necessity. You may believe
that I have not forgotten you and that I have more than enough
will to help achieve your contentment; I will not fail to aid you
in whatever way I can. At present my concern is to carry out
my old desire for that hostelry, and when that is done I will not
lack will, as I say. I do implore and charge you to help Urtuño
de Avendaño in arranging the income for the hostelry. And
since he considers you his friend, you consider him so in return,
because he is faithful and of good will. I owe him much and
view him as a brother.

As the provincial superior father fray Francisco del Castillo
writes me, it appears that Sancho García wants to be the patron.
They say he is going to start a lawsuit, maintaining that I made
him a donation of the patronship so that he would stay with the
wife he has. He didn't deserve her for all the money he took
back from here; let him spend that and more, before he should
have the patronship, even though the document were valid, and
all the more so because it is not, but false, just the way that
Juan Ochoa de Egurbide and he saw fit to arrange it, as will be
seen. And as St Gregory says, he who is not grateful for benefits
received makes himself unworthy of those yet to come. You
know well and are a good witness of who Sancho García was
and what his worth and potential were before he came here,
against my will and through your solicitation and industry –
because I knew him already. Now that he finds himself in the
house and position of your wife's father, they tell me he has
become a Lucifer, and it would be a burden on one's conscience
to give more wings to his arrogance. You know how he has
treated milady your mother-in-law; now he wants to start a suit
against me, and you must have found out by now how he
thanks you for what you did for him. Time will show what will
happen.

I was greatly sorrowed by the death of your son, coming as
he was highly recommended and well outfitted in Jáuregui's

ship, which ran aground; many who were in it died and a great sum of property was lost. We may believe that his soul was saved, and he is better off with God than in Biscay or Mexico City. God knows what He does, and we do not know what is best. I beg your wife to do what she can to console Mariñíguez, and have pity on her for having been given such a poor husband. My greetings to your sisters.

Martín de Urquiaga is able by now to help you marry off your daughters, because, aside from a chaplaincy that pays him 100 ducats, he earns more than 200 at the mines of Sultepec, where he is now. Since starting to say mass he shows much promise. We will see what can be done.

And tell the holy ladies on my behalf that I don't know why they are demanding the money from Urtuño de Avendaño. It was never my intention to have the money given them directly, but to have the income devoted to them so that they could furnish necessities to friars who come as guests. Let them have patience, since in the past they have lived without income, and in the future they will have a certain amount of help, even if they do have to provide for the friars. And since I have done my part, let those there make a good effort to arrange the income promptly, so that I can see this plan carried out before my end. And I charge you to aid Urtuño and the father provincial superior, in whom I place all my confidence. In this you will put me much in your debt.

May our Lord make you fortunate and give you his grace, that we may see each other in paradise. From Mexico City, 26th of April, 1548.

Your fellow in prayer,

Fray Juan, Bishop of Mexico City

[1] Archivo General de Indias, Justicia 1011, no. 2, ramo 2, pieza primera.

34. The Franciscans and the Indians

Fray Pedro de Gante, in Mexico City, to the emperor, 1532[1]

> ... There are very good scribes and preachers or speakers of great fervor, and singers who could sing in your majesty's chapel choir ...

Either secular priests or friars could man the ecclesiastical component of the encomienda, taking the chief encomienda town as a headquarters and from there instructing the Indians of the region in Christianity. In the Mexico of the first generation, friars of the mendicant orders were most associated with this function, and of these the Franciscans were preeminent. Arriving in the country first, they evolved methods which the other orders followed by and large, building great monastery churches and cloisters which became the primary public places of the Indian towns and even, since they often contained three or four friars and served a corresponding number of encomienda districts, tended to free the order from too great a local dependence on any individual encomendero. The rural monasteries were satellites of the even larger ones in the cities, above all Mexico City.

In the larger centers there took place the most famous episode in early Spanish American cultural history: a concerted Franciscan effort first to learn Nahuatl, and then using this tool to teach a selected number of Indians the refinements of European culture, including writing, grammatical and rhetorical principles, all the arts and crafts, sometimes even Latin. It is quite hard to get a proper perspective on the success of the program. The achievements are formidable. The monasteries, if they as works of art are considered part of the effort, dominate the Mexican countryside to this day. Literacy in Nahuatl was another result with lasting significance; the first generation of notaries whom the friars taught taught others in turn, so that a self-sustaining Nahuatl literacy and record-keeping continued to flourish in the Indian towns until the end of the colonial period.

But if such were the results, one must wonder if the well-developed Mesoamerican traditions of glyphic-pictorial writing and prolific monumental building were not the most important causative factors. In discussing the general progress of acculturation in central Mexico, one must remember how few people in how few places were involved in such programs, and that the effort slacked off to almost nothing in a generation or two. General acculturation was carried out by the interaction of the Indians with the total Spanish civil population. Spanish artisans in the long run doubtless had much more to do with the spread of European crafts than did the friars, and they often played an essential role in the building of monasteries as well. The differential in speed of cultural change between Mexico and Peru had ultimately to do with things as basic as their respective geographies, the hospitable Mexican plateau allowing the Spaniards to concentrate in the midst of the Indians, whereas with Peru's more extreme topography the capital and the bulk of the Spaniards were on the coast, far removed from the mass of the Indian population.

At any rate, the monasteries, the functioning Indian record-keeping and history-writing, and much else, were unique to Mesoamerica. Let us let Flemish fray Pedro de Gante give the Franciscan view of the program and its success, in the following famous letter.

Sacred Catholic Caesarean Majesty:

I greatly wish that your majesty could be informed of what I am going to say by a letter of my superior, without my having to be so bold as to say it myself and to beg your majesty to condescend to our petition, for though it is pious I am not worthy to ask it. Nevertheless, your majesty, by his license and order I am compelled to do so, and even reprehended for not having told and reported on it before, so that your majesty would have known of it earlier, since it is something so much in the service of God and your majesty. It seemed fitting to my superior that I should be the one to write this, as the person who has most performed the function of Martha in this connection, and therefore I dare speak to your majesty, believing also that your majesty, removed from personal considerations, will look not at the letter or the insufficiency of him who sends it, but at the substance of what is begged of your majesty and with humility is asked in alms.

Your majesty, I am a lay brother, companion of fray Juan de Tecto, who was father guardian in Ghent when your majesty sent him, along with another friar and myself, to these shores nine years ago, as your majesty may already be aware. Fray Juan de Tecto and the other friar went with the Marqués del Valle don Hernando Cortés to the cape of Honduras, and died on the way back, from the storms and hardships of the journey. In the time since we entered this land, through the work of the Lord I have labored middlingly, as a useless servant, at the conversion and instruction of the natives. My task has been and is to teach them Christian doctrine generally, conveying it to them in their language, at first in Texcoco and Tlaxcala, and for the last six years in Mexico City and the surrounding towns, and other towns farther away, making tours and seeking to destroy the idols and idolatries.

Aside from this and other tasks of different kinds relating to conversion, which would be too long to tell, I have had and have charge of teaching boys of different ages to read, write, preach and sing; since I am not ordained, I have had more time and opportunity for all this. Because of that, and because there is a reasonable ability for these things in the people, fair progress has been made; without falsifying I can say that there are very good scribes, and preachers or speakers of great fervor, and singers who could sing in your majesty's chapel choir, so good that perhaps if it is not seen it will not be believed. To teach and indoctrinate these boys, a school or chapel has been made within the site or enclosures of our house, where continually every day five or six hundred boys are taught.

Next to our monastery we have built an infirmary for the sick among the natives, where besides those who are being taught in the house, others come for treatment, which is a great comfort for the poor and needy, and aid in their conversion, because they come to know the charity that is practiced among Christians, and are attracted to the faith and to liking us well and conversing with us.

For all these things I always try to seek what alms I can, but they are hard to obtain, since most of the natives are poor. The Spaniards, though they perform charities, have other necessities of their own which they are more obliged to meet. If your majesty would order that this work be entirely yours, you could grant us alms that would relieve us of hardship and satisfy all the necessities of your new subjects and vassals; it would be a great augmentation of our holy faith and very much in the service of God our Lord and in earnest of your majesty's salvation. If your majesty would grant three or four thousand bushels of maize each year, a thousand five hundred for the school and the rest for the infirmary and the patients, that or whatever your majesty should grant would be just and very good and a great example so that the natives will believe that your majesty loves them and considers them your children; and indeed they are recognizing it more every day by the rectitude which they see that now, more than in other times, is being maintained in matters of justice, and they are more favored on your majesty's part and by your command, for these people know how to distinguish the good from the bad, and thus they would wish to be subjects of your majesty alone rather than being distributed among the Spaniards.

Our God preserve your Sacred Catholic Caesarean Majesty in your imperial estate and increase your life and illumine you always to do His holy will. Amen. From Mexico City here in New Spain, the eve of All Saints, year of our Lord 1532.

Chaplain and least vassal of your majesty,

Fray Pedro de Gant

In the infirmary that I mentioned there are always many patients, at times three or four hundred.

[1] Published in Spanish in *Cartas de Indias*, pp. 51-3.

35. The Dominican attack

Fray Andrés de Moguer, in Mexico City, to the
Council of the Indies, 1554[1]

> ... Consider what sort of indoctrination they can
> give them! ...

In Spanish American secular society there were conflicts
between the first conquerors with their large encomiendas, and
later arrivals attempting to get some share for themselves. This
was just as true in the ecclesiastical world, and first-comers had
just as great an initial advantage. Myths formed around the
Twelve, the first party of Franciscans to arrive in Mexico, and
the order quickly established itself in the largest towns of the
central part of the country. The later-coming Dominicans and
Augustinians were forced into relatively peripheral or secondary
situations. They resented it, protested, and carried on various
kinds of skirmishes until finally, again as in the secular world,
some accommodations were made, though overall Franciscan
predominance was retained.

The Dominicans were the greatest scourge of the Franciscans,
not only because they were second in seniority and strength,
but because of the propensities of the two orders. The Franciscans were pragmatic builders, converters and baptizers; the
Dominicans, the Order of Preachers, were intellectuals inclined
to higher education, thorough preparation, and doctrinaire positions. Thus power politics and conviction coincided in their
constant complaint that Franciscan ambition and compromise
were leading to the dilution of Christianity through haste; time
should be taken to instruct both ecclesiastics and Indians before
general application of the sacraments, the ratio of ecclesiastic
personnel to Indians should be reduced, etc. All of this both
suited the Dominicans' taste, and would hamstring their rivals
until they could catch up with them. Very basic human attributes often surface in these debates. Note the portrait of fray
Pedro de Gante, so different from his elaborate humility in
Letter 34. A childlike Franciscan pride in numbers, and a

responding childlike Dominican jealousy, are prime factors in the continuing debates. Of course these things varied from region to region; in Peru it was the Dominicans who were first and strongest. The characteristics of the orders, however, are relatively universal, and thus the whole Dominican-dominated body in Peru was more doctrinaire, less energetic in building and teaching.

The 'one language' that the Franciscans are criticized for using is of course Nahuatl, and although it is true that there were many languages in New Spain, Nahuatl's widespread use in preconquest times as a lingua franca gives the Franciscan practice much justification.

Very powerful lords:

To the glory of our God and Lord and His honor and with royal favor, we have here in New Spain nineteen houses of friars in Indian towns, with four to six friars in each one, and even in the smallest one two friars, not counting three other houses that we have in the Spanish towns, which are here in Mexico City, in Puebla and in Oaxaca; in these three houses the friars are numerous and there is higher instruction in the necessary sciences, and we teach the faith and good customs that are necessary to instruct and indoctrinate the natives. In these houses we also treat the friars who fall ill in the Indian towns, and punish those who are delinquent because, with our weaknesses, everything is necessary.

Following the counsel of the oldest and wisest, that those who have taken the habit in this country should be taught before they teach, it has been necessary to occupy ourselves in that effort for some time, and during that time the very reverend Franciscan fathers, imitating the holy apostles, have taken and occupied three fourths of the country, though they do not have enough friars for it, because in towns where ten or twelve ministers are needed they content themselves with having one or two. In most places they are content to say a mass once a year; consider what sort of indoctrination they can give them! His lordship the archbishop, wishing as pastor to remedy the situation and give ministers to his flock, has given some towns to others, but the natives have not been willing to obey them or give them food, on the advice, it is said, of a fray Pedro de Gante, lay brother of the order of St Francis, and the archbishop in annoyance had four or five of them given a lashing in jail, but even then they will not obey him.

We wish you to know that existing, as indeed there exist, such high abilities in the order of Saint Augustine, and in ours of Saint Dominic, and desire to learn these languages, the friars of Saint Francis have occupied a land as large as the Mexican using only one language, where more than two hundred languages are necessary, and they prevent the entry of other friars; this is clear, because the Indians say they want no others than the fathers of Saint Francis, and will not feed those whom the archbishop sends. As it concerns the royal conscience, they should be ordered not to intrude in more than they can accomplish, since we all preach one God and one faith, and not to permit so many souls to go to perdition because they cannot give them sufficient instruction, and to obey his lordship the archbishop as prelate and pastor that he is of all, and for the ministers his lordship assigns to be received, since he was given their governance. And you should write to the provincial superior of Saint Francis who resides here in New Spain, giving him these orders. From Mexico City, 10th of December, 1554.

Your highness' servant and chaplain,
Fray Andrés de Moguer

[1] Published in Spanish in *Cartas de Indias*, pp. 123-4.

36. The Franciscan reply

Fray Toribio de Motolinia, in Tlaxcala, Mexico,
to the emperor, 1555[1]

> ... If Las Casas called the Spanish residents of
> New Spain tyrants, thieves, robbers, murderers and
> cruel assailants only a hundred times, it might
> pass ...

Letter 35 is the merest hint of the great campaign, carried on
above all by Dominican fray Bartolomé de las Casas in thousands of scalding pages, opposing not only the Franciscans, but
the encomienda, the conquest, even the very notion of a Spanish civil occupation of the Indies. Renewed again and again in
Spain, the debates swirled in one area after another of Spanish
America, always after the conquest was well past and a Spanish
presence fully established: in the Caribbean in the second de-
cade of the century; in Mexico in the middle decades; and in
Peru yet later. The attacking parties were, when not Dominicans, usually lawyers, late-comers, or people still in Spain; the
defenders were Franciscans, settlers, sometimes viceroys and
governors. Las Casas himself was in Spain far more than in the
Indies. In view of this and also considering that former Licentiate Las Casas' favorite genres were the treatise and the brief,
not the letter, we include as representative of this kind of
invective a well-known letter by Franciscan fray Toribio de
Motolinia, defending views much like those of the ordinary
settlers to whom most of this volume is dedicated. Fray Toribio, one of the Franciscan Twelve, changed his earlier name of
Benavente to a Nahuatl form meaning 'one who is poor or
afflicted,' since the Indians are supposed to have uttered the
word repeatedly on seeing the Franciscans in their simple hab-
its. Motolinia became one of the principal powers among the
Mexican Franciscans, taking his turn in all the more important
posts and becoming (as he does not fail to make clear) the best
of the first generation of Franciscan writers on Nahua culture
and history.

The letter is the product of a thoroughly exasperated man. Having written page on page and brought the letter to a conclusion, Motolinia got notice of yet further infuriating publications by Las Casas, and returned to write almost as much more. One understands the exasperation. The arguments were necessarily deflected ones. The basic Las Casas position, at times at least, was that Indian lives and civilization should be preserved intact at all costs, changed only by voluntary adherence to a well-understood Christianity. Actually, European diseases and techniques alone would have prevented such a result, but few understood this (Motolinia comes close), and in any case it did not make good propaganda. Las Casas found it necessary to blame everything on the evil actions of individuals, to put all emphasis on destruction rather than creation. The Franciscans were not oblivious to the destruction, but had also been creating mightily, as we have seen. Motolinia was at the peak of his career, ready to bask a bit in the extraordinary achievements of himself and his order, and here was someone spoiling it all with unbounded criticism and no recognition.

The great basic Franciscan and settler reply is well stated here: They know nothing, they have done nothing. We have been here, we have done much and learned a great deal; we have built and taught and studied. We are concerned with real problems, from the daily instruction of our flock, through moderation of tributes, to the evangelization of Florida; they care more about arguments than about Indians. The scathing tale of how Las Casas, on doctrinal grounds, would not baptize an extremely desirous and fervent Indian of Tlaxcala gives us the quintessence of the Franciscan perception of the Dominican position. This part of the argument is impressive, if inevitably inconclusive. Motolinia also contests Las Casas' facts, points out that other humans than the settlers have been known to sin, and delights in the existence of a less doctrinaire, more Franciscan-like wing of the Dominicans in Mexico, represented by fray Domingo de Betanzos. Wandering a bit from his points at times, Motolinia is not as sharp a scholastic debater as some, but he does have an excellent grasp of the essentials of the controversy, as well as of other things.

There is quite a bit more in the letter than vitriol and clash of opinion. Much of what is said on depopulation and Spanish land use is Motolinia's special brand of penetrating common sense. We also have an example of his preaching style in the extended metaphor of the statue and the history of empire. The letter gives the appearance of being a whole year's correspondence, and it contains some staples of ecclesiastic writing not closely related to the controversy, such as petitions for aid for the churches and for more friars to be sent, as well as some 'governor's talk': an overconcern about defense and complaints about the high price and scarcity of food (note that many settlers' letters and even Letter 37 say the opposite).

As Motolinia concludes (for the second time), he presents a portrait, already strongly legendary despite the fact that he himself had taken part in much of the action, of Cortés as a God-sent bearer of Christianity. The Franciscans would long continue to elaborate this theme, deifying their old ally as a pointed way of expressing that the conquest with its accompanying phenomena took place by divine will, and that accommodation to it was the course of reason and morality.

Sacred Caesarean Catholic Majesty:

Grace and mercy and peace *a Deo patre nostro et Domino Jesu Christo.* Three things principally move me to write your majesty this letter, which I believe will be enough to remove some of the scruples of conscience that this Las Casas has proposed to your majesty and the members of your councils, all the more in the things he is now writing and having printed. First I must tell your majesty that when the Spaniards entered New Spain here, it had not been ruled for very long from Mexico City, nor by the Mexica, and the Mexica themselves had won and usurped dominion through war. The first and original inhabitants here in New Spain were a people called Chichimecs and Otomis, who lived as savages and had no houses, but huts and caves in which they dwelt. They neither sowed nor cultivated the earth, rather their food and sustenance were herbs and roots, and the fruits they found in the fields, and the game they took with their bows and arrows, eating it dried by the sun; nor did they have idols and sacrifices, beyond considering the sun to be God and invoking other creatures. After them came other Indians from a distant land, called Culhua; they brought maize and other seeds, and domesticated fowl; they started to build houses and cultivate the earth and clear the forests, and since they began to multiply and were people of more ability and capacity than the first inhabitants, little by little they became the rulers of this land, whose right name is Anavac or Anauac. After many years had gone by, there came the Indians called the Mexica, who took this name, or were given it, because of an idol and important god they carried with them called Mexitli, also named Tezcatlipoca, and through all this land this was the idol or demon most generally worshiped, before whom a great many men were sacrificed. Through wars these Mexica came to rule New Spain, but the principal dominion was first in the hands of the Culhua, in a town called Culhuacan, which is two leagues from Mexico City, and then later, also through wars, rulership came to rest with a lord and town called Azcapotzal-co, a league from Mexico City, as I wrote at greater length to the Count of Benavente in an account of the rites and antiquities of this country.

Your majesty, when the Marqués del Valle entered this land, God our Lord was very offended with it; people suffered the cruelest of deaths, and our adversary the demon was very pleased with the greatest idolatries and most cruel homicides there ever were, because the predecessor of Moctezuma, lord of Mexico, called Ahuitzotzin, offered to the idols in a single temple and in one sacrifice that lasted three or four days, 80,400 men, whom they brought along four streets, in four lines, until they reached the sacrificial block before the idols. And at the time when the Christians entered New Spain, more than ever before there was sacrificing and killing of men before the idols in all the towns and provinces. Every day and every hour they offered human blood to the demons, in all the towns and districts of all this country, aside from many other sacrifices and services to the demons that they performed, not only in the demons' temples, of which almost the whole country was full, but on all the roads and in all the houses; all the people were devoted to the service of the demons and the idols. Now these and many other abominations, sins, and offenses made publicly to God and neighbors have been prevented and removed, our holy Catholic faith implanted, the cross of Jesus Christ and the confession of his holy name raised everywhere, and God has brought about a great conversion of people, in which many souls have been saved and are being saved every day; and many churches and monasteries have been built, with more than fifty monasteries inhabited by Franciscan friars alone, not to speak of our monasteries in Guatemala and Yucatán, and this whole country is in peace and justice. If your majesty could only see how the church festivals are celebrated all over New Spain and with what devotion the rites of Holy Week are observed, and all the Sundays and holidays, you would give praise and thanks to God a thousand times. This Las Casas is wrong in what he says, writes, prints and urges. It will be necessary that I tell where his zeal and works lead and what they end in, and whether he aided the Indians or vexed them.

And I humbly implore your majesty, for the love of God: now the Lord has revealed the land of Florida to us, so near to here that from the river of Pánuco, part of this jurisdiction of Mexico, to the great rivers of Florida, where Captain Soto wandered for more than five years, there are no more than eighty leagues, which in our times, and especially in this land, is like eight leagues. The towns subject to your majesty go beyond that river of Pánuco, and there are also many towns between there and the river of Florida, so that the distance is even less. For the love of God, your majesty, take pity on those souls, have compassion and sorrow for the offenses against God being committed there, and prevent the idolatries and sacrifices being performed there to the demons; order, with the greatest speed and in the best way available to you as the anointed of God and captain of his holy church, that the holy gospel be preached to those Indian infidels. Not in the way ordered by Las Casas, who gained nothing more than 2,000 or 3,000 pesos in costs to your majesty for providing and outfitting a ship in which some Dominican fathers went to preach to the Indians of Florida with the instructions he gave them. The moment they touched land half of them were killed, right at the port, before reaching the town; the others went fleeing back to the ship and came here to tell how they had escaped. But your majesty need not spend much, nor send much from Spain, beyond your order, and then I trust in God that a great spiritual and temporal gain will ensue. Here in New Spain are all the means required, because there are experienced friars who, given orders, will obediently go and expose themselves to all risks to help in the salvation of those souls; also there are many Spaniards here, and horses and livestock. All the survivors of Soto's company who came here, and there are quite a few of them, wish to go back there because of the goodness of the country. And to have people leave here would be very good for this land because of the many idlers here whose trade is to think and do evil. And this is the second thing that I, poor person that I am, implore your majesty on God's behalf.

The third thing is to beg your majesty, for the love of God, to order the learned men of your councils and the universities to look and see if the conquerors, encomenderos and merchants here in New Spain are in the proper state to receive the sacrament of penitence and the other sacraments without issuing a public document before a notary and giving their sworn word. Las Casas affirms that without these and other legal acts they cannot be absolved, and he sets so many scruples before the confessors that all that is lacking is to send them to the inferno. It is necessary that the High Pontiff be consulted in this matter, for what will it help those of us who have baptized more than three hundred thousand souls each, and performed an equal number of marriages, and confessed another great multitude, if because of having confessed ten or twelve conquerors, they and we are to go to perdition? Las Casas says that everything the Spaniards have here is evil gain, though they should have acquired it through enterprise; there are many farmers and craftsmen here, and many others who make a living by their work and sweat. And so that what he says or prints may be better understood, may your majesty know that about five or six years ago I was ordered by your majesty and your Council of the Indies to collect certain confessionals that Las Casas left here in New Spain, handwritten, among the friars. I sought out all those to be found among the Franciscans and gave them to don Antonio de Mendoza, your viceroy, and he burned them, because they contained false and scandalous statements. Now, in the last ships to reach New Spain, there have arrived the same confessionals in print, which has caused a great outcry and scandal throughout the land, because many times he gives the conquerors, encomenderos and merchants the names of tyrants, robbers, violaters, ravishers and thieves. He says that always and every day they are oppressing the Indians; he also says that all the tributes from the Indians have been and are being taken evilly, unjustly and tyrannically. If that were so, a fine state your majesty's conscience would be in, since your majesty draws from half or more of the most important towns and provinces of New Spain, and the encomenderos and conquerors have only what your majesty orders them to be given. And as far as the Indians receiving moderate tribute quotas, and being well treated and looked after, through the goodness of God today they almost all are; and as to justice and religion being administered to them, that is what is being done. Even so, this Las Casas maintains what he has said, and more; his principal insult or insults are to your majesty, and he condemns the learned men of your councils, often calling them unjust and tyrannical. And he also insults and condemns all the men of the law that there are and have been in all New Spain, whether ecclesiastic or secular, and your majesty's Audiencias and their regents. Certainly the Marqués del Valle, and Bishop don Sebastián Ramírez, and don Antonio de Mendoza, and don Luis de Velasco, who governs now with the Audiencia judges, have ruled and governed both commonwealths, Spaniards and Indians, very well, and continue to. Surely, for the bit of canon law that Las Casas studied, he dares too much; his confusion appears great, his humility small. He thinks that all err and he alone is right, because he also makes this statement, which follows word for word: 'All the conquerors have been robbers and ravishers, the most qualified in evil and cruelty that there ever have been, as is manifest to the whole world.' All of the conquerors, he says, without making a single exception. Your majesty already knows the instructions and orders that those who go to new conquests carry and have carried, and how they work to observe them, and are of as good life and conscience as Las Casas, and have a more upright and holy zeal. I am amazed that your majesty and those of your councils have been able to bear for so long with a man so vexatious, unquiet, importunate, argumentative and litigious, in a friar's habit, so restless, so poorly bred, insulting, prejudicial and troublemaking. For fifteen years I have known Las Casas, since before he came to this country. He was going to Peru, and not being able to stay there, he was in Nicaragua, and was not calm there for long, and after that he was among the people of Oaxaca, where he felt as little repose as in the other places. After he came to Mexico City he was in the Dominican monastery, but he soon had enough there too and went back to wandering and going about with his tumult and unrest, always writing indictments of other people, seeking out the crimes and bad things that the Spaniards had committed through this whole land, to exaggerate and make worse the evils and sins that have occurred. In this he seemed to do the work of our adversary, though he thought himself more zealous and more just than the other Christians, including the friars; but he had hardly anything to do with religion here. Once he was talking to some friars and told them what he did was little, that he had not endured as much nor spilled his blood, and that the least of them was a greater servant of God, and watched over souls and virtue and religion more than he, by far. All of his affairs have been with some troublemakers who tell him things to write, agreeable with his impassioned animosity against the Spaniards, to show how much he loves the Indians, and that he tries to defend and favor them more than anyone else, though here he spent very little time at it, except loading them down and fatiguing them.

When Las Casas was still a simple friar, he came once to Tlaxcala, bringing behind him twenty-seven (or was it thirty-seven?) Indian porters, whom they call *tamemes* here. At that time some bishops and prelates were examining a bull of Pope Paul concerning marriage and baptism, and we were then forbidden to baptize adult Indians. One Indian had made a three- or four-day journey to be baptized, and had demanded baptism again and again; he was very well prepared, catechized and instructed. Then I and other friars greatly begged Las Casas to baptize that Indian, because he came from so far, and after a great deal of begging he made many conditions of preparation for the baptism, as though he knew more than anyone; for certainly the Indian was well prepared. When he finally said he would baptize him, he put on a surplice with its stole, and three or four of us friars went with him to the door of the church, where the Indian was waiting on his knees. Then I don't know what came over him, but he didn't want to baptize the Indian after all, and left us and went away. At that I said to Las Casas: 'How is this, father, all this zeal and love that you say you have for the Indians is exhausted in loading them down and going around writing about Spaniards, and vexing the Indians, since your grace loads down more Indians than thirty friars? And since you won't baptize or instruct an Indian, it would be well if you would pay those that you so load down and tire out.' At that time, as I said, he had either twenty-seven or thirty-seven Indian bearers, I can't remember the number exactly, and most of what those Indians carried was indictments and writings against Spaniards, and trifling knick-knacks. And when he was going back to Spain to become a bishop, he had 120 Indians loaded down, without paying them anything. And now he is trying to get the Council of the Indies to order that no Spaniard here could have Indians carry loads for him, even if they are well paid, as is done everywhere now. And all the Spaniards demand now is three or four Indians to carry their food and bedding, since they are no longer available along the roads.

After this, Las Casas always went about troublemaking and

representing the affairs of important personages; but all he negotiated in Spain was to return as bishop of Chiapas. Since he failed to carry out what he had promised here that he would work for, father fray Domingo de Betanzos, who knew him well, wrote him a long letter, which everyone knew about, in which he told him in so many words how all his life he had made trouble and noise, and what mischief and damage he had caused wherever he went, with his reports and his indiscreet zeal, and especially how he had been the cause of many scandals and deaths in the land of Peru. And being there in Spain now, he has not ceased to do the same, feigning to do it from zeal for the Indians. When someone writes him a letter from here, not always truthfully, he shows it to your majesty or your councilors, and on account of one individual thing that they write him, he solicits a general decree, and disturbs and destroys the government and the commonwealth here. This, then, is what comes of his zeal. When he came as a bishop and arrived in Chiapas, seat of his diocese, the citizens received him, as being sent by your majesty, with much love and all humility; they took him to his church under a canopy of honor, and lent him money to pay the debts he brought from Spain. Then within a very few days he excommunicated them, imposed fifteen or sixteen laws and conditions for confessions, and left them and went his way. Referring to this, Betanzos wrote him that the sheep had turned into goats and that he was such a good carter he had put the cart before the oxen. Then he went to the kingdom of Verapaz, of which he had said that it was a grand thing with infinite people. This land is near to Guatemala, and in going about inspecting and instructing there I have come very close to it, since it is only two days' journey away, and it is not a tenth of what they have said and represented there in Spain. There are single monasteries here in Mexico which instruct and serve ten times as many people as there are in the whole realm of Verapaz, and the bishop of Guatemala is a good witness to it. I saw the people, unimpressive and sparser than others. Afterwards, Las Casas returned to his troublemaking and came to Mexico to ask the viceroy's license to return to Spain; and though it was not given to him, he did not fail to go without it, leaving his flock and the souls entrusted to him without recourse, Spaniards as well as Indians.

There would be reason, if reason were enough for him, to make him return here immediately, so he would stay with his flock even two or three years; since he is more holy and wise than all the bishops there have ever been, and he says the Spaniards are incorrigible, he could work with the Indians and not leave everything ruined and abandoned. Four years ago some friars passed through Chiapas and saw how, on Las Casas' orders, they were refusing to absolve the Spaniards who requested confession, even when on the point of death, and there was no one to baptize the Indian children who requested it in the towns, though the friars whom I mentioned baptized many. Las Casas says in that confessional of his that the encomenderos are obliged to instruct the Indians entrusted to them, which is true, but in saying further on that they have never dreamed of doing it, he is wrong, because many Spaniards have instructed their Indians, in person or through their employees, the best they could, and many others, when there were not enough friars, have put secular priests in their towns; almost all of the encomenderos have obtained friars to take to their towns, where they can give instruction and administer the holy sacraments. There was a time when some Spaniards wanted neither priest nor friar near their districts, but now for a long while many Spaniards have sought friars, and their Indians have built monasteries and maintain them in their towns, and the encomenderos provide the friars with food, clothing, and ornaments. It is no wonder that Las Casas doesn't know about it, because he never sought to know the good, only the bad, and he never settled down here in New Spain, nor learned the Indians' language, nor deigned to apply himself to instruct them. His function was to write indictments, to condemn the sins that the Spaniards have committed everywhere; this is what he enlarges upon, and surely this alone will not carry him to heaven. What he writes thus is not all certain nor very well established, and if one looks and notes the sins and atrocious crimes that have occurred in the city of Seville alone, and which the officers of justice have punished in the last thirty years, one will find more crimes and evil deeds, and worse ones, than everything that has happened in all New Spain ever since it was conquered, which was thirty-three years ago. One of the things in this whole land that arouses the most compassion is the city of Chiapas and its province, which since Las Casas went there as bishop, has been destroyed in the temporal and the spiritual, he so inflamed everything. Please God that it not be said of him that he left his souls in the hands of the wolves and fled, *quia mercenarius est et non pastor, et non pertinet ad eum de ovibus.* When some bishop gives up his episcopate, leaving the church that he received as a spouse, where he has a great obligation and bond, greater than with a profession of lower estate, as seen in the great solemnity with which it is given, why then, to leave and abandon it there must be the greatest cause, and where there is not, such a resignation had better be called apostasy, apostasy from the high and perfect episcopal estate, rather than anything else. If it were for reason of very great illnesses, or to enter a very strict monastic retirement, never again to see human beings or mundane affairs, even then we do not know if such a bishop would be very secure before God; but in order to make oneself a solicitor at court, and to solicit, as he now does, that the Indians demand him as Protector! When the letter in which he asked for this was seen in a congregation of Franciscans, they all laughed at it, nor could they think what to say and respond to such delirium. There in Spain he will not be seen with a letter from a chapter or congregation of Franciscans, while he asks them here to send him money and affairs. Who could think well of such things? I believe your majesty will abhor them as a clear temptation of our adversary, for the unrest of yourself and others. Your majesty ought to order him to be shut up in a monastery so that he would not cause greater evils; if not, I am afraid he will go to Rome and be the cause of perturbation at the Roman court.

As to the overseers, tribute-collectors and miners, he calls them executioners, soulless, inhuman and cruel. And granted that some have been greedy and of ill repute, certainly there are many others who are good Christians, pious and charitable, many of them married and of good life.

The same will not be said of Las Casas as of St Lawrence, who for giving half of his burial place to the body of St Steven was called the polite Spaniard. Las Casas says in that confessional that no Spaniard in this country has acted in good faith concerning the wars, nor the merchants either, for having brought them merchandise to buy; and by this he judges people's hearts. Likewise he says that no one bought and sold slaves in good faith, but he is wrong, since for many years they were bought and sold in the squares with your majesty's brand, and for some time many Christians acted bona fide and in invincible ignorance. He also says that to this day they are still oppressing the Indians, which also goes against your majesty. Well I remember some years ago, after your majesty sent don Antonio de Mendoza, the lords and nobles of this land assembled and solemnly, voluntarily renewed their obedience to your majesty, finding themselves in our holy faith, free of wars and sacrifices, and in peace and justice. Las Casas also says that of everything the Spaniards have, there is nothing that is not stolen; in this he insults your majesty and everyone who has come here, those who brought property with them as well as those who have bought and acquired it justly, and he dishonors them in writing and in print. Are the Spanish nation and its prince then to be thus insolently defamed, so that tomorrow the Indians and other nations may read it? And he also says that in all these years there has never been a just conquest or war against Indians. God provides the things to come, and he alone knows them, or such persons as his divine majesty should wish to reveal them to; now Las Casas in the things he says wants to be a soothsayer or prophet, but he will not be a true prophet, for the Lord says: this gospel will be preached in all the universe before the end of the world. Thus it is your majesty's mission to give haste to the preaching of the holy gospel through all these lands, and with those who will not willingly hear the holy gospel of Jesus Christ, let it be by force, for here one can apply the proverb 'better good forced on you than bad you desire.' By the word of the Lord, he who finds treasure in the field should sell it all forthwith and buy the field; and now without giving a great deal your majesty can buy and acquire this treasure of precious pearls that cost the very rich price of the blood of Jesus Christ, because if your majesty does not favor this, who is there here who can or may gain the precious treasure of souls that are scattered over these fields and lands? How can Las Casas say that all the tributes are and have been wrongly taken? We see that when they asked the Lord if tribute should be given to Caesar or not, he answered yes. If we look at how the rule of the Roman empire came to be, we go back to find that first the Babylonians, in the time of Nebuchadnezzar the Great, took the kingdom of the Assyrians by war, and that empire endured, according to St Jerome, more than 1,300 years. This kingdom of Nebuchadnezzar was the golden head of the statue that he himself saw, according to the interpretation of Daniel, Ch. 2, and Nebuchadnezzar was the first monarch and head of empire. Afterwards the Medes and Persians destroyed the Babylonians in the time of Cyrus and Darius, and this kingdom was the chest and arms of that same statue; there were two arms, that is, Cyrus and Darius, and the Persians and the Medes. Afterwards the Greeks destroyed the Persians in the time of Alexander the Great, and this kingdom was the statue's metal abdomen and thighs. Such was the resonance of this metal that it was heard through all the world, except in this land, and the fame and fear of the great Alexander grew until it was written: *soluit terra in conspectu eius.* And when he had conquered Asia, the people of Europe and Africa sent ambassadors who went to Babylon to wait on him with gifts and give him obedience. Afterwards the Romans subjugated the Greeks, and they were the statue's feet and legs of iron, which consumes and erodes all metals. And afterwards the stone that was cut from the mountain without hands cut down and diminished the statue of idolatry, and this was the kingdom of Jesus Christ.

During the rule of the Roman emperors, the Lord said that tribute should be given to Caesar. I will not try to decide whether our wars are more licit than theirs, or which is the more licit tribute, theirs or ours; let your majesty's councils decide. But note what the prophet Daniel says in the same chapter: that God alters the times and the epochs, and changes kingdoms from one rule to another, because of sins, as is seen in the land of Canaan, which God gave to the children of Israel with great punishments of the Canaanites, and later he gave the kingdom of Judea to the imperial Romans for sins and the death of the son of God. I appeal to your majesty on behalf of the fifth kingdom, that of Jesus Christ, signified by the stone cut from the mountain without hands, which is to fill and occupy all the land, and of which kingdom your majesty is leader and captain. Let your majesty order everything possible done so that this kingdom may be fulfilled and widened, and the gospel will be preached to these infidels, or to those nearest, especially those of Florida, who are here at our door.

I would like to see Las Casas persevere for fifteen or twenty years in confessing ten or twelve sick, ailing Indians daily, and an equal number of healthy old ones who never confessed before, and see to many other things, many of them spiritual, concerning the Indians. A fine thing it is that there in Spain, to show his zeal, he says to your majesty and those of your councils: So-and-so is no friend of the Indians, he is a friend of the Spaniards; do not believe him. May it please God that he manages to be a friend of God and of his own soul. What he is concerned about there is harm done to the Indians, or lands the Spaniards request here in New Spain, or livestock rights granted them prejudicial to the Indians. This is no longer the time that was, because now he who does harm worth two pesos pays four, and he who does harm worth five pays eight. As to giving lands, your majesty could very well grant excess, empty or untilled lands to Spaniards who are settled and want to apply themselves to farming the land, when it is without prejudice to others. Since for the past ten years there has been great mortality and pestilence among the Indians, there are far fewer of them; even where there has been the least loss, two thirds are gone, in other places four fifths, in others seven eighths. For this reason there are excess lands in many places, aside from the uncultivated land and the war grounds that they left unplanted. These were fields that they left between one province and the next, between one ruler and the next, where they came to make war on each other, as, before they entered the faith, they did continually, because almost all the people they sacrificed to the idols were taken in the wars, and for that reason they thought more of capturing one than of killing five. They did not farm these lands, and there is room there. When there is just need, your majesty might make grants there, if the Indians have not by now occupied and cultivated some of them; your majesty could grant them with less prejudice than others, indeed with none at all.

As far as the stock farms are concerned, almost everywhere the stock which were doing damage, especially the horses and cattle, have been removed, not for lack of large fields, but because they were running untended; since they were not gathered in at night to sleep in pens, they ran everywhere and did damage. But now they have been assigned times for summer pasture, when they are to enter and leave, with penalties for not complying, for here by the goodness of God there are officers of justice to see to these things, and also other people who are as concerned about it as Las Casas. For sheep or goats, there are fields and lands everywhere; even very near to the great city of Tenochtitlan-Mexico City, there are many enterprises for livestock of all kinds, both large and small. Likewise near to the cities of Puebla and Tlaxcala, and in the towns of Tepeaca and Tecamachalco, in all these towns and their districts there are great fields and pasture grounds where great numbers of livestock can graze without harm, especially sheep and goats; after all, at home in Spain they often graze near the grainfields, and the owners pay for any damage they do. Here there are many vacant lands and large fields where far more animals than now exist could run; whoever says different either does not know about it or has not seen it. The province of Tlaxcala alone is ten leagues wide, in places eleven, and fifteen to sixteen leagues long, measuring over forty around; the province of Tecamachalco is nearly the same size, and many other towns have many vacant lands, because the Indians occupy less than a fifth of the districts. And since livestock are so advantageous and necessary, and both Spaniards and Indians use them, cows and oxen as well as horses and the other kinds of stock, why not grant out something that exists in excess and let the animals graze in peace, since it is for the good of all?

And since many Indians are now using horses it would be well for your majesty to order that license to have horses be given only to the principal lords, because if the Indians get used to horses many of them will become good riders and in time will want to equal the Spaniards. This advantage of having horses and cannon is very necessary in this land, because it gives force and advantage to few against many. Let me tell your majesty that all New Spain here is deserted and abandoned, without any defense or fortress at all against the dangers, discords and wars that our enemy and adversary forever wishes and tries to raise up among us; defense is needed though it were only because we are here in an alien land, and there are many blacks, who at times have conspired to rebel and kill the Spaniards. There is no better situated place in New Spain to build a fortress than the city of Puebla, where it could be done at less cost because of the many good materials available, and it would mean security for the whole country.

The towns to which your majesty owes most in all New Spain here are Texcoco, Tacuba and Mexico City, because each of these was a kingdom, and the ruler of each had ten provinces and many towns subject to him. Besides this, among these principalities were distributed the tributes of a hundred and seventy provinces and towns, and each of the rulers was no small king. These lords, as soon as the Christians arrived and challenged them to receive the faith, gave obedience to your majesty, and Texcoco and Tacuba aided the Spaniards in the conquest of Mexico. The other lords of the land still have and possess their principalities, and pay tribute to your majesty because you are their king and lord and because you administer religious instruction, sacraments and justice to them, and keep them in peace; your majesty gives them more than you receive from them, even if Las Casas will not believe it. But the lords of Texcoco, Tacuba and Mexico had some of the hamlets subject to their main towns taken away and distributed to others. They would be content if your majesty would order some small or medium-sized town to serve the ruler of Texcoco, and the same for the ruler and town of Tacuba.

This as to temporal matters; as to matters of the spirit, these souls cry out for ministers. Since many friars have left Spain for these lands, and continue to every day, let your majesty send some of the many friars in Flanders and Italy who are servants of God, learned, desirous of coming to these parts and working in the conversion of infidels. There have been friars of those nationalities in this land, and to this day there are still some servants of God who have given a very good example and worked much with the natives. Besides this, the main church of Mexico City, the metropolitan, is very poor, old and patched together; it was built only provisionally, and that twenty-nine years ago. It would be right for your majesty to order its construction to begin and favor it, since it is the head, mother and mistress of all the churches of New Spain. And your majesty should order that this church and the other cathedrals of New Spain each have a town to serve it, as they did before; there would be no encomiendas put to as good a use in all New Spain. They have much need of such towns, to help repair, maintain, clean and adorn the churches and the houses of the bishops, which are all poor and indebted. Shoemakers and blacksmiths have held encomiendas here, and still do; the churches need them much more, since they are without income and have very little.

I say all this with desire to serve and inform your majesty of what I have felt and seen of this land in the course of thirty years since we came here by your majesty's order bearing the bulls and briefs of Leo and Adrian which your majesty had solicited. The Cardinal of Santa Cruz, fray Francisco de Quiño-nes, and father fray Juan Clapión, may God rest him, were to come here and bring the bulls. Of twelve of us who came here to begin the conversion of these people, there are only two now left alive. May your majesty receive this letter in the spirit in which I write, and let it be valued only as far as it conforms to reason, justice and truth. I remain, as least chaplain, praying to God that his holy grace always dwell in your majesty's blessed soul, so that you always do his holy will. Amen.

After what I said above, I saw and read a treatise that Las Casas composed on the subject of the Indians enslaved here in New Spain and on the islands, and another one concerning the opinion he rendered on putting the Indians in encomiendas. He says that he composed the first on commission of the Council of the Indies, and the second by your majesty's order. No human being of whatever nation, law or status could read them without feeling abhorrence and mortal hate and considering all the residents of New Spain as the most cruel, abominable and detestable people there are under the sun. This is the effect of writings that are done without charity, that proceed from a spirit alien to all piety and humanity. I am out of touch with the climate in old Spain, because it has been more than thirty years since I left it, but I have often heard from people just coming from Spain, pious friars and Spaniards who are good Christians and God-fearing, that they find here more Christianity, more faith, more practice of the holy sacraments, and charity and alms to the poor of all kinds, than in old Spain. May God pardon Las Casas for so gravely dishonoring and defaming, so terribly insulting and affronting these communities and the Spanish nation, its prince, councils, and all those who administer justice in your majesty's name in these realms. And if Las Casas will confess the truth, I ask him to bear witness what numerous and large donations he received here, and with how much humility people suffered his overbearing temperament, and how many persons of quality entrusted many important affairs to him, and when he offered to keep faith with them, gave him large sums, though he hardly fulfilled a thing of what he promised. The servant of God fray Domingo de Betanzos, among others, complained of this in the letter already mentioned.

It should have been enough for Las Casas to give his vote and opinion on what he felt about giving encomiendas of Indians to Spaniards, and to put it down in writing, without printing so many insults, slanders and vituperation. It is well known what a sin it is to defame one person; more to defame many, and much more to defame a commonwealth and nation. If Las Casas called the Spanish residents of New Spain tyrants, thieves, robbers, murderers and cruel assailants only a hundred times, it might pass, but since he calls them that a hundred times a hundred, aside from the little charity and less pity that he shows in his writings, and aside from the insults, wrongs and affronts that he makes to everyone by speaking thus to your majesty in that treatise, there would be much reason for him to adopt moderation and speak with some tincture of humility. Of what advantage and edification can words be that are said without pity or humanity? Surely little. I don't know why it is that Las Casas should want to condemn a hundred for what one person does, or attribute to a thousand what ten committed, and defame everyone who is or has been here. Where have so many good people been condemned for a few bad ones? If the Lord had found ten righteous men in the time of Abraham and Lot, he would have pardoned many. Because in Seville and Córdoba there are some thieves, murderers and heretics, are the inhabitants of those cities all evil thieves and tyrants? Mexico City-Tenochtitlan and the other cities and towns of New Spain have not shown less loyalty and obedience than they, which is the more to be appreciated the more distant they are from the king.

If the things Las Casas writes were true, certainly your majesty would have great reason to complain of all those you have sent here, and they would be worthy of great punishments, the bishops and prelates, who would all be obliged to lay down their responsibilities and appeal to God and king to conserve their flocks. Yet we see that the good bishops of New Spain persevere in working at their tasks and duties, hardly resting day or night. And your majesty would have grounds to complain of the judges and presiding officers that you have appointed to Audiencias everywhere, with high salaries; in New Spain alone there are Audiencias in Mexico City, New Galicia, and Guatemala, and all of these sleep soundly, content to have resting on their consciences so many sins of others as Las Casas says. (Your majesty is not so careless or inattentive as Las Casas would have it, nor do you neglect to penalize and punish those who do not keep faith with you. A thing worthy of note is the punishment that your majesty ordered given to an Audiencia that had hardly taken office, when the judges were imprisoned in Spain and the president, the governor of New Spain, was here in the public jail for more than a year, and then went to Spain to finish paying for his guilt.) And your majesty should also be indignant with the councils of New Spain, those of the churches as well as those of the cities, since all are appointed by your majesty to rule and care for your vassals and towns, if they do not do what they should. And your majesty would have the same complaint of the friars of all the orders whom your majesty sends here with much cost and work bringing them from the provinces of Spain, with orders to erect monasteries, giving them chalices and bells, and some have received valuable ornaments. With reason your majesty could say, why are they all like voiceless dogs, allowing the land to be destroyed without barking or crying out? But no, instead almost all are at their tasks, doing what they should.

When I found out what Las Casas had written, I was unhappy with the royal council for allowing such a thing to be printed. Later, on consideration, I saw that it was printed in Seville at the time when the ships were about to leave, like something surreptitious and underhanded. I believe that God permitted it so that people would know and respond to Las Casas' opinions, though with more moderation and charity than his writings deserve, so that he would be converted to God and give satisfaction to all those he has harmed and falsely defamed, and so that in this life he could do penance; also so that your majesty might be informed of the truth and might know the services that Captain don Hernando Cortés and his companions have performed, and the great loyalty, surely worthy of reward, that New Spain has always shown your majesty. And your majesty may be sure that the Indians of New Spain are well treated, and they pay less tribute and tax than the farmers of old Spain, each in his own fashion. I will not say this of quite all the Indians, because there are a few towns where the tribute quota was set before the great pestilence and whose tributes have not yet been modified. Your majesty should order these quotas to be revised. Today the Indians understand their quotas very well, and will not pay a penny more under any conditions, nor does the encomendero dare ask for a cacao bean more than is in his quota, nor will his confessor absolve him without restitution, and the officers of justice will punish him if they find out about transgressions. That neglect and oppression that Las Casas so often mentions do not exist here because, glory be to God, there has been much care and zeal here among the preachers, and vigilance among the confessors, and, in those who administer justice, a spirit of obedience to execute what your majesty orders concerning the good treatment and defense of the natives of this land; in all truth, what I say is so.

During the last ten years the natives of this land have diminished greatly in number. The reason for it has not been bad treatment, because for many years now the Indians have been well treated, looked after and defended; rather the cause has been the great diseases and plagues that New Spain has had, so that the natives continue to decrease each day. God knows the cause; his judgments are many and hidden from us. Whether or not the great sins and idolatries that took place in this land cause it, I do not know; nevertheless I see that those seven idolatrous generations that possessed the promised land were destroyed by Joshua, and then the children of Israel populated it in such a fashion that when David counted the people, he found 800,000, counting only strong men fit for war, in the ten tribes, and in the tribe of Juda and Benjamin 500,000. And afterwards, in the time of King Asa, 580,000 warriors from the two tribes took part in the battle that Zara gave to the king of the Ethiopians, and the land was so populated that one reads of over 150,000 citizens in the city of Jerusalem by itself; now in all that kingdom there are not half as many citizens as there once were in Jerusalem alone.

As to the cause of that destruction, or that of this country and the islands, God knows it. Your majesty and the Catholic Monarchs of holy memory have ordered all the measures and remedies humanly possible, but human council and human power have not been enough to remedy it. It is a great thing that so many souls should have been saved, as they continue to be, and that so many evils, idolatries, homicides and great offenses against God should have been halted and prevented. What is very important at present is that your majesty should provide stability for this land, for as it now is, it suffers greatly. Your majesty has already received sufficient information and you know what is best; in your majesty's councils there are many reports adequate for establishing stability quickly, which will be in the service of God and your majesty. It is needed by both commonwealths, Spaniards and Indians. As in Spain for the conservation of peace and justice there are garrisons, and in Italy an army, and on the borders always men of arms, it should be no less so in this country. Don Antonio de Mendoza, viceroy of this land, used to say: 'If this land is not given stability, it cannot last long – ten or twelve years, dragging things out painfully; but if things go quickly, it will not last that long.'

This whole country is extremely expensive to live in and short of foodstuffs, which used to be very abundant and cheap, and if people were poor at least they had enough to eat. Now among the poor and indebted Spaniards there are many idle people hoping for the least occasion in the world to rob the natives, because they say that the Indians are rich, and the Spaniards poor and dying of hunger. Your majesty can readily see what can happen in a land that has its king and government two thousand leagues away, and that stability here is more necessary for the Indians than for the Spaniards. I will not go further into the reasons, to avoid prolixity, and I know that your majesty has the good will, knowledge and experience to give stability to this land; there is no lack of prayers that God give you his grace. I am confident that you will do the right thing and that with what your majesty should decide, God will be served and this land saved.

In the treatise that this Las Casas or Casaus printed, he errs, among other things, principally in three: that is, in the manner of enslavement, in the number of slaves, and in their treatment. As to enslavement in New Spain, he gives three ways of doing it, none of which is as he writes. It is easy to see that he knows little of the rites and customs of the Indians of New Spain. In that book I wrote, in the 4th part, in Chs. 22 and 23, one will find eleven manners of enslavement, which are the ones we gave to the bishop of Mexico City. Three or four of us friars have written of the antiquities and customs of the natives here, and I have what the others wrote. Since it cost me more work and time, it is no wonder that I should have compiled and understood it better than others. Las Casas also writes of enslaving Indians during wars, and wastes a great deal of paper on it, and here too it is seen that he knows little of what went on in the wars of the natives, because they did not make slaves in wars nor ransom any of the captives they took in them, but kept them all to sacrifice, for generally speaking these were the people sacrificed all through this land. Very few were sacrificed except those taken in war, for which reason the wars were continuous; to do their duty to their cruel gods and to solemnize their festivities and honor their temples, they went about everywhere making war and assaulting people in order to sacrifice them, offering hearts and human blood to the demons, in which many innocents suffered. There seems to be no small cause to make war on the oppressors and killers of the innocent, who with screams and clamoring asked God and man for succor, since they suffered death so unjustly. As your majesty knows, this is one of the reasons for which war may be waged. And they had the custom that if one of the lords or noblemen taken in war escaped, the very people of his town would sacrifice him, but if he was a man of low estate, called a *macehual*, his lord rewarded him with gifts of cloth. This and the rest of what went on in the wars appears in the same book, in the 4th part, Chs.

14, 15 and 16.

As to the number of slaves, on one page he writes that 3 million were enslaved, on another page 4 million. The places and provinces where Las Casas says all this happened are Mexico, Coatzacoalcos, Pánuco, Jalisco, Chiapas, Guatemala, Honduras, Yucatán, Nicaragua, the coast of San Miguel, and Venezuela. It would be well if he also put, even just out of humility, the coast of Paria and Cubagua, since he was there, and would tell how it went with him there. Almost all the places he puts are here in New Spain; I have added up the provinces and places where he says enslavement took place, making larger rather than smaller estimates (to avoid length I will not go into detail), and all together it does not make 200,000. And showing this number to others who have experience and have been here longer, they assure me that there were 150,000, or not over 100,000; I myself believe there were 200,000. As to the number of 3 million, it is 2,800,000 too high, and the number of 4 million is 3,800,000 too high. So it is with many of the exaggerations with which Las Casas greatly troubles your majesty's conscience and badly injures and dishonors his fellow men in print. This number of slaves is something that could be established by examining your majesty's record books of the taxes you received.

As for treatment, I speak for New Spain, where almost all have been set free. According to my understanding, there may be about a thousand Indian slaves left in the world, and these are being liberated daily, so that inside a year there will hardly be one left in the land. Your majesty did all that was needed to free them when you ordered that owners of Indian slaves should prove they had been enslaved justly, which was almost impossible, and indeed by law the contrary should have been the case; yet what your majesty ordered was best, because very few were properly enslaved. Las Casas says that in all the Indies there was never just cause to enslave a single person; how does he know? He himself says that he is not acquainted with Mexico City and its surroundings, so it is no wonder he should know little about it. He was in this land about seven years, and of those he spent five pressing causes. There have been friars in New Spain who have gone from Mexico City to Nicaragua, 400 leagues, and in not two towns the whole way did they fail to preach, say mass, give instruction, and baptize children and adults, few or many. So the friars here have seen and know a bit more than Las Casas about the good treatment of slaves. The officers of justice and the friars as preachers and confessors (for there were Franciscans from the beginning, and later came those of other orders) have always taken great care that the Indians, especially the slaves, should be well treated and instructed in Christian doctrine and knowledge of God, the principal worker of all good. Before long the Spaniards began to instruct their slaves and bring them to the churches to be baptized, instructed and married, and Spaniards who did not do this were not absolved. For many years now the slaves and servants of Spaniards have been married *in facie ecclesiae*, and I have seen many, here in the region of Mexico City, and in Oaxaca and Guatemala and other places, who were well married and good Christians, living in their houses with their children and their personal property. It is not right that Las Casas should say that service to Christians is heavier than a hundred towers, and that the Spaniards esteem the Indians less than the beasts or the manure in the squares. It seems to me a great load on his conscience to dare say such a thing to your majesty; and speaking with the greatest temerity, he says that the service that the Spaniards take from the Indians by force, being insufferable and most rigorous, exceeds the tyrannies of the world, equaling that of the demons and surpassing that of those who live without God or law.

Such a thing should not be said. God deliver me from anyone who would say such a thing! The branding iron for slaves, the one called of your majesty's trade, arrived here in New Spain the year of 1524, in the middle of May. As soon as it reached Mexico City, Captain don Hernando Cortés, who was governing at the time, met in the Franciscan monastery with the friars and men of letters who were there in the city, and I was present. I saw that the governor was sorry the iron had arrived, and he opposed its use; when he could do no more, he placed limits on the license that came with it to brand slaves. The enslavement beyond the limitations occurred in his absence, when he had left for Honduras.

And as to those who murmur against the Marqués del Valle, God rest him, and who try to blacken and obscure his deeds, I believe that before God their deeds are not as acceptable as those of the Marqués. Although as a human he was a sinner, he had the faith and works of a good Christian, and a great desire to employ his life and property in widening and augmenting the faith of Jesus Christ, and dying for the conversion of these gentiles. He spoke of this with much spirit, as one to whom God had given this gift and desire, and had placed as the unique captain of this land of the Occident. He would confess with many tears and receive communion devoutly, putting his soul and property in the hands of his confessor, to order and dispose of all of it as was necessary to relieve his conscience. And thus in Spain he sought out very learned confessors, with whom he ordered his soul and made great restitutions and large charities. God visited great afflictions, travails and illnesses on him to purge his guilt and purify his soul; I believe that he is a child of salvation, and that he has a larger crown than others who denigrate him.

After he entered New Spain, he did much to bring the Indians to an understanding of the true God and to have the holy gospel preached to them. He told them that he was your majesty's messenger in the conquest of Mexico, and while he went about this land, he tried to hear mass every day, observed the fasts of the church, and fasted on other days out of devotion. God furnished him two interpreters in this land: a Spaniard named Aguilar, and an Indian woman named doña Marina. Through these he preached to the Indians and informed them who God was and who their idols were, and thus he destroyed the idols and all the idolatry he could. He tried to tell the truth and be a man of his word, which was greatly to his advantage with the Indians. The banner he carried was a red cross on a black field, in the midst of some blue and white flames, and the device said: 'Friends, let us follow the cross of Christ, and if there is faith in us, in this sign we will conquer.' Whenever he arrived at a place, he immediately raised a cross.

It was a marvelous thing what energy, spirit and prudence God gave him in everything that he undertook in this land. Very much to be noted are the daring and strength that God gave him to destroy and throw down the principal idols of Mexico City, which were statues over fifteen feet high. Clad in heavy armor, he took a bar of iron and raised himself up so high that he managed to hit the head and eyes of the idols. When he was about to bring them down, the great lord of Mexico, Moctezuma, sent him a message not to dare touch his gods, because he would kill him and all the other Christians forthwith. Then the captain turned to his companions with much spirit and half weeping, said to them: 'Brothers, for all we do for our lives and interests, now let us die here for the honor of God and so that the demons will not be worshipped.' And he responded to the messages that he wished to place his life at stake, and he would not stop what he had begun; that those were not gods, but stones and images of the demon, and let them come ahead. And though there were only 130 Christians with the governor, and the Indians were without number, God and the spirit they saw in the captain so struck them with terror that they dared not stir. When the idols were destroyed, he put an image of Our Lady there.

At that time there was a lack of rain and the maize fields were drying out; the Indians brought many dry stalks of maize and told the captain that if it didn't rain they would all perish of hunger. Then the Marqués gave them confidence, saying they would pray to God and St Mary for rain. He asked all his companions to prepare themselves, and that night they confessed to God and implored his mercy and grace; the next day they went out in procession, and the captain received communion at mass. And though the sky was clear, suddenly there came such a torrent that before they could reach their lodgings, which were not very distant, they were all drenched. This was a great edification and preachment to the Indians, because from then on it rained regularly and was a very good year. Whenever the captain had opportunity, after giving the Indians news of

God, he would tell them to consider him their friend and the messenger of a great king in whose name he came, and that on his behalf he promised them they would be loved and well treated, because the king was a friend of the God that he preached to them.

Who has loved and defended the Indians of this new world like Cortés? He often admonished and begged his companions not to touch the Indians or their things, and though the land was full of maize fields, there was hardly a Spaniard who dared to pick an ear of maize. Because a Spaniard named Juan Polanco entered an Indian's household near the port and took some clothing, he had him given a hundred lashes; another, named Mora, who took a turkey from peaceful Indians, he ordered hanged, and if Pedro de Alvarado had not cut the rope, his life would have ended there. Because two blacks of his took two blankets and a turkey from some Indians, he ordered them hanged, at a time when there was nothing else of such value as blacks; he had another Spaniard publicly disgraced because he lopped off the branches of a fruit tree and the Indians complained. He wanted no one to touch the Indians nor to have them carry loads, under penalty of 40 pesos. The day I disembarked, coming from the port toward Medellín, near where Veracruz is now, since we were on a stretch of sand and in hot country, and the town was three leagues distant, I asked a Spaniard who had two Indians with him to have one of them carry my cloak for me, but he dared not do it, affirming that they would fine him 40 pesos, and so I carried the cloak on my back the whole way. Where war could not be avoided, Cortés asked his companions to defend themselves as best they could without striking back, and when they could not help it, he said that it was better to wound than to kill, and that a wounded Indian inspired more fear than two left dead on the field.

The Marqués always had rivals and opponents in this land, who tried to obscure the services he did God and your majesty, and there was no lack of enemies there in Spain either. If it weren't for them, I know your majesty would always have had special affection and love for him and his companions. Through this captain, God opened the door for us to preach his holy gospel, and it was he who caused the Indians to revere the holy sacraments and respect the ministers of the church. Since he is now deceased, I have gone to this length to defend his life in some measure.

May the grace of the Holy Spirit always dwell in your majesty's soul. Amen. From Tlaxcala, 2nd of January, 1555.

Humble servant and least chaplain of your majesty,
    Motolinia, fray Toribio

[1] Published in Spanish in *Colección de documentos inéditos relativos al descubrimiento, conquista y colonización de las antiguas posesiones españoles en América y Oceanía*, VII, pp. 254-89, and elsewhere.

37. The petty administrator

Bartolomé Pérez Guillermo, deputy governor of Zinapécuaro, Mexico, to his nephew Gregorio Sánchez de Moscoso in Calzadilla de los Barros, Extremadura, 1577[1]

> ...and the main thing is, she comes of very important parents...

We conclude Part III with two letters from lower members of the governmental and ecclesiastic hierarchies. The writers seem more immersed in the society and economy of their immediate surroundings than in their respective organizations, and they reveal themselves in most aspects as settlers like any others. In both cases the famous nephew in Spain is a central figure, as so often in the messages of settlers in Part II: in this letter, soon to arrive; in the next, fervently hoped for.

Not only did the encomenderos have to learn to share the economic exploitation of their districts with other Spaniards, they also soon saw their informal jurisdictional-administrative dominance there challenged by representatives of the civil administration entering the countryside. Sooner in some areas, later in others, but eventually almost everywhere, there came to be officials stationed outside the Spanish cities, appointed for short terms, to administer justice locally and collect royal tributes from the gradually increasing number of Indian towns which were placed directly under the crown rather than in encomiendas. With various titles, from the resounding *corregidor*, through *alcalde mayor*, perhaps the most common term, to the more modest *teniente (de gobernador)* as in the present case, these administrators had their seats in the largest Indian towns of jurisdictions containing on the order of five encomiendas or so. Though among the lowest direct appointees of viceroys or governors, they did have staffs, consisting of some constables, secretaries and retainers.

Like the estates of the non-encomenderos, the institution of the alcalde mayor was a manifestation of the thickening Spanish web, a congeries of interests and counterinterests no longer so easily dominated by a few individuals. And just as the encomenderos found advantages in the economic invasion of their territories, and long retained a more subtle kind of dominance, so they did in the sphere of rural government. Part of the pressure to appoint alcaldes mayores came from the old need of the governors for patronage, for meaningful posts to give the followers they brought from Spain. Corresponding pressure existed on the part of the encomendero families, a quickly multiplying group. Only the eldest son could inherit the encomienda; something else had to be found for the others, and a post as alcalde mayor was one solution, though a temporary one. Thus we see two principal types in local administration. First, the outsider, a governor's man, often directly from Spain, indebted from his trip, wanting a quick profit to wipe out the debt and to save something for himself during his brief term in office. Second, the insider, usually belonging to one of the encomendero families of the area. Particularly in smaller or poorer jurisdictions, nothing is more common than to see younger brothers and uncles of the local encomenderos taking turns as alcalde mayor. Either way, the encomenderos retained great influence. With their junior relatives this is clear, but they also, being permanent and deeply rooted, had the advantage over temporary outsiders, who needed the encomenderos' help to make a success of their economic ventures. Even the staffs of the alcaldes mayores were often long-time residents of the area, having long since made their accommodation with the local powers.

Bartolomé Pérez Guillermo seems to be a mixture of the two types. He is an outsider who has chosen the way of the insiders. He is fairly new from Spain, apparently from a family associated with the lower levels of law enforcement (his nephew is constable in their home town), and he most likely came to be appointed through the viceregal machine – he certainly makes much of the fact that the viceroy forwarded him a letter. He may have been one of the few who decided not to aim for quick wealth and then leave the area, not to push textile or hide production or to speculate with the king's maize; notice his indirect criticism of those who do. At least, unlike most outsiders, he has chosen to take root and ally himself closely with the encomienda families. The Juan Velázquez de Salazar whom he praises so highly was one of New Spain's greatest encomenderos, and part of his grant was close to Pérez Guillermo's jurisdiction, if not within it. Pérez Guillermo has now married into Velázquez de Salazar's household, and is the next thing to his dependent. He suggests that his nephew actually enter the encomendero's service. Note also the typical distinctions in title among the women involved. Pérez Guillermo is very proud of his new wife's connections and background, and indeed her surname has a good ring; but she is not a *doña*, and the encomendero's wife most emphatically is.

The reader may think it strange that Pérez Guillermo speaks of the Augustinian order as being the most powerful, when we have previously spoken of the priority of the Franciscans in Mexico. The statement is to be taken as applying to the locality. Zinapécuaro is in the west, in Michoacán, near such great Augustinian establishments as Yuriria and Cuitzeo.

Very magnificent sir:

On the last day of September of this year of '77 I received by way of his lordship the viceroy your letter written May 28. It gives me great joy, as reason requires, to know that you want to come to this land just to see me. Certainly my spirit has long desired to see someone from home here in this land; only a son of Andrés López, who used to live on the corner of the street of the Martyrs, has come here, to a province they call Zacatecas. And also Juan Nicolás, son of Cristóbal Sánchez, who used to live next to the square, came to this country looking for a brother of his called Benito Martín; it was he who told me of this son of Andrés López, and also that you are now chief constable of the town, and that my brother Alonso Pérez is a widower and in hardship since he has no one left there but milady sister Ana Domínguez and Teresa Alonso. I don't know why my brother Mr Alonso Pérez doesn't write, since I wrote him. If he is in need, then let him come along with you to this land, and I will give him enough from what I have to live in great honor, because I have no one here I can trust to send money by, and there in Spain money often doesn't reach the right destination, and for this reason one can't send it.

I have arranged here for you to come very comfortably in the fleet that will sail the year of '78, as you say in your letter. It chances that a very important cavalier named Juan Velázquez de Salazar is there in Castile now, having left here to go to the court as a representative of New Spain; he is a person who can do much and is worth much, in that country as well as this, and he has more than 10,000 or 12,000 pesos in yearly income from vassals. Milady doña Ana de Esquivel, his wife, is writing to tell him to bring you back in his service, to do me a favor. I am also writing myself to Mr Juan Velázquez, asking his grace to do me the favor of taking you into his service to bring you to these shores. So as soon as you see this, leave immediately to seek him out, and try in every way to see him and speak to him and offer yourself for his service, because he is a very important cavalier, and for his great goodness he is highly considered there in Spain; he will be at the court or in Seville. And if perhaps you and my brother Mr Alonso Pérez come, I am writing him to do me the favor of lending you 100 pesos for the trip, and I will pay him back as soon as you get here. And milady doña Ana de Esquivel is writing the same also, and since her grace is writing, I think everything will be all right, since she is very much my patroness and wishes me well.

The Lord saw fit to take from this present life my wife Isabel
Ponce, God rest her soul, who left me two children, one of
them a boy, the other a very pretty girl. I married again in the
household of milady doña Ana de Esquivel here. I wanted to
tell you this so you would understand that there is obligation
on the part of Mr Juan Velázquez to take you into his service,
and if you come in that way you will gain a great deal, because
serving him will oblige him to do what he can for you in this
country. I married a young lady of great honor, of very noble
parents, since she has three brothers who are friars, two of them
Augustinian, who are the ones who are powerful here and have
much at their command, and the other one is Dominican, all
three very important people. And thus you see that I married
very much to my advantage, my wife being so noble and so well
related. She sends you her greetings, because she saw the letter
you wrote me, and read it, since she knows how to read and
write, and is sagacious, and the main thing is, she comes of very
important parents, may they be in God's heaven, for they are
dead now. Her father was named Cristobal Pérez Lozano and
her mother Catalina de Contreras, and my wife's name is Isabel
Pérez de Lozano.

I never did get the letter that you say you sent me by a canon
of Michoacán.

My brother-in-law Mr Rodrigo Ponce sends greetings, and also
milady Ana Vanegas, my mother-in-law, and another sister of
my late wife, called Ana Vanegas too.

I have done everything possible to have this letter go to you
by way of a dispatch-boat his lordship the viceroy is sending to
Spain, because he was the one who channeled your letter to me,
since I am at present his majesty's lieutenant in this town of
Zinapécuaro and in another called Ucareo; there must be about
eight leagues of jurisdiction. I have been here for more than
three years, and I even was when I last wrote, but didn't care to
write you about it, and wouldn't now either if there weren't the
occasion that his lordship the viceroy did me the favor of sending me your letter. And I am well liked hereabouts, since I am

more proud of my honesty than of the profit I can gain from the office. There are many things I could write you about this land, but I will mention only one, which is that here men who know how to work and give themselves to virtue make a living, and those who don't, don't. There are as many vagrants here as there. What causes it is the great luxuriance of the land, because wherever a man goes he will find someone to feed him, though it is true that things are getting tighter than they used to be.

I greet those gentlemen my brothers and cousins and relatives, and beg them to write me by you. May our Lord guard your very magnificent person and raise your estate as both you and I, your uncle, desire. From this town of Zinapécuaro, the 6th day of the month of October of 1577.

Your uncle kisses your hands,
Bartolomé Pérez Guillermo

[1] Published in Spanish, with comment, in Otte, 'Die europäischen Siedler.'

38. The parish priest

Bachelor Francisco de la Calzada, in Potosí, to his sister María de la Calzada in Valencia de Don Juan, Old Castile, 1577[1]

... The priests and friars who have a nephew whom they can trust are very rich ...

Bachelor Calzada gives us in this letter a good object lesson in the economic situation of the secular clergy. The regular orders had general funds, endowments and estates which could shield friars from overt individual activity for economic gain. But secular priests were practically free agents, with no institutional support, and Calzada is not exaggerating much when he says their salaries were 'not enough for drinking water.' Even to maintain himself in the style the community expected, much less to save anything for retirement, a priest had to have supplementary sources of income. One of the best such sources was a chaplaincy, paying the priest from an endowed fund for saying periodic masses on behalf of the patron. These plums, however,

went largely to relatives of the encomenderos and other prominent local people who endowed them. Priests in the countryside
commonly worked for their encomenderos as trusted, high-level
managers or inspectors, and also began to acquire estates of
their own; in towns they invested in whatever was most likely
to show a profit, whether commerce, real estate, or here, mines.
They ordinarily received certain supplies and labor from the
Indians in addition to their salaries, from the same source as
encomienda tribute, and indeed the encomenderos were long
responsible for seeing that they got it. The products and services
were often not of a kind they could use directly; instead they
sold the products and employed the labor on their estates. In
this way they acquired capital for more lucrative enterprises
within the Spanish sector of the economy. These additional
emoluments are the 'rations' that Calzada refers to as being
worth 2,000 pesos a year, far more than the salary proper, and
that the viceroy has taken away. This measure, had it stuck,
would have been the death of Christianity in Peru; but it did
not, and rural priests especially continued receiving their rations, in Peru as elsewhere, until the end of the colonial period.

Calzada's ambition is to buy a refining mill using 'this new
invention of mercury.' Even at Potosí the richest deposits, those
which could be exploited through smelting, were not inexhaust-
ible. By this time they had become depleted, and the introduction (hardly invention) of the amalgamation process was making
possible a new boom, greater and longer lasting than the original
one. To operate his mill Calzada would need help, not so much
because it would be unbecoming in an ordained priest to manage a mill personally, as because his basic position is that of
priest to a parish, and there is no reason to think that he neglected his mission. The post, after all, generated the capital for
his enterprises.

Secular priests were just that, secular. They had to be and
were expected to be. The tendency extended to friars as well, as
Calzada hints. Therefore it is natural that Calzada should be
concerned very much with the question of whether to return to
Spain or retire in Peru, the same as other settlers. And if he

seems a little crass in looking forward to not having to 'go about instructing Indians, which is surely a great travail,' this is after all a remark made within the family, and if we think about it, implies a sustained effort on Calzada's part.

Dear sister:

Since I have been in this realm of Peru I have written many letters, over fifteen of them, to you and to my nephew Próspero de Viso. And I have received only two from you, and one from my nephew, which I so prize and guard that they will accompany me when I return to Spain, if God permits.

I have always begged you to get my nephew Pedro de la Calzada started on his way here, since it would be greatly to my advantage and his. He has been so missed that if he had come I wouldn't be surprised to see us on the road to Spain within two years, because Potosí is more prosperous now than it has been since the world began. With this new invention of mercury, there are many men I know who less than three years ago were penniless and 3,000 or 4,000 pesos in debt, and now some of them have 50,000 pesos, others 40,000, and others who came only two years ago have 10,000 or 12,000 pesos.

The priests and friars who have a nephew whom they can trust are very rich, both groups of them. And those of us who have no one to trust have nothing but our parish salaries; there we spend more than we earn. This viceroy has done us a bad turn by reducing our salaries and removing our rations, all of which was worth over 2,000 pesos, and allowing us only 600 pesos of assayed silver, which is not enough for drinking water. If we don't devise other businesses or dealings, we can't outfit ourselves to go to Spain; but anyone who has someone to help him can leave very quickly. If my nephew had come, I would have bought him a mercury mill, that is, where silver is extracted through mercury, and with that, in less than two years we could leave with 6,000 or 7,000 pesos each. As it is, I don't know when I will be able to leave, because I am involved in spending so much in this and that endeavor that though I wish to cut down, I can't.

I was about to send three or four bars of silver, worth 1,500 ducats there, but here we have heard such bad news of everything in Seville being taken for the king, that I decided not to. And many who were about to leave for Spain are staying for the same reason. Also some tell of such misfortunes of wars and successions and many other troubles, that it clips the wings of men who want to go to Spain. Many buy properties and possessions and marry here, intending not to see Spain again. I don't know what I will do. Surely my desire is to die not here, but where I was born. If I am to go, it will be within three years, even if I take only 4,000 or 5,000 pesos with me. If I decide to stay, I will buy a very good farm or *chácara*, with a vineyard of 10,000 or 12,000 stocks and many trees, Castilian and local, that will support me when I want to retire and rest, and not go about instructing Indians, which is surely a great travail. But, as I said, if I can I would rather go to Spain, because I am very gray and fat, and this life is hard on me.

I beg you always to write me and advise me of the health of yourself and all your household, of my nieces and nephews, and all the news you get about things there and about our relatives. Here I have been told that Rodrigo de la Calzada's wife is dead, and also his son, the oldest, Antonio de la Calzada. I was greatly grieved that we are diminishing this way. I have heard nothing of our relatives the canons of León and Astorga. Keep me posted on everything.

I stay well, praise our Lord. Luis Alvarez, son-in-law of Luis del Cerro, is here in Potosí, and is applying himself to earning a living from mercury. Licentiate Gómez Hernández, brother-in-law of Licentiate Flores, is corregidor here. He is a citizen of Arequipa, and is very rich. He would like to know of his nephews, and whether Licentiate Flores is alive. Nothing else presents itself. Our Lord, etc. From Potosí, 15th of January, 1577.

Milady sister, your least brother kisses your hands,
Bachelor Francisco de la Calzada

[1] Published in Spanish, with comment, in Otte, 'Die europäischen Siedler.'

BIBLIOGRAPHY

The texts of the letters of this volume are of course translations. They are as accurate as we can devise, but they are cast in a colloquial American English meant to speak to the present rather than to be rigorously literal or quaint. We feel we have taken few liberties, but, for example, Spanish has a way of running on indefinitely without either mentioning the grammatical subject or losing the clarity of reference, and in such cases we have not hesitated to supply an intended name more often than in the original. We have also expanded where appropriate, as in rendering *fundición* as 'melting down of gold.' Perforce we have altered the categories of the originals, whether for simple lack of true English equivalents, for clarity, or in accordance with twentieth-century scholarly conventions, as in our blanket use of 'encomienda' when the originals have both *encomienda* and *repartimiento*, and indeed the latter more frequently than the former. For the purposes of strict scholarly investigation, or simply for the reader interested in learning as much as possible about the categories of thought, level of education, and subtleties of style of the writers of the letters, there is no substitute for close perusal of the originals. It is in fact our hope that readers will be encouraged to search out original texts, not only of the letters we publish here, but of many other comparable ones. To that end we offer a list of some relevant publications. All of the items under Otte's name contain comment as well as letters, much of it considerably more detailed and technical than what we have presented here for a more general audience. The two most substantial of Otte's collections, with the most extensive explanatory material, are 'Die europäischen Siedler' and 'Cartas privadas de Puebla,' from which many of our selections are taken.

We also list some publications with mainly public and official correspondence. Of these the *Cartas de Indias* has served us most as a source. And since our ultimate interest is not merely in letters per se, but in using fresh, individual, intimate material on human lives as a means to grasp broader patterns and trends, we list some recent works of social history which contain a strong biographical element. Among these, Lockhart's publications on Peru contain further details and background on several of the writers of the letters in this volume.

1. Publications with private correspondence

Helmer, Marie. 'Un tipo social: el "minero" de Potosí.' *Revista de Indias*, XVI (1956), 85-92.

Otte, Enrique. 'Cartas privadas de Puebla del siglo XVI.' *Jahrbuch für Geschichte von Staat, Wirtschaft und Gesellschaft Lateinamerikas,* III (1966), 10-87.

'Die europäischen Siedler und die Probleme der Neuen Welt.' *Jahrbuch für Geschichte von Staat, Wirtschaft und Gesellschaft Lateinamerikas,* VI (1969), 1-40.

'La Nueva España en 1529.' *Historia y sociedad en el mundo de habla española: homenaje a José Miranda.* México, 1970, pp. 95-111.

'Los mercaderes vascos y los Pizarro. Cartas inéditas de Gonzalo Pizarro y Hernando Pizarro y su mayordomo Diego Martín.' *TILAS*: Bulletin de la Faculté des lettres de Strasbourg (May–June 1966), 25-42.

'Mercaderes burgaleses en los inicios del comercio con México.' *Historia Mexicana,* XVIII (1968), 108-44, 258-85.

'Mercaderes vascos en Tierra Firme a raíz del descubrimiento del Perú.' *Mercurio Peruano,* nos. 443-4 (Libro Jubilar de Víctor Andrés Belaúnde) (March–April, 1964), 81-9.

'Nueve Cartas de Diego de Ordás.' *Historia Mexicana,* XIV (1964), 102-30, 321-38.

'Semblanza espiritual del poblador de Indias (siglos XVI y XVII).' *Verhandlungen des XXXVIII. Internationalen Amerikanisten-kongresses* (1968), III, 441-9.

—, and Conchita Ruiz-Burruecos. 'Los portugueses en la trata de esclavos negros de las postrimerías del siglo XVI.' *Moneda y Crédito,* no. 85 (June 1963), 3-40.

2. Publications with other types of correspondence

Anderson, Arthur J. O., Frances Berdan, and James Lockhart, eds. and trans. *Beyond the Codices.* UCLA Latin American Center and University of California Press (forthcoming).

Cartas de Indias. Madrid, 1877.

Colección de documentos inéditos para la historia de España. Madrid, 1842-95.

Colección de documentos inéditos relativos al descubrimiento, conquista y colonización de las antiguas posesiones españolas en América y Oceania, Madrid, 1864-84.

Pérez de Tudela, Juan, ed. *Documentos relativos a don Pedro de la Gasca y a Gonzalo Pizarro.* 2 vols. Madrid, 1964.

Porras Barrenechea, Raúl, ed. *Cartas del Perú (1524-1543).* Lima, 1959.

Las relaciones primitivas de la conquista del Perú. Paris, 1937.

3. Works on Spanish America related to social-biographical history

Bowser, Frederick P. *The African Slave in Colonial Peru, 1524-1650.* Stanford, California, 1974.

Brading, D. A. *Miners and Merchants in Bourbon Mexico, 1763-1810.* Cambridge, 1971.

Ganster, Paul B. 'A Social History of the Secular Clergy of Lima During the Middle Decades of the Eighteenth Century.' Doctoral dissertation, University of California, Los Angeles, 1974.

Góngora, Mario. *Encomenderos y estancieros. Estudios acerca de la constitución social aristocrática de Chile después de la conquista, 1580-1660.* Santiago de Chile, 1970.,

Los grupos de conquistadores en Tierra Firme (1509-1530). Santiago de Chile, 1962.

Hunt, Marta Espejo-Ponce. 'Colonial Yucatan: Town and Region in the Seventeenth Century.' Doctoral dissertation, University of California, Los Angeles, 1974.

Lockhart, James. *The Men of Cajamarca: A Social and Biographical Study of the First Conquerors of Peru.* Austin, Texas, 1972.

'The Social History of Colonial Latin America: Evolution and Potential.' *Latin American Research Review,* VII (1972), 6-45.

'Spaniards among Indians: Toluca in the Later Sixteenth Century.' In: Franklin W. Knight, ed. *Creole Societies in Africa and the Americas.* The Johns Hopkins University Press (forthcoming).

Spanish Peru, 1532-1560. Madison, Wis., 1968.

Super, John C. 'Querétaro: Society and Economy in Early Provincial Mexico, 1590-1630.' Doctoral dissertation, University of California, Los Angeles, 1973.

INDEX

continued

continued